OUR LADY OF UNITY'S CO-FOUNDER'S FORMATION AND MISSION HANDBOOK

The Official Manual of Her Religious Order

Romeo Deiparine

Order this book online at www.trafford.com
or email orders@trafford.com

Most Trafford titles are also available at major online book retailers.

This book truly prepares those responders to our Lady's calling to participate in Her last and greatest mission in uniting all God's people by bringing them home to where we all belong to the only and one true church established by Her Son, Jesus Christ our Lord and God. By one's membership to Her Religious Order truly prepares and strengthens the responder into the long and difficult journey to our divine destiny. This book's foundation was rooted in Sacred Scriptures, Church Tradition, Church teaching and from Her Inspiration and guidance so we can and will imitate Our Lady's and our Lord's Life to perfection. Let it be known that our Lady was and is the greatest worker in God's Vineyard and she promise to Her Co-Founders that triple crown reserve for those who abide and obeys the rules of Her Order. This book's publication primary provides responders the holy methodology in shaping and forming their soul into the likeness of the Founder and to Her Divine Son.

Print information available on the last page.

ISBN: 978-1-4907-9477-8 (sc)
ISBN: 978-1-4907-9485-3 (e)

Trafford rev. 04/18/2019

www.trafford.com

North America & international
toll-free: 1 888 232 4444 (USA & Canada)
fax: 812 355 4082

Contents

PART ONE

PART TWO

PART THREE

PART FOUR

PART ONE

Our Lady of Unity

The History

In the year 2008, a lowly Third Order Carmelite was inspired by our Lady of Mount Carmel of the necessity and essentiality of establishing a religious community calling it, Our Lady of Unity.

She give instruction to go on a mission to gather devout and faithful Catholics inviting them to join Her religious Order. Without any clear and concise idea as to what are the purpose, goal and charism, Her calling was not answered promptly thinking it was a delusion. All the religious Order of the Catholic Church have their own charism defining their calling in helping the Body of Christ in its mission saving souls. No action was taken from Her calling completely ignoring it but every now and then the thought of establishing Her community kept coming back as an irresistible force that constantly troubled him. Praying fervently and unceasingly, our Lady slowly revealed to Her boy (servant) that everyday tens of thousands souls are lost to eternal damnation and there is that greatest need of fervent and faithful servants of God to intensify their prayer life so many souls will be save. And as the real Body of Christ, we baptized in the true Church had the greatest responsibility in performing our mission in helping Her and Her Son saving soul. So many meaningful messages was relayed to Her "boy" why the establishment of the Order of our Lady of Unity is so essential and necessary in sustaining the life of the world.

Gradually, she revealed to Her "boy" that so very few are responding to the call of holiness and perfection and sadly she pointed that even those who were called and chosen to the high offices of the clergy had failed miserably in living the Life of Her Son to perfection. And even more disturbing are the many thousands of priests whom She loved who were chosen and called to the highest life have also failed miserably in their vocation to be the living Christ. And worst, are the Body of Christ who were baptized as Catholics have made a mockery of the true religion by their lacked of commitment in following His teachings and the teachings of the Church. Simply said, there is the greatest need in healing the wounded Body of Christ.

How could the establishment of Her Order can make such impact when the billion members failed in their vocation as Christians? The boy's question was answered through the Scripture of which she encouraged him to read and ponder.

"And he said, Oh let not the Lord be angry, and I will speak yet but this once: Peradventure ten shall be found there. And He said, I will not destroy it for ten's sake." (Genesis 18:32).

Weak in interpreting, the Holy Spirit came to enlightened the "boy's mind. Despite the increasing religiosity of the Christian, Islamic, Jewish faith and other religions, so very few truly seek the life of holiness and perfection and by establishing Her chosen community there is still that chance through Her guidance that many will generously respond to such calling of becoming the living and perfect sacrifice acceptable to the Triune God that would bring healing to the severely wounded Body of Christ. Every one is called and this is the only opportunity one will ever have to be consecrated to the Most Holy Trinity where the soul is temporary or permanently sealed to become His very Own special possession. Such lofty thoughts were revealed to this poor "boy" and that the responder will have the greatest chance in earning the triple crown reserved to those who are consecrated to the Triune God.

Our Lady of Mount Carmel also lead the "boy" to the real truth that salvation is not that easy contrary to most of our belief that it is easy and simple by simply believing that Jesus Christ is Lord and Savior and we will be save. She, however showed the "boy" to the following passages showing that salvation indeed takes more than faith. It takes all our strength, energy, effort, conviction, commitment, courage and most importantly, it takes the indwelling of the Triune God in the soul to even have the chance of inheriting and possessing the kingdom of God. The "boy" searched diligently and found the following passages confirming what the Lady of Mount Carmel's message that our salvation must be taken seriously not casually. And to do so, we have to give our all as we were warned by the first Pope of the true Church established by Christ.

"And if the righteous scarcely be saved, where shall the ungodly and the sinner appear?" (Peter 4:18).

Indeed, this is a very serious passage that we all must meditate for this is the truth of our salvation. This is not a threatening passage but an actual saving standard for our salvation.

And by consecrating ourselves to the Triune God one has the greatest chance obtaining our salvation. As the world is closing in for its curtain to close, our Lady of Mount Carmel wants the establishment of Her religious Order the Lady of Unity as Her last Marian mission where its consecrated members will be greatly involved in the conversion of the Jewish and Islamic faith and those other religion where Her Divine Son is not accepted nor received as the Messiah. As she was a member of the Jewish faith, Our Lady revealed that the whole world and all of humanity owed to the Jewish religion since they shared to us their true and living God and it is the greatest responsibility of the Catholic Church to return the favor by praying and interceding not only for the

Jewish religion but to all religion who missed the truth that only through the Son that one can be save.

Again, this is Her revelation why we can not take the free gift of our salvation casually or carelessly. Or simply by faith. She supported heartily Paul's preaching that we can not take the gift of our salvation for granted and the absolute necessity to be very serious in seeking our salvation by working diligently in obtaining it. Remember, we have only one chance.

"Wherefore my beloved, as ye have always obeyed, not as in my presence only, but now much more in my absence, work out your own salvation with fear and trembling." (Philippians 2:12).

This is the greatest reason why Her religious Order must become the center of true spirituality that can bring our salvation into the reality knowing the degree of difficulty that each one of us must face and encounter while we waited with the greatest hope that we will obtain it. Since it is our Lady's last Marian mission, she is revealing to all God's children that they all should cultivate that close intimacy not only to Her Son Jesus but to the other Two Persona of God. By cultivating and pursuing such spirituality, our unity with Triune God will become our witness that we did participated with Him in obtaining our salvation and the triple crown awaits those who did so. It is only through this unity that we did followed this transforming commandment that most of us never paid attention to. Our Lady emphasized that we can never become like God nor we are worthy of Him if we ignore this powerful passage.

"Be ye therefore perfect, even as your Father which is in heaven is perfect." (Matthew 5:48).

The "boy" complained that only God is holy and perfect and we could never reach the heights of holiness and perfection like God and such passage seems unreasonable. Quickly, Her Spouse, the Holy Spirit enlightened his poor and shallow mind by His revealing Light.

"We know how grossly unholy and imperfect you are. I taught my followers to work very hard and very diligently to imitate me. This is one of the greatest reason why I came down so I can teach and show you how to be holy and perfect. By not trying it would be impossible for anyone to obtain salvation. Your rewards is Ourselves and we can not describe what awaits to those who truly loves us and truly gives its all to us. True, in your wretched condition, there is no way one will become like us. Only we are holy and perfect. But, we set such highest standard because by doing so, powerful graces will be given to those who truly tried to become holy and perfect. Millions lost their soul because they never tried to become holy and perfect. Most even assumed that only the chosen one will become a saint. They have become a victim of their own deceiving thoughts carefully planted by the evil one. They have forgotten that I have given my

Own Life for them so they can have Mine. They have forgotten that I created everyone to be Mine. So very few are chosen because so very few responded to my calling to be holy and perfect. Those who won salvation were the most imperfect the most wretched and hopeless sinners but they became saints because they chose to become holy and perfect. True, they became holy and perfect because I rewarded them for their sincere efforts giving them abundant graces transforming them beyond themselves. It is I who took over when one truly desire to seek holiness and perfection and the Three of Us will be the one who will ensure that one will receive the triple crown"

Now, the "boy" received the greatest enlightenment that only through the involvement of the Triune God that one will become like God. To become like Him, one must be baptized in the Catholic Church simply because our Lord and Savior is literally present with His Own Body, Blood, Soul and Divinity and by the sacred and holy rite of baptism one will immediately become a part of God. Sad to say and sad to inform other Christian Churches that their own baptismal rites although acceptable in His Sight but will not make them a legitimate member of His Body. It was revealed to this ignorant "boy" that they have separated themselves by their own conception by marginalizing the greatest promise of our Lord that anyone who eats His flesh and drink His Blood will have eternal life. They have reduced the Real and True Presence of the living God during Holy Communion as merely a symbol. Such disbelief will be rewarded in accordance to what they think and in His perfect justice what they sow they will reap. Sowing a symbol also reap the symbol. Meaning to say that they have refused to believe in His promise to eat His real Flesh and drink His Real Blood and they will have the greatest difficulties in transforming themselves to become God. Still salvation could still be theirs but possibly in a symbol not the real salvation.

By being baptized, confirmed by the Catholic Church one will have the greatest opportunity to become God because our Lord Jesus did brought His Body (the true church) to the new heaven where He is seated at the Right hand of the Father unceasingly praying for His Body so the graces of our transformation be granted to those who wants to be holy and perfect. This is our greatest hope and consolation that the Son of God and man is now enthrone in the new heavens while here on earth we the pilgrim or militant church perseveres in our race so we can be united with our Head now being glorified by the Father. As His very Own Body, our Lord although in the new heavens He did fulfilled His promise to the Catholic Church that He will remain in them by instituting the Blessed Sacrament where He reduced Himself to the lowest form to make Himself accessible and available at all times giving blessings and graces to those who constantly and regularly come to do homage to Him. And in the Blessed Sacrament and His ever presence in the Catholic Church one who is a member of His Body will have the greatest weapon of salvation and transformation and that the seven powerful sacraments that our Lord had provided for His Body so they can be properly and effectively arm against all the enemies of our salvation. Our salvation is very very difficult and we all should believe that it is so when He enlightened Matthew to sent the message to us.

"For I say unto you, that except your righteousness shall exceed the righteousness of the scribes and Pharisees, ye shall in no case enter into the kingdom of heaven." (Matthew 5:20).

Theologians and spiritual masters and gurus surely knew how the scribes and Pharisees practices their religion by their strict observance of God's laws and commandments. They did spent their lives living their religion to the fullest and we really have to asked ourselves if we are that serious and committed in entering the kingdom of God which is widely and openly available to all of us. The Lady of Mount Carmel instructed the "boy" to become Her apostolic administrator of Her religious Order, Our Lady of Unity. Thus, by Her inspiration, the book titled, "Our Lady of Unity" was written and completed in a few weeks. In addition, the "boy" also wrote the community rules for Her Order and she promised to those who answered the call eternal happiness by simply obeying the Rules of the Order.

"Because strait is the gate, and narrow is the way, which leadeth unto life, and few there be that find it." (Matthew 7:14).

She emphasized to Her "boy" to meditate day and night about this message that the salvation of our soul is truly very difficult and challenging that if we are nonchalant in receiving God's greatest gift to us then we should be in grave danger of the judgement.

"I know thy works, that thou art lukewarm, and neither cold or hot, I will spue thee out of my mouth." (Revelation 3:15).

Finally convince of his calling as Her apostolic administrator, this "boy" an active member of the Old Carmelite Order as a Tertiary answered to become a servant to the Mother of the Church, Mother of salvation and Mother of all God's creation.

Thus, the history of our Lady of Unity's religious Order begins and its final mission will not end until the end of time.

The Founder

The Founder is a She. Our Lady of Mount Carmel had informed Her "boy" that the arrival of rapid technological advances in all area changes drastically our lifestyle threatening our spiritual growth and awareness of the things eternal. And she already knew that it will become seriously worst as we enter into the twenty one century where technological advances in the sciences will threatened the existence of religion and worst losing God completely from our lives. The love of the world and its treasures and pleasures had drawn most of God's creation to desire less of the things of God and heaven. They have found the new garden of Eden where wealth, comfort and pleasure became the standard of happiness thus losing the desire for God. To climb the heights of spirituality is no longer appealing since the life in our new world had become very appealing to our flesh. The imitation of the life of Christ could no longer compete with what our modern and advance world had provided. As the number of holy and perfected souls had diminished, threatening the existence of the world, Our Lady of Mount Carmel came to intervene as she had done countless times for our sake so what happened in Sodom and Gomorra will not be repeated. She could have save that city but she was not there. Billions will never have a clue how the Blessed Virgin has the greatest and powerful influence to the Almighty God because they do not belong to the true Church established by Jesus Christ Himself. Only the baptized members of His Body knew how many miracles did she performed throughout the world and how many millions can testify how the Blessed Virgin Mary obtain for them powerful help both corporally and spiritually.

The world has to be reminded all the time that it is the Blessed Virgin who works the hardest in our Lord's Vineyards. And she alone by the fullness of God's grace bestowed on her had performed and produced the greatest harvest in His vineyard. The world should know how she told a lowly native to erect a chapel for Her and with the help of Juan Diego, our Lady of Guadalupe became the greatest harvester of souls by converting millions to the Catholic faith. Anyone who visited the Virgin of Guadalupe in Mexico will be spiritually touch by the graces of which our Lady possesses. It is not only in Mexico but in Portugal specially in Fatima where she dazzled the whole world by her dazzling appearance converting millions back to the true faith. And also millions and more comes to the holy shrine in Lourdes where thousands were physically healed. From France and to the long lists of our Lady's appearance in all the parts of the world millions more experienced conversion to God because she keeps appearing and pleading to change our lives and to embrace repentance, penance, fasting and prayer. Who is she that can change the condition of the world? Who is this woman that brought millions to their knees and obeyed her wishes to repent and to seek God? The miracles and conversions she displayed should overwhelmed us into believing that this woman who is just like us can possess such powerful influence unmatched even the miracles recorded in Sacred Scripture. This woman was chosen to possess such powers because God fully invested all His graces on Her knowing she will use all of it for our sake but most importantly to give the Most Holy Trinity the greatest glory and honor. Mary obeyed and understood Her Son's pleading.

"Woman behold your Son."

Jesus knew His mother was the recipient of the fullness of God's graces and how He valued us by what He had to undergo so we will be saved. Even though He is the Redeemer, Jesus was asking Her help in saving many more souls knowing God the Father and God the Holy Spirit was intimately united with Her and like at Cana, she cannot be refused by the Triune God simply because she never refuse anything God asked of Her.

Then, on the other side of the coin, our Lord look upon His beloved disciple John.

"Son, behold your mother."

Our Lord was asking not only John but all of us to take great care of Her knowing how powerfully precious she is in the mission of salvation. We can take great care of the Mother of God and Mother of the Church by our obedience to God and to the precepts of the Church by always doing what His Son tells us. We can take great care of God's Mother by accepting and embracing Her as our very own. By doing so, we can now look and behold this woman clothe with the sun and the moon under her feet crown with stars and magnificent to see what the great good God had entrusted to us. His mother and our mother.

Billions could not see nor appreciate what the great good God had given us - His very Own Mother. They refused to honor Mary as our mother when our God honored His Mother. Have we ignored this commandment to honor our father and mother? Yes, we all honor our Father in heaven but how about the other part, the mother? If we failed to do so then we have greatly failed the Triune God by not honoring this Great lady of our own.

Thus, the Founder entrusted to the "boy" a small mission of proclaiming to the whole world the essentiality and necessity of establishing Her religious Order to make known to all that the Mother of God and our very own mother needed help so she can help us make through this most demanding and difficult journey in transforming ourselves to be one with God. There is no need of an argument or settling theological rhetoric that Jesus alone save simply Mary possesses all of the Triune God's graces so she can help us come to Jesus so we can be save. She also entrusted to Her community to make sure that Christians separated from the real Body of Christ come back to the true church otherwise they are at risk of losing that greatest inheritance prepared to those who truly loves Christ. No amount of preaching or praying can compensate being baptized in the Catholic church. Yes, salvation is still possible for our revolting Christian brothers and sisters but they are in a much greater risk since they are deprived of the Church powerful and potent sacraments and most important was their deprivation of the help of the Mother of God, the only begotten daughter of the Father and the holy spouse of the Holy Spirit. The "boy" reasoned that it would create more problems and more alienation of other faith and religion by such proclamation that all should be baptized in the Catholic Church. To which came the enlightenment from Her Spouse that the truth must be known not to be concerned about division and alienation and the boy was lead to the passage of Scripture that our Lord came not to unite but to divide. Father against son, mother against daughter and brother against sisters. Two thousand years passed since our Savior came but His prophesy stood the test of time as we can see how we keep dividing and fighting each other even in our religiosity. And it will remain that way until the end of time since His Words are purely the truth.

The religious Order of our Lady of Unity will be established not only for the sake of our Protestant brothers and sisters but to the special children of Abraham in faith. Our Lady had the greatest love and affection with the Jewish faith since she and her beloved Son belongs to this holy religion. As the Jewish religion did shared their God to the whole world, all of humanity should be grateful and appreciative of them otherwise we will never know who God is. What they shared to us all is indeed priceless. The Jewish people and their faith as children of Abraham truly were chosen for the sake of the future of all humanity. They shared their God to their separated children of Abraham where Muhammed founded the Islamic faith and they have spread rapidly where billions are practicing the Muslim religion. As the spouse of the Holy Spirit, Mary is the seat of wisdom where she confided to the "boy" that both the Jewish and Islamic religion will encounter the greatest difficulties of being united to the Triune God and their transformation to become like Him is not possible. She revealed that in their monotheistic religion they are deprived of the Trinitarian concept of God where the Three powerful Persona must come into the transforming equation of making as one with Him. All Christians knew the situation that there is no salvation except through Christ the Lord for He had taught that no one can come to the Father except through Him. Concerned for the lost of billions of soul, the "boy" was inconsolable thinking how could the great good loving and merciful God allowed such sorrowful situation. Aside from the Jewish and Islam religion, there are the Hindus, Buddhist and hundreds other religion where our Lord Jesus is not accepted and received as our Lord and Savior. And there exists in our world where in so many areas that religion is not even practice. How could they be save?

Thus, She called Her "boy" as the instrument in establishing the Order of Our Lady of Unity where the Lady of Mount Carmel will be its founder. She called one of its lowliest member of this illustrious Order to be Her apostolic administrator to facilitate and put into operation the last Marian mission where Holy Mother Church will be greatly involved in inviting and gathering all God's people into One Body of Christ. One faith and one church. As the Founder gave us the Son for our salvation, in Her last and final mission, the Founder with the help of Her Co-founders and with the powerful participation of the Catholic and apostolic Church will gave to the Triune God all that belongs to Him. This is and will be Her greatest and last mission to gather all Her children so she can give all of us to the Triune God.

Preface: Fundamental Constitution

As the Blessed Virgin Mary brought the Prince of Peace to the land of our exile ending enmity with God, we owe to our Lady of peace our greatest gratitude for her response to become the Mother of God and the only one qualified to be the ark of the new covenant. Pure logic dictates that without her, there is no Messiah and there is no salvation for us. She is honored, revered and respected greatly by the Catholic Church knowing her role to our salvation and sanctification. Unfortunately, billions are clueless that this Great Lady of our race are given by the Son of God to be our mother also as our greatest helper in the salvation of our soul. A holy and wise thought by a saint should make us think when he professed "It is truly wise and smart to have both Jesus and Mary on our side knowing the great difficulty we all are facing in saving our soul. There is no argument that two is better than one."

"Honor thy father and thy mother" This is one major command by God. We who believe in God does honor Him as Father but what about the mother? Are we not accountable if we failed to honor the mother? To disobey any of this commandment one disobeys all. Clearly, anyone who refuse to embrace, honor, revere and respect God's mother will surely face severe consequences. This is simply God's command. In His dying moment on the cross, He gave us the greatest inheritance, the Holy Mother of God.

"Son, behold thy mother."

God gave us His mother to be our greatest helper for the salvation of our soul is not an easy matter. We need all the help we can get even though Jesus our Savior solely saves, He too needed the Father and the Holy Spirit as a symbol of unity in the community of our integration to the Holy Trinity. The Savior of mankind was asking her help in His dying moments knowing this Great Lady was given the fullness of God's graces.

"Mother, behold thy Son."

She immediately knew what He wanted and despite all her pains and sorrows watching her beloved Son suffering the greatest torments, Mary at the foot of the cross prayed for the two crucified criminal knowing that both were about to lose their soul to damnation.

"Father forgive them for they know not what they are doing" She repeated His Son's prayer and the good thief salvation was granted.

"Today you will be with me in paradise."

Both Jesus and Mary is truly needed to greatly improve the chances of our salvation.

Thus, it was commanded to the "boy" to write the Order's Fundamental Constitution as the last and saving agenda for all God's people specially those who are deprived of knowing that the Messiah, the only begotten Son of God had already come and that the new heavens is now freely wide open and freely available and assessable to those who truly love and give itself wholly to the Triune God. This very simple document expresses the great desire of our Lady of Unity who is in great need of our help so she can help all of us get to our heavenly home.

The Fundamental Constitution

I

The purpose of the Order was and is to invite everyone to become our Lady of Unity's great helper and partner by participating in her last Marian mission evangelizing the whole world that only through the Messiah the Son of God and the Son of Mary that salvation is possible. This is the absolute truth and anyone who refuse to accept or deny this truth will suffer the greatest loss - the possession of God for all eternity. By one's participation as Co-founder of the Order of our Lady of Unity, she promise the greatest reward of sharing the glory and splendor of the Most Holy Trinity.

II

Help me help you. This was Her request to the "boy" the essentiality and necessity in establishing Her religious Order calling those who are really and truly serious committed soul to respond this one and only opportunity in giving the Triune God the greatest glory and honor by helping Him through our Lady in the final and closing mission of the Church uniting the children of Abraham in faith whose religiosity does not bring them to true salvation because of their spiritual stagnancy being deprived to enter into intimate relationship with the Most Holy Trinity. They have remained with the Father depriving themselves with the two powerful Persona of God where they could not be fully transform into His true Likeness. He had come and by missing the Son of God, the Jewish, Islamic and all other religion in no way will earned that coveted triple crown reserved only to those who are consecrated to the Triune God. Responder will receive abundant blessings and graces fueling the intention of the Triune God in fulfilling His will of uniting all His flock under the one true shepherd.

III

Our Lady of Unity, founded by our Lady of Carmel is the only religious Order of the Catholic Church where the Blessed Virgin Mary is intensely involved since this is Her final Marian mission in helping the Triune God drawing, gathering and guiding His creation to the fullness of the truth of our salvation. Many souls are deceived for there are thousands of false shepherds using the Word of God as an attractive means in luring innocent and ignorant souls into their own flock. It is the responsibility of the Order to inform that true salvation can be obtain by the true Church which teaches the fullness of God's truth.

IV

True salvation is not and never be an easy matter that most if not all of us had taken for granted. Like Esau traded his birthright for a meager meal, we too had traded the kingdom of God and heaven to the worthless and useless things of this deceptive world we live in. Specially in this new technological age where most of us are drawn into wasting precious time and resources leading to the decline of our spirituality. Knowing that tens of thousands of souls are lost each day and more will be in the future, Our Great Lady like she had done in the past two thousand years is now become very more active and in need of help revealing to the "boy" that Her Order must be established so many faithful devout souls will give their helping hand to their mother and most importantly to the Triune God.

V

As the Holy Trinity needed help from each other's Persona and as the Triune God needs help from the lowly creature like Mary so does the glorious Queen of heaven and earth needs our help so the most holy will of God will be done in us. As Mary earned the crown of God she promised to those who respond to Her calling as Co-Founder of the Order a crown coveted by many but given to the chosen ones who made the choice in joining the community of our Lady of Unity.

VI

The chosen ones are those members who truly come to serve and not to be serve. To answer Her glorious calling one must truly do it solely for the love of the Triune God and to obey the holy rule of Her community so Our Lady's promise will be fulfilled. She had instructed that members to be professed and consecrated during Holy Mass will definitely receive signal graces and the soul will on the way to true salvation. True salvation can only be taught and achieve by how one can follow perfectly the teacher of truth which is Jesus Christ the only begotten Son of the father and the only Son of Mary. Non Catholics are clueless how powerful is our Lady's intercession to the Triune God that our Savior left us an inheritance that the whole world can not give. Billions sadly ignored the Mother of Salvation rejecting Her powerful help in their salvation. The Order's mission was to make known to all so we can accept and embrace Her to be our very own mother.

VII

The Order's purpose was willed by our Lord and Savior Jesus Christ that we received and embraced His Own mother as our very own. Beloved by the Father, Son and Holy Spirit, the Blessed Virgin Mary was specially chosen to received all God's graces so the mother of salvation and the mother of the Church will be God's greatest helper and humanity's much needed helper in fulfilling and finishing God's greatest handiwork. Without Her perfect obedience there will be no Emmanuel and humanity will never be reconciled and restored to the One who created us.

VIII

And in the history of our salvation none can come close to what our Lady has done in bringing soul's back to the Most Holy Trinity giving Her Father, Her Son and Her Spouse the greatest glory and honor and by doing so Our Great Lady was given the triple crown of God for she was very deserving of such glorious reward. Not only Queen of heaven but also here on earth our Lady was crowned with glory and honor since she brought to the Triune God the greatest honor and glory a lowly creature could ever gave.

IX

To the responder of Her call one becomes Her helper Her Co-Founder and Co-worker and to labor as an evangelizer in promoting how one can earned the triple crown that she received from the Most Holy Trinity.

X

Our Order involves teaching and preaching that only the Catholic Church can bring true salvation to the whole world for this is the only one true Church established by our Lord Jesus Christ when He ordained, appointed and anointed Peter to be His Vicar once He ascended to the new heaven. Only by our integration to the Body of Christ through holy baptism that true salvation is possible. The Blessed Virgin Mary, our lady of Unity is enthroned in all Catholic Churches as its most prominent member and also its mother. Professed and consecrated members of Her Order will be active participant of the Church mission of unity and will always be in perfect obedience to the Holy Father.

XI

Co-Founder of Her Order will be involved in the ministry of teaching, preaching and promoting our Great Lady as that unknown powerful force in our salvation. Unknown to many because only the Catholic Church knew how powerful she is in pleading to the Triune God and because he was entrusted the fullness of God's graces. Tracing Her history, the works of our Great Lady was the greatest reason why billions of souls embraced the true church established by Her Son and the only begotten Son of God where our salvation made possible.

XII

All are called to participate and join our Lady of Unity's last mission as prominent member of Her Order where one have the greatest opportunity in receiving what was promised to the Carmelite "boy", the triple crown of God. By one's profession and consecration to the Most Holy Trinity the most coveted crown of the Triune God will certainly be the greatest reward one will ever hope to receive.

The Vision

The expectation that all Catholic parishes will fully support and cooperate by inspiring practicing and devout Catholics to answer the calling of our Lady of Unity. Full support from all Bishops by inspiring parish priest to become a Co-Founder with our Lady since they were chosen and called to become the living Christ setting a shining example of their divine dignity as Her Son's brothers. As she was Her Son's greatest helper, our Lady is also in need of great help from Her Beloved Son's brothers knowing their powerful influence on the faithful will draw many to the Order. As our Lady's last and greatest mission, Her pleading for help must not be ignored nor delayed for we members of Her Son's Body have this great accountability in participating in fulfilling and completing the marvelous works of the Most Holy Trinity in transforming us to become like Him. There should be no hesitation in helping our Beloved Mother knowing how much we owed Her by all the helps we received from Her.

As a tribute and to honor Her last and greatest mission in uniting all God's flock under one shepherd, every diocese all over the world should named one of their parish church, Our Lady of Unity where all professed and consecrated Co-Founders will congregate once a year sharing its gifts and talents. They will share together "The Last Testament" housed and revered in the parish of Our Lady of Unity. This yearly celebration will be held on the Feast Day of Our Lady of Unity which will be revealed by Her apostolic administrator.

Since this is the only religious Order founded by our Great Lady, it is expected that this will be the largest and biggest religious Order of the Catholic Church and it has to be since billions revered and loved Her. Most importantly, she is pleading all our help helping Her in the final phase of our existence and that is an abundant harvest of souls. As the greatest worker of God's vineyard, she is calling for our help knowing that billions more soul are in great risk and for every responder to Her calling can become contributor in bringing more souls to God.

As we labored mightily in this life to reap a rewards that is worthless, how much we labor for the kingdom of God determines our contribution and the value of the treasures we reap recorded by the Book of Life. Thus, what is our involvement with our Lady's greatest mission determines what will be our eternal lot.

The year 2022, will be the Order's first special audience with the Holy Father for his apostolic blessings for all consecrated and professed Co-Founders and with special permission those who are in their formation stages. This special audience with the Pope will be made in year 2024, 2026, 2028 and every two years until the end of time. Perfect was and is the obedience of our Lady to the Holy Trinity and so must the Co-Founders to imitate Her in this beautiful virtue of obedience specially to the Vicar of Christ, the Pope for he is our visible head. It is recommended that Co-Founders made the trip to Rome unless of course restraint with health or financial reason.

For each professed and consecrated Co-Founder of Her Order, she promises that at the moment of one's particular judgement, she will be present facing our Eternal Judge and Her pleading will be our greatest consolation and blessed hope that we will spent eternity with our Lady of Unity enjoying the beatific Vision of the Blessed Trinity. Members of Her Order will have the greatest advantages and benefits because the Founder and the Co-Founder are one and such unity can not broken unless the Co-Founder renounces and rejected the holy Rules.

Remember this lofty thoughts, better and greater is our chances of gaining God and heaven if we have both Jesus and Mary on our side.

The Co-Founders

The calling of our Lady of Unity is our greatest opportunity to truly fathom the mystery of the Triune God. The responder will also reap the greatest benefits as being a Co-Founder with the Great Lady and such unity with the great Mother of God in essence guarantees that our immortal soul will be safe. She promised and guaranteed union with the Triune God if one is in perfect obedience to the Rules of Her Order. Once the soul is in unity with the will of the Holy Trinity then They will made their dwelling place in this faithful and obedient soul. Soon to be the biggest and greatest religious Order of the Catholic Church, the Co-Founder will also reap the treasury of grace stored by the Founder Herself which will be dispense in accordance to the merits gain. Knowing to be transformed into God, our journey to eternal life will be very difficult and demanding, we desperately need those graces necessary and essential in our transformation from dust to divinity. Thus, the lofty thoughts makes the greatest sense to have both our Lord Jesus and our Mama Mary to be with us always in this most perilous journey to eternity where we are judge according to our faith and the works we have done in our lives. The Order simply preach and teach what is truly truth about "real salvation" instructing the ignorant and innocent and to rebuke false teachers and pretentious shepherds who teaches the partiality of the truth. Responder to Her calling are the ones who are really serious and sincere about the salvation of their one and only immortal treasure.

Qualifying the Co-Founders:

Only the most Holy and Almighty God can make us qualified. Anyone who truly wants to give its all to the Holy Trinity surely qualifies to become Her Co-Founder. This is the greatest qualifier.

Secondly, one is and must be baptize in the Catholic Church and have practiced their faith. There is no age limitation but one must be at least 21 years old and in good mental and psychological health.

Thirdly, one must be in the state of God's grace and if not must work out that one will be.

Most importantly, the office of the clergy specially bishops, priests and deacons are much needed by our Lady of Unity for they are the light of the Church and Beloved brothers of Her Son. How pleased will be our Mother when the prominent spiritual leaders and models of His Son's Church answered Her greatest calling for help.

Responders will undergo two years formation program (one classes per month 3 hours or less). Formation book will be provided and the truly serious and sincere soul should always attend all of its classes. (24 in two years)

Profession and consecration to the Most Holy Trinity will be solemn and sacred and will be performed during Holy Mass where it will be witnessed by our Lady and she will be the one who will present to the Most Holy Trinity.

After three years profession and consecration the Co-Founder after deliberate discernment can make perpetual its profession and consecration and will have the option to serve the SOS Missionaries in the most difficult and most challenging mission. The SOS Missionaries are our Lady's chosen ones who are willing to give its all for the greatest glory and honor of the Most Holy Trinity.

May the Holy Spirit guide you to serve our Lady, Mother of God and ours.

Introduction

This book is not only for the highest and greatest good of those responder to become Co Founder to our Lady's Religious Order but also to those who devotedly embrace and practice what was taught in the Formation Classes. Most importantly, if one perfectly obeys all the Holy Rules of Her Order then one's sincere effort to grow into the likeness of our Lady and Her Divine Son certainly be on the way to one's greatest transformation from being dust to divinity.

Saints were transformed from its lowest baseness to the highest form of the divine simply because of their formation program made possible by the teachings of Sacred Scriptures, Church teachings, Tradition and even private revelations. Although private revelations attract skeptics into buying what was revealed one simply can not deny nor even argue that private revelations from God is an ongoing process that will make our transformation perfect and complete. Even though Sacred Scriptures is the Word of God it is not completed and much like the existence of the imperfect and incomplete Church Militant, it is so necessary and essential that God never stops in revealing what was and is to come. Such was the point why our Lord Christ upon completion of His Works sent the Third Persona of God so He can finish the imperfect and incomplete Works of the Two Persona. Therefore, the Holy Spirit as Its mission was to complete our transformation into His Own as sons and daughters of the Triune God. Thus, as the final phase of our transformation the Holy Spirit's responsibility was to enlightened the Church what is Its mission and its own responsibility in making possible the seemingly impossible in making us like God. Thus, the Holy Spirit never stops in Its Own mission not only renewing the phase of the earth but most importantly renewing fallen humanity and raising it so God's greatest Works be completed and perfected.

There is never no doubt that the greatest methodology in transforming ourselves to the higher life was the formation program embraced and practiced. Obviously, Sacred Scriptures transformed many to seek and desire to follow our Lord's teachings which resulted in attracting billions of souls in embracing and practicing Christianity. Even those who did not believe in Christ as Messiah, the Jewish and the Islamic faith hold on to their own formation program through the Old Testament Books as their own methodology in climbing to the heights of divinity. Other religions obviously received enlightenment from the Holy Spirit by leading them to live a life of goodness and godliness making themselves presentable and acceptable to God though deprived of knowing and embracing His Second Persona who was and is the only way to the Father. Since the ways of God unfathomable, those other religions where the Messiah was and is not received, revered and honored but did lived a life where the principle of God's love was practiced then obviously they were formed by none other than His Third Persona, the Holy Spirit who was responsible in forming God's Life to all creation. Even though Jesus is the only way to the Father salvation is always possible to other religion if they have been formed by the Holy Spirit who was sent by none other but by the Messiah so that even though they missed His glorious coming by His redemptive Love the Third Persona extended the works of our Lord Jesus so those who are outside the Church will also be save. But, believe it or not, the Catholic Church is the only true church that brings salvation to all God's people because of the seven transforming sacraments forming its member into the real living Body of Christ. In this one and only true saving Church each sacrament forms member soul transforming it into a higher level of life where the presence of the Holy Spirit is actively involved in shaping and forming to a completed masterpiece designed by our Supreme Architect.

Since His ascension to the Father and mystically bringing us home with Him (His Body, the Church) though still separated, there is that greatest need for the Holy Spirit to become the hardest worker in our salvation. Our Father did His job well so does the Son but it is the love of the Father for His Son and us and the love of the Son to His Father and us that the Holy Spirit must enter into this final formation process making us one with the Son where we are transported now fully united with our Lord Jesus and we too are seated also on the Right Hand of the Father. Such sacred privilege was promised to us by our Lord when He told His followers that He will prepare such place (In my Father's house were many mansions). This absolute truth is the Christians greatest hope that once we are done in this life we will have an eternal dwelling place where no one can described the joys and perfect happiness waiting for those who truly loves the Triune God. And if we truly are serious about such sacred promise then there is no time to daily dally about this delectable destiny offered to everyone. If procrastination kills the cat so does our soul if we continue to ignore God's calling so we can obtain what was promised.

This formation and mission book will put the responder in a much greater position in fulfilling our greatest destiny transforming our baseness into the sublime heights of divinity where we can live that blessed hope into reality. Once become Co Founder with our Lady one becomes one with the Father, one with the Son and one with the Holy Spirit and such union with the Triune God is achieved here on earth then we are already in heaven. And it is the Mother of God, the Mother of our Savior and the Spouse of the Holy Spirit and the Lady of Unity that will ensure the professed and consecrated Co-Founder who will bring us to such sublime union with the Blessed Trinity. This is the greatest privilege to those who will help our Lady of Unity in its final mission gathering and uniting all God's people into the true Ark of the Covenant.

PART TWO

Formation Program

Year One
(12 Classes)

First Class: (3 hours or less)
Hymn: Sing Together, Glory and Praise to our God
Opening Prayer:

Introduction to Religion

Leader will read the Scripture passage.

"If any man among you seems to be religious, and bridleth not his tongue, but deceiveth his own heart, this man's religion is vain. Pure religion and undefiled before God and the Father is this, To visit the fatherless and widows in their affliction, and to keep himself unspotted from the world." (James 1:26-27)

After the reading spent five minutes in silence by slowly reading and meditating the message below.

To be religious is God's gift to us. It is His Holy Spirit drawing us to Him. Wherever we are religion is always be a part of our life and such sacred activities is the greatest evidence that God is indeed present in the world but most importantly in each one of us. God wants us to know Him and religion is the first step so we can enter a relationship for this is His holy will. All kinds of religion existed because we have that hidden and unfulfilled desire trying to find Him and to be united with Him. This is our heaviest cross, our separation from God. And religion bring us the greatest hope and expectation that eventually we will be one with God. Therefore, to be religious is indeed good and to be irreligious put itself in peril in completely losing God forever.

However good and noble it is to be religious, Scripture warns us that all kinds of religion has no value unless one live its life in accordance to God's holy will. How many hours we spent praying has no value at all if we live our lives in the flesh and not on the spirit. What good religion is if we keep our tongues spreading bad news in gossiping, slandering and lying. Our mouth should be spreading the good news of our salvation by sharing love and unity. Most importantly, our heart should be purely motivated in giving all of our love to God and specially to our own neighbor. Thus, religion becomes pure and holy and acceptable to God if we exercise charity to all specially the most needy like the orphans and widows. If one is religious and its deeds is full of love then God will be most pleased.

After the 5 minutes of silence, the LEADER slowly read the message.

Then, together the community pray slowly:

"Holy Mary, mother of our salvation, obtain for us members of your community the graces to become religious but most importantly the graces that each one of us present before you will always be charitable to all those who truly needed help. As you were very kind to your cousin Elizabeth during your visitation obtain also the graces that we will always practice the virtue of kindness to every one we met. Pray for your community that each one of us present here will become God's instrument of fulfilling His holy will."

Pray the Our Father, Hail Mary and Glory be slowly.

Then Sing "Immaculate Mary"

THE THREE MAJOR RELIGIONS:

The Jewish Religion

Leader reads the following message:

In all religion, the Jewish religion is the noblest and the greatest. Why? Because this is the religion where God Himself revealed to us. All other religion are worthless unless its model are the writings and teachings of God's prophets. We can find God revealing Himself on the Old Testament. We can say God introduces Himself to us through His chosen people. We all should be grateful to our Jewish brother for sharing us their God. Thus, it is not good or profitable to hate or curse God's chosen ones for it was written in Sacred Scriptures that He will bless those who blest the children of Israel and curse will be upon them that curses them. But before we proceed about the Jewish religion let us examine that in ancient Egypt before God revealed Himself, The Egyptian Pharaoh had already possessed in their hearts that after their death, they will live eternally and with such thoughts they preserved their bodies. Others worship the sun, the moon and even any object because they have a soul thirsting for the living God that is hidden within itself. Each one of us is truly seeking and searching for God because we belong to Him. If you heard someone calling themselves an atheist do not believe them for in reality they have the greatest hunger and longing to be with God. In their anger and frustration of not finding Him or being deprived of His grace and light they resented and give up their quest in seeking God. As Co worker of our Lady of Unity, we should look with pity and compassion for those who claimed unbelievers for God is within them and it only take a little light and grace to find themselves in love with God.

Religion is so crucial if we want to be close to God but in our religiosity it is so essential and necessary to supplement it with godliness. These two elements should be together otherwise it is very difficult to get close to God. A religious with no godliness and godliness without religion does not make the cut. And in our formation as Co worker with our Lady of Unity we should always keep in our hearts to be religious and godly. This was God's command to Moses the greatest prophet of the Old Testament when He revealed Himself to us. Of course, His revelation at first was only for His chosen people and those who did not belong to the tribe of Israel were completely deprived of knowing Him. Thus, God command to Moses was to love Him with all our hearts, mind, soul and with all our strength. Our religiosity in essence is an important first step in fulfilling His greatest commandment but again only a single step in a long and difficult journey in reaching and uniting ourselves to God. Then, God commanded us to love our neighbor as self as the second greatest commandment. Godliness can be fulfilled in how we treat everyone and it is the virtue of charity that perfected our love for neighbor. It is our goodness, kindness, generosity, compassion and concern for them that makes us perfect in fulfilling the second greatest commandment of God. Thus, it is of the greatest importance for each member to know and memorize God's Ten Commandments for this will be the standard of our daily life. We pleases God by doing so and in His just ways one will receive much more blessings and graces that eventually if we persevere and not quit God will surely be our reward. There was a survey that less than five percent can recite correctly God's Ten Commandments and such disturbing news makes us wonder how God felt knowing we do not treasure and revere His precious Commands. And how foolishly we kept complaining about the condition of our world and in our own lives that we blame the good and loving God for the mess that we created. Therefore let us ask ourselves what did we do for Him? Quoting President John Kennedy's word, "Ask not what God can do for you but what you can do for Him?" Replacing country with God makes perfect sense in how we can please God. Ask yourself, how often you think of Him during the day and during the night. Did you pray enough? Did you worship Him? Praise Him. Adore and revere Him. Did you give thanks to Him always or only sparingly. Did you live a holy and blameless life? We have to asked more of ourselves about our greatest responsibility to our good God and to our neighbor. Thus, the true religion begins with the Jewish religion for in the children of Israel, God made known to us who is He and what does God wants of us.

Together, sing a hymn. "Hail Mary"

The Islamic Religion:

The second major religion is the Islamic religion where there are a billion members and they are most present all over the world. They have become one of the fastest growing religion in the world but dominant throughout Asia and Africa. The largest population of Muslims are in Indonesia, Pakistan, Bangladesh and India. As the Jewish religion revered and honored the teachings of the Old Testament, the Muslim have their own and the Quran is revered and taught to the faithful as to how to live their lives. They believe that the Quran is the unaltered and final revelation of God. Islam meant submission to God. The Quran was God's word revealed to their prophet Muhammad. They believed in one God and called

Him Allah and they revered and honored their prophet as the greatest. They believed that God is just and each one of us is accountable for our injustices and they believed in heaven and hell as our final destination after our judgement. The Islam religion devoutly practices prayer by doing it five times a day during dawn, noon, afternoon, sunset and evening. They practiced charity by helping the truly needy. Fasting is essential and necessary in their religious practices during daylight hours in the month of Ramadan and most important each Muslim must make a pilgrimage to Mecca at least once in their lifetime unless restraint by financial or physical reason.

Both the Jewish and the Islamic religion are monotheistic meaning that there is only one God.

They both revered Abraham as their father and the contents of the Quran are also found in the Old Testament. Some historians and researcher discovered that before he became a prophet Muhammad was a merchant constantly on the move and he was always in constant company with Jewish merchants where he was introduced to the teachings of the Old Testament. Muhammad had also many Christian merchants friends where he learned some teachings of the New Testament. As an intelligent man and wise merchant Muhammad saw an opportunity that most Arabs were irreligious and needed spiritual guidance inspiring him to gather followers teachings them about God or Allah. He presented the Quran as the final revelation from Allah and that he was His chosen prophet to gather his countrymen descendants of Ismael. With his confession that an angel Gabriel appeared to him and that he will be the final prophet. Biblical scholars studied the Quran and analyzed its contents and messages and concluded that mostly was derived from the Old Testament and some elements from the New Testament. Such findings were logical since Muhammad probably had learned from his constant interaction with both Jewish and Christians. Whatever be the truth God only knew but what he did was admirable since he made the Islamic religion grew into one of the biggest religion. Possibly, God allowed it to flourish because what the Quran taught is simply what His chosen people taught.

The Christian Religion:

Christianity, the world's largest religion attracts about thirty three percent of the world's population. Its followers believe in the teachings and life of Jesus Christ. God gave us Jesus, the truth. He formed the twelve apostles and they in return, went out to preach the good news to the ends of the earth.

"Freely ye have received, freely give." (Matthew 10:8). Jesus gave the power and authority to these chosen twelve and what He had accomplished the apostles did too. They bore witness to everything that He did but what finally strengthened their faith and belief was witnessing His cruel death on the cross and His subsequent resurrection from the dead. His followers thought He had failed in His mission but they were really stunned when Mary Magdalene told them that she had seen the risen Jesus.

"Now when Jesus was risen early in the first day of the week, he appeared first to Mary Magdalene, out of whom he had cast seven devils." (Mark 16:9). They could not believe that Jesus rose from the dead, but indeed it was not within the realm of reason that a dead person can rise. It is not possible to rise from the dead, but with God all is possible. (Matthew 19:26; Mark 10:27 Luke 18:27.) They had forgotten that just before He was crucified, Jesus raised Lazarus from the dead witnessed by so many. (John 12:1).

"And this is the will of Him who sent me, that everyone who sees the Son and believe in Him may have everlasting life; and I will raise him up at the last day" (John 6:40).

The resurrection of our Lord from the dead defies human logic but the power of God is beyond logic. Science cannot explain the mysteries of God. Had Jesus not risen from the dead, the apostles and His disciples would never had risen again from the depths of their fears. Christianity would have never flourished. In fact, it would have died and buried with Him on that cross. Now, the Christian cross is exalted and revered all over the world giving us the greatest hope to be with God forever.

When the risen Lord showed Himself to the apostles, not only were they risen from the darkness of their doubts and fear, they were also raised in body, spirit and soul. The resurrection of Jesus is not symbolic or fabricated but witnessed by many and recorded by history. The fact is that truly Jesus rose from the dead and even spent many days with His apostles and disciples teaching them more about the kingdom of God.

Which religion one belongs is a matter of free will. All religion are good for our living soul because it teaches us that God truly exists and that we have a real purpose in our existence. Religion brings God into our hopelessness and helplessness as we try to fulfill His will in bringing us all back to Him where we truly belong. As we live, struggle and suffer in a land of exile religion gives us hope and strength to persevere living until we are done here and return to Him that created us. Humanity needs religion otherwise, without it, the world would be much worse that it is now. Our God perfectly ordained the miseries and burdens in our lives so we will seek a better world and a much better life. Such assumption is logical because each one of us will have no other option but to seek God to fulfill the longing of our soul that originated from Him. We should never stop in praising and giving thanks to God for giving us religion because it will lead us back to where we belong. Religion introduces God to everyone. Rich or poor. To the innocent and ignorant and to the intellectual. Believers and unbelievers. Thus we should put religion as our highest priority for the religious soul who sincerely and fervently seek God will not be denied for His generosity one receives blessings and graces.

Break is recommended after an hour. 5 to 10 minutes. Leader and members decides the time.
After break community sing the hymn "Hail Holy Queen"
Prayer:

Holy Mary mother of God full of grace pray for us your community and make each one of us your powerful instrument in making you known as mother of salvation. There are many religions with different teachings which divided God's children even leading to many conflicts causing extreme division and chaos which is a contradiction to God's will. As Patroness of Unity obtain from us from the Holy Trinity all the graces that we can participate in promoting unity and harmony to all His people that we will be united as one flock under one shepherd. Obtain from your holy Spouse, the Holy Spirit that He will always guide and lead Pope Francis I in reaching out those who are not in communion with the Holy See.

Our Father, Hail Mary and Glory be.
Group Discussion:
Not more than fifteen minutes:

Discuss the similarity of the Jewish and Islam religion. What are they?

Why is it that the Christian religion is so different from Islam and the Jewish religion?

The Buddhist and the Hindus have made themselves an appealing and attractive religion. Discuss why. What are their primary teachings.

Christianity is still the most appealing and most desired religion. What are the reason why?

Why are the Christian are so divided? There are thousands of Christian churches all over the world and some its founder even proclaimed that they are the real and true church.

Is the Catholic church really the one true church?

Discuss if it is possible that unity be achieved that we be under one shepherd.

After discussion leader will continue to discuss religion and its true origin.

The origin of true religion can be traced from its roots. The Jewish faith is the root of all true religion because God who is truth revealed Himself to His chosen people. True religion meant that what we seek, what we desire and what we want is the One True God who created us. Thus, if we seek other gods then it is false religion. For example, Hindus believed that there is reincarnation and they believed that to them cows are sacred. Primitive Indians worshipped the sun and other unknown spirits. The Romans made many statues for their many gods. The Buddhist monks practiced extreme denial of the desire of their flesh focusing primarily in living in the spirit that some can even levitate as a result of their powerful spiritual meditation. Devil worshippers obtain demonic powers through their own religious rituals and incantations. Voodoo practitioners can truly inflict injury and even death and of course witchcraft have their own religion. False religion was with us for a long time and it is still dominant in every part of the world. True religion is nothing else but to seek the one true God where one can worship, adore, revere and love Him. And it was Moses who received from God the Ten Commandments where true religion begins where He made known to us that we all should give all our love to Him. And also most importantly, to love our neighbor much like God's love for us.

In conclusion, true religion then is to seek, to know, to love and to serve the one true God who made us strictly for Himself. Thus, the Jewish religion, the Islamic religion and the Christian religion are true religion because its followers are in pursuit for God whom we can not see nor touch but knowing He exist and that God is always in our midst active in helping and guiding us back to Him for we all belong to Him. Divisive we are in the flesh but by God's goodness and kindness His Spirit never stop working into our very own spirit so our immortal soul can be enlightened and even purified for our sanctification and salvation.

Thus, the three major religion although different and even divided have one thing in common and that is they are offsprings from the great patriarch Abraham. The Jewish, Islamic and Christian religion are the branches from the roots of Abraham whom God made the covenant that he will be the father of many nations. Putting this three major religion together validates that indeed God's own promise was fulfilled when these three religions dominates the world.

However, what separates the Christian religion from the others is that Christ Jesus, the Incarnate Word, the Crucified Lamb and the Risen Lord was not a part in their religion. When this happens, they have missed what is truly love and yes, they have missed God in the flesh and they have missed His first visit to our forsaken world.

In closing the first class, slowly read the Scripture passage why the Christian religion is the one that surpasses all religions.

"All things are delivered unto me of my Father: and no man knoweth the Son, but the Father; neither knoweth any man the Father, save the Son, and he to whomsoever the Son will reveal him." Matthew 11:27.

Both the Jewish and Islamic religion does not know Jesus that He is the Son of God. Such deprivation of the God-man create a vast void in their religion. They only believe in the Father but the Christians have His Three Persona but One God. They have no clue that if God has only one Persona God can never complete His masterpiece. Jesus, the Second Persona is needed for our justification and redemption and without the Third Persona which is the Holy Spirit the works of the Father and the Son cannot be completed. It is the Holy Spirit who sanctifies and finishes the works of the Holy Trinity. And Christians indeed received the greatest gift of knowing and having Jesus as their Lord and Redeemer.

"Jesus saith unto him, I am the way, the truth, and the life: no man cometh unto the Father, but by me." St. John 14:6.

Clearly, Christians have the greatest advantage over any religion because we have Jesus, God Himself who alone can ransom us from the slavery of sins. Before Jesus coming, it was the blood of animals shed on altars as sacrificial offering but such sacrificial ritual could never redeem us. It should be the blood of both God and man that would satisfy the perfect justice of God. For such reason, our Lord testified that only through Him that we can come to our heavenly Father. Simply said, salvation can come only through Jesus. And He did showed us the way through His teaching of the fullness of truth. How could salvation come to other religion without knowing our Lord Jesus can only be answered by our Judge. But the truth He had spoken that only through Him that we can come and enter the kingdom of our heavenly Father where we will reign with Him for eternity. Therefore, Christians should always be grateful to God that they know His only begotten Son and to treasure such Divine dignity that we have freely given through His grace. And since much was given to us like being a Christian then we have also the greatest responsibility of truly living the life of Christ in us otherwise if we claimed to be Christian in name only salvation then is not possible.

Closing Prayer:
Hymn: Salve Regina.

Second Class: (3 hours or less)

Together Sing Hymn, "How Great Thou Art"
Opening Prayer:

Dissecting The Catholic Church

Leader will read the Scripture passage.

"When Jesus came into the coast of Caesarea Philippi, he asked his disciples, saying, Whom do men say that I the Son of man am?" Matthew 16:13.

Our Lord was initiating an interview who will be chosen to be His representative once His mission is done. As God the Father sent Him to be seen in the world so now Jesus must also chose someone who will be His vicar once He return to the Father. As the Jewish people were chosen among all nations for His revelation, so also must Jesus chose among His disciple to represent Him as the visible head of His universal church.

"And they said, Some say that thou art John the Baptist: some, Elias; and others, Jeremias, or one of the prophets." Matthew 16:14.

No one knew that Jesus was the Messiah, the Son of the living God. Of course, when our Lord came the whole world did not knew Him that is why they crucified Him. Even His chosen apostles who were with Him all those times also did not knew Him. They were just obedient follower to Jesus listening to all his teaching and witnessing all His good works and even those miracles He showed during His ministry. But they have no idea that God himself was their constant companion.

"He saith unto them, But whom say ye that I am?" Matthew 16:15.

Jesus pitied them for their ignorance but understood their childish innocence knowing it takes grace and enlightenment from the Holy Spirit for someone to know Him. Even today though we knew that He is our God and Savior our faith with Him contradicted our works.

"And Simon Peter answered and said, Thou art the Christ, the Son of the living God." Matthew 16:16.

Boldly and confidently, Peter with no hesitation proclaimed Him as Lord and God. How could a very simple and ordinary fisherman with no education and with no theological background was able to proclaimed that Jesus was the long awaited Messiah?

"And Jesus answered and said unto him, Blessed art thou, Simon Barjona: for flesh and blood hath not revealed it unto thee, but my Father which is in heaven." Matthew 16:17.

In the scene, is the involvement of the Three Person of God in choosing the one who will represent God visible in our flesh, our very own as the one and only Head of God's church.

It was the Heavenly Father sending the Holy Spirit to reveal to Peter that the Second Persona of God is in their midst. With the approval and blessings of the Triune God, Jesus found the one.

"And I say also unto thee, Thou art Peter, and upon this rock I will build my church; and the gates of hell shall not prevail against it." Matthew 16:18.

Long before His coming to our world, the Triune God had already conceived the perfect plan in helping us to our difficult journey to eternity by establishing His invincible church as the most powerful means in defeating the enemies of our salvation. The coming of the Messiah had two most important mission. First, our redemption and justification and second was to establish His church. Knowing how weak and fickle we are there is that greatest necessity and urgency in building that invincible Church where God Himself is always present till the end of the world. God remembered our fickleness when Moses left them when he went up the mountain to receive the Ten Commandments and after so many days that he was gone, God's chosen people without the presence of their spiritual leader went astray by making an idol for their God (false religion). Without Moses presence, without a visible leader God's own chosen have lost their faith. From such experience, it was decided by the Triune God that His church His kingdom on earth must be established to ensure that we will always have His presence. That our leader is always with us. Not only the establishment of His church kingdom but to have a new Moses so to speak but always present and always visible so we will not go astray. Once they founded Peter, in unity the Triune God decided to appoint and anoint him. And Peter was given much and now he bore the greatest responsibility for he was given the keys of heaven. As no one can come to the Father except through the Son and so with the keys given to Peter for heaven then no one can enter heaven except through the keys of Peter.

"And I will give unto thee the keys to the kingdom of heaven: and whatsoever thou shalt bind on earth shall be bound in heaven: and whatsoever thou shalt loose on earth shall be loosed in heaven." Matthew 16:19.

Next to the annunciation where Mary was to become the mother of God, Peter's appointment and anointment was and will be the greatest event of our salvation history. Without the yes of Mary, there would be no Jesus and without the appointment of Peter there is no Catholic and no universal church to guide and guard God's flock. Mary and the Church were God's greatest instrument for our salvation. Without the two no salvation. This is the fact and the truth. Therefore, in the Catholic church spring salvation. With other churches and religion salvation is only possible by God's justice and mercy. When the Catholic church declared that only through this church that salvation can be achieve controversy rages among Christian churches and even to other religion. In order to promote unity and peace, the Catholic church soften its stance but in mystical theology, without the Catholic church there is no salvation. For this is the only one true church appointed and anointed by our Lord Jesus and He established it to be His official Body where He will draw everyone as its members and He Christ Jesus be its head. That is the reason why when He started His ministry Jesus presented Himself for baptism so that everyone who wants to be a part of His Body (Church) must also be baptized so one can be integrated to the real Body of Christ. And when His mission was done, Jesus before He ascended to His Father in heaven specifically instructed His apostles and disciples that they should go to the ends of the earth baptizing them in the name of the Father, the Son and the Holy Spirit. Clearly, baptism is essential and necessary for the salvation of our soul. For the unbaptized simply could not be in heaven unless with no fault of their own and God the perfect Judge will have the final say.

"He that believeth and is baptized shall be saved; he that believeth not shall be condemn." Mark 16:16.

Peter, the first pope, in his first sermon, delivered on the day of Pentecost, declared that Jesus of Nazareth is the Messianic king. The means of salvation which he indicates is baptism and that only by entering the church can we participate in the redemption wrought for us by Christ. The church alone dispenses the sacraments and the seven powerful sacraments can not be obtained from outside the church thus salvation could be very difficult if one does not belong to the true church. Again, conflicts and unending arguments and debates will never end because the protestant church will remain with their own stance that they too are the Body of Christ for they have also been baptized in the name of the Father, the Son and the Holy Spirit and with their growing numbers as independent Christians submission to the Papal Office will never on their agenda. Since Martin Luther formerly a devout Catholic priest bolted from the church and succeeded in gathering vast followers protestant churches have spread like wild fire and with so much freedom everybody can build its own church and appointing themselves as pastor. Thus, they the protestant churches have divided themselves to all kinds of denomination with their own freedom to teach and preach about Christ without any restraint. What is so dangerous when there are so many teachers teaching and showing the way, the truth and the life can be disastrous and catastrophic like what happened in Guyana where the reverend Jones drove his followers to commit suicide. Rev. Jones preached the Gospel and he did attracted many followers but sadly and tragically they became victims of false prophets. In Waco Texas, February till April 1993 tragedy struck when more than eighty people were killed during a standoff between Federal agents and followers of the religious sect, Branch Davidian. The late David Koresh was its leader proclaiming himself as the final prophet again, drawing and deceiving others because he had memorized the Bible. Radical Muslims willingly wrapped bombs to their bodies and blowing others believing that by doing so for Allah they will received the rewards of their martyrdom. The history of destruction and death is too long to be listed but this is the sad truth when there are so many teachers or shepherds who tried to guide and teach other about salvation can be very dangerous. Our God know this will happen that is why He only wants one church and one teacher to shepherd His flock.

“Beware of false prophets which come to you in sheep’s clothing, but inwardly they are ravening wolves.” Matthew 7:15.

In His wisdom, God wanted only one shepherd to guide and lead His people. He chose Peter to be God’s anointed and visible shepherd of His flock. Such sublime responsibility can only be entrusted to just one teaching authority so there will be no confusion and chaos but only unity and harmony. The way to perfection and holiness is difficult and God knows this when He reminds us.

“Because strait is the gate, and narrow is the way, which leadeth unto life, and few there be find it.” Matthew 7:14.

Thus, we need all the help we can get and we need all of God’s graces to reached our heavenly homeland. The Catholic church teaches holiness and perfection knowing this is what God wants from us.

“Be ye therefore perfect, even as your Father which is in heaven is perfect.” Matthew 5:48.

Perfection is the real goal for those who truly love God. The excuse that no one is perfect is a complete cop-out coming from our self love with our own ill will. We are imperfect but inspired to be perfect to measure the depth, the length, and the width of our love for Him. Perfection is always possible if we really prioritize in becoming one. It is no doubt and very difficult to be perfect but we have a lifetime to work on it. A lifetime of practicing perfection is so cheap a price to pay for the rewards that God promises us. Perfection is the only way we can get to heaven and there is only one who can teach perfection and that is God Himself who can help and show us how.

The way to perfection is very difficult and only one is qualified to teach.

“Be ye not ye called Rabbi: for one is your Master, even Christ; and all ye brethen”

It is clear that God shall be our only teacher because He is perfection. He know and lives perfection. If the teacher is not perfect then the student is shortchanged since the teaching are compromised. Therefore, it is to our greatest benefit to have the true shepherd teaching us the way to perfection otherwise we will be following blind shepherds who will led us to the wide path of perdition.

"Let them alone: they be blind leaders of the blind. And if the blind lead the blind, both shall fall into the ditch." Matthew 15:14.

Perfection is God. We are commanded to strive for it otherwise we cannot be like Him. Perfection is God's standard. He will not demand unless it is possible. He came to give us that true religion teaching the fullness of truth and the way to perfection. The reality of why He demanded for holiness and perfection is that, we are so grossly imperfect and despicably unholy and actually we can never be holy and perfect unless one is united with Him. He demanded us to reach for the moon (perfection and holiness) and knowing we can never reach such heights at least our sincere efforts we can reach the star. But if we do not try to be holy and perfect we become stuck on earth and chose to be content being dirt and to return to dust where there is no hope to spent eternity with God in the highest heaven.

Break 10 to 15 minutes.
After the break, together slowly pray:

Holy Mary, mother of the church, pray to the most Holy Trinity that all His children will know the fullness of truth. You gave us your Divine Son, our Lord Jesus as the true teacher of God's truth and He gave us the mother God as our powerful intercessor in all our needs. Do not be deaf to our cries and obtain all the graces that all your children scattered, deceived and divided be united into the Body of Christ your Son so by their integration to the church salvation may be theirs. We pray for the sake of God's greater glory, majesty and honor. Amen

Our Father, Hail Mary and Glory be.
Our Lady of Unity pray for us.
Sing the Hymn: Amazing Grace.

When our Lady appeared in Fatima she revealed that every day tens of thousands souls are lost to hell. So very few directly entered heaven and saved souls who fell short of holiness and perfection are in purgatory. Everyday most souls goes to purgatory and hell and this the primary reason why our Lord instructed us to be holy and perfect even though difficult because if we do not listen to Him what will happen to us when our time is done? Hell or purgatory. Do not listen and believe at funeral when someone said, O he is now in a better place in heaven. But sorry such statement is so far from the truth. He could be if he did listen to our Lord and indeed he work out his salvation with trembling and hard work. If he did, yes you can say he is in a better place because there is no way he can be in hell. When you sincerely seek holiness and perfection for the love of God it is most certain salvation is obtained even though how far we are from being holy and perfect. The sincere effort to strive for holiness and perfection will be more than enough to be saved. But to those who never listen to our Lord's instruction about holiness and perfection will be in grave danger of losing God and heaven. No amount of good works will save the soul unless God saw something worth saving. But to those who truly tried to become holy and perfect it is guaranteed that it will be in heaven or in purgatory. The Catholic church had been attacked and abused about the doctrine of purgatory but they are simply clueless because their own teachings come from their egotism and pride. Protestant pastors tried to erased purgatory from their teaching trying to attract more people into their fold promising something that is far and short from the fullness of the truth. What pride they have to think that they can go directly to heaven when God is holy and perfect. Do they really think they are already holy and perfect because of their commitment in serving the Lord through their great preachings? Do they truly believe that they are holy and perfect already because they can quote Scripture and impressively wowed their flock? We should realized the holiness and purity of God that all of us made of dust and made of flesh have the audacity to stand in His majestic presence face to face? No. No one can stand in His presence and no one can see God face to face unless one is holy and perfect like Him. Once we die, we will see the light of God and from such vision we will see and know our destiny. We will know if we have attained holiness or perfection and once we saw that light we proceed to the place deserving of us. We will know that we fell short of holiness and perfection and realizing how filthy and deformed we are, we willingly and lovingly plunged ourselves into that beautiful fire of purgation knowing that by doing so we can start taking shower so to speak so we can become so clean and fresh worthy to present ourselves to Him. Yes, do not be afraid nor dread purgatory because you have attained salvation and you are indeed destined to be in heaven once you have completed the perfect process in making you holy and perfect. Yes, holy and perfect like God and in purgatory once the process is completed one becomes like God. If ever you entered purgatory rejoice for you are on the way to become like God.

Thus purgatory was God's greatest invention as the final phase of our purgation so no stains or speck of sin remains. We all know that even the most holy in us does fall at least seven times a day what more the majority of us swimming in sin. Although we did received purgation here on earth, it does not completely remove all the stain, all the filth and all impurities and this is the greatest logical reason that purgatory was so essential and necessary to make us perfectly cleansed and purified making us ready to face our God. The Catholic church were wrongly accused that purgatory was its own invention but the truth is no man could ever come up with such brilliant idea for our greatest and highest good but God.

In all religion only the Catholic church revealed that without purgatory so few can enter heaven. But God found a way so that more will get into heaven through this final purifying process. God wanted all to get to heaven that is why He commanded creation to multiply so there will be an abundant harvest. That is why He came down from His throne in heaven for the redemption of all and that is why God build a church as our guide and the gates that opens to heaven. The Catholic church is the real deal. She had everything because God provided her with every weapons and tools for our protection and defense against the enemies of our salvation. The Catholic church can never be destroyed for Jesus is truly and always present in all the tabernacles in every place on earth. For over two thousands years all her enemies kept trying to destroy it but they failed all the time. Let us dissect the reason why.

When He ascended to heaven Jesus promised to sent the Holy Spirit to help us win our salvation. Not only that, Jesus must remain with us although He is seated at the right Hand of God as our Eternal high Priest knowing that without His real Presence we all be in trouble. Just like the trouble of the tribe of Israel when Moses was gone and during his absence, they fashioned their own god to replace their lost leader. By instituting the Blessed Sacrament in every Catholic churches all over the earth, the faithful will never look for another god knowing that Jesus their Lord and Savior is always with them. That is the Real Presence of Jesus in the Blessed Sacrament. Where ever you visit Him in the Blessed Sacrament you will see the faithful and devout Catholics in company with their Lord adoring, worshipping, praising, thanking, talking, praying and pouring out to Him whatever problems and burdens they have. Such faith in the real Presence of Jesus in the Blessed Sacrament is the greatest reason why no one can destroy God's one and only church He commissioned.

Thus, the Eucharist is the sacrament which contains the true Body and Blood of Jesus Christ, together with His Soul and Divinity, the entire living and glorified Christ under the appearances of bread and wine. As long as there is a consecrated Host in the tabernacle Christ is personally present there. He is the same Jesus Christ, true God and true Man, who walked the streets of Galilee and Judea. And we received Him at Holy Communion, He actually comes as our very personal guest entering in our whole being giving us the grace to persevere and endure until we are called to meet Him face to face. The protestant never believe what the Catholics believe and for leaving the true church they have also abandoned their Lord. Just think of what they will be missing. We have the real Presence of God in our midst and they chose not to believe what was taught as truth. Rather, the protestant never accepted the teachings about the Real Body and Blood of Christ during Holy Communion because grace was lost by abandoning the true church of Christ. They only see Jesus real Presence as bread and wine. By doing so they are deprived of the tremendous benefits of having the Real Jesus in our being. They preferred His Words rather than Himself. God's Words are powerful but compared to the Real Presence of God and His Words are quite different. Moses received the Words of God engraved in stone but what a difference to have Jesus presence with His apostles. This is why the Catholic Church separates Herself from other religion. This true Church is above and beyond all religion put together because of the real Presence of God.

In addition, the Seven powerful sacraments is what make salvation in the Catholic more sure and secure for in each of those sacraments truly and really God is present.

For example, the sacrament of baptism where one automatically become a part of His Body where one will have easy access to the other sacraments.

The sacrament of confirmation where the Holy Spirit confirmed and sealed the baptize as real member of the Body of Christ.

The sacrament of vocation where one enter into servitude to God by either entering holy orders as a priest, deacon, nuns or lay religious or the sacrament of matrimony where couple entered into a holy union of body and soul and by creating a family of believers.

The sacrament of reconciliation is one powerful means of purifying the stain if sin in our soul. This is what truly separates us from every religion because of our easy access of forgiveness of our sins. Knowing the most holy will at least fall seven times a day, the sacrament of reconciliation easily restore the image of God in us through the absolution given by the priest to the penitent.

And the most important is the reception of the Real Body, Blood, Soul and Divinity of Jesus at Holy Communion if received worthy by the communicant will receive abundant blessings and graces but to those who receive it in the state of mortal sin will be accountable for its irreverence and disregard of His commandments.

Finally, the Sacrament of anointing of the sick or extreme unction where one is in danger of death where the priest anoint the sick to bring comfort and assurance that God came to bring healing not necessarily the body but most importantly the healing of the soul.

All the seven powerful sacraments are weapons of salvation. No one should live without it.

And then, only the Catholic church saw that the Blessed Virgin Mary will be our greatest helper saving our soul. She is full of grace and she can easily obtain from the Triune God whatever she wants in accordance to His will. The church taught the faithful to embrace Mary as its second intercessor for our salvation.

And then, only the Catholic church recognized how powerful are its saints in heaven as another powerful intercessor in helping us obtain the grace of our salvation.

And then, only the Catholic church taught how the souls in purgatory can obtain graces from God with their intercession for the Catholic church.

And then, the secret powerful hidden army of the Catholic church who kept providing faithful and loyal followers in infusing fresh fighters against Her enemies. Example, the Franciscan Orders constantly did penance in behalf of the church by their lives of simplicity and poverty. The Dominican Order with their preaching of the truth will be the Church defender. The Carmelite Order where its members live a life of contemplation supplying the church with gifted writers and unceasing prayers. There are many many more religious Orders of the Catholic church that its existence can be called another powerful church inside the most powerful Church. Rightly so, it should be since this church truly belongs to Christ our Lord. Contrary to accusation of many of its enemies the Catholic church is not man made. It is made by God.

Break 5 to 10 minutes.
After the break slowly pray:

Our Lady of Unity most prominent member of Holy mother church do not forget your faithful children laboring for the conversion of heretics and for the salvation of souls by your powerful intercession by obtaining graces of fortitude and courage to persevere in our calling. Amen.

Our Father, Hail Mary and Glory Be.
Our Lady of Unity pray for us.
Sing the Hymn, Servant Song.

Group Discussion: 15 minutes

Discussion about being a Catholic. Is she the one and only true church? Is the Pope the only one teaching authority? Why is it that salvation is only through the Catholic church? Discuss why the protestant are resentful against the Catholic church, their attacks. Muslims and other religion not knowing Christ can still be save through the Catholic church, in what way.

Closing Prayer:
Hymn: Salve Regina.

Third Class: (3 hours or less)

Hymn: Let There Be Peace On Earth (Sing together)
Opening Prayer:

The External Life

Leader will read the Scripture passage:

"Even the Spirit of truth; whom the world cannot receive, because it seeth him not, neither knoweth him: but ye know him; for he dwelleth with you, and shall be with you. I will not leave you comfortless: I will come to you. Yet a little while, and the world seeth me no more; but ye shall see me: because I live, ye shall live also." St. John 14:17-19.

After birth the child cried. We wonder if the child was happy or sad. Is it a cry of joy or pain? Born in the flesh, the child experienced for the first time both side of what life will be all about. We all experience its joys and pains and born and living in the flesh everyone of us does not want any pain. Pain can be described as physical, emotional and mental. We want to have joy. Joy will be define as worldly happiness all of us seek. We want the better things in this world. We need to have a god job so we can have better wages so we can have what we needed in life. Various needs unending will be stored in our heart where all our desires are. But going back to the cry of the child, two reasons why it cried. First, the cry of joy. After many months in total darkness contained in so little space of the mothers womb, finally cried for joy seeing for the first time the marvelous light of the world which was an amazing sight to see. Finally darkness is over. The child experienced for the first time the freshness of life's beginning and what a mighty difference a space the world provides. What a world that I belong and it will be all mine. The child felt the comfort of its mother's loving arms as she hold it and love was introduced. Second, the cry of pain. The child felt hunger and thirst and cried for its need. The child becomes uncomfortable from the cold or heat in its new environment and there is a need and it cried. The child cried sensing abandonment and unattended by the one whom it trust. From its cry the child became a prophet that life will be filled with two things. Pain and joy, that is worldly joy or happiness. The child had no idea that the world it dearly embraced is the land of our exile and it does not know that our real home is in heaven.

Born in the flesh, this is our external life.

The world will be our oyster. Indeed the world is ours because we belong to it. If the Spirit of Truth is not present in the child, the child will not love it nor have any desire for it for in the world will be its only desire and God is remotely out of the equation. This is the main reason why so many souls are lost because of our preoccupation that this world is our oyster that we can have everything our hearts desires. This is the reason why the things of heaven and God became secondary and not the primary goal. This is the reason why our Lady of Unity is pleading to the faithful and devout to intensify its prayer life and to live a holy and perfect life for the sake of saving souls. And as part of the world, one cannot receive God and the message of the Gospel are repulsive to them. Those poor souls have become so comfortable in their darkness that any little light of truth became irritable and annoying. For them, heaven and the promise of eternal happiness with God is far from the reality of their lives. Since light and darkness is not compatible, is the reason why the world is one of the greatest enemy of our salvation. Indeed, the world is so powerfully attractive. It is filled with treasure and pleasure. Specially in our times when technology's advancement had made our lives more comfortable, more tolerable and even more pleasurable to our physical senses. That is why we were warned that those who loves the world has no love for God. Like our Lady's warning at Fatima that tens of thousands of souls are lost everyday, our time is becoming worse that the souls lost to hell everyday can no longer be numbered. This is the reason why Our Lady of Unity are calling and inviting all to join Her community to become religious specially lay people and to make their lives a sacrificial offering to the Triune God so many souls will be spared from eternal death. With what the new world are offering with all its progress it had truly drawn billions of souls to the trappings leading to the wide path of perdition which compelled our Lady of Unity to work even harder calling us to Her community to counter the severe and vicious attacks of Her enemies. Indeed, our external life is our greatest threat in our journey to our God and heaven.

Silence for 5 minutes and do the reflection of the world and with our own lives.

After reflection together the community pray slowly:

"O most Holy Trinity, Father of Love, Prince of Peace and our Sanctifier hear our prayer as we call and cry out to our merciful and loving God for the graces that we will become productive workers of Your vineyard. Guide and protect us from all the enemies of our salvation. Behold, we Your children in exile captivated by the allurements of this world, victimized by the deceitful devises of the devil and the assaults of our own corruptible flesh are in so much need of Your Mercy and Grace to make us holy and perfect as You are. Unworthy we are, make us one with Your Three Persona so we can live Your Life as our very own. We humbly pray for your greater honor and glory and for the conversion and salvation of sinners. We pray in the Name of Jesus our Lord who lives and reigns with You and the Holy Spirit now and forever.

Our Father, Hail Mary and Glory Be.
Our Lady of Unity, pray for us, your devoted community. Amen.
Sing together, the Hymn, "Hail Holy Queen"
Resume Classes:
The External Life:
Class discussion: Limit 25 minutes.
Leader presides:

What is in the world that we are so attracted to. List each one that the community presented to the leader. Discuss the listed attraction one by one. List which attraction is sinful and what is not. New survey showed that majority: the love of money came in first, next position and power, prestige, popularity and being love. There are more lesser things mention. After discussion, spent 3 minutes and ask yourself if your own attraction to the world will be a great or lesser impediment in your spiritual life. Grade them from 1 to 10. One being less and 10 as the greatest.

After 25 minutes of discussion resume. Leader reads the following Scripture message below.

"For what shall it profit for a man, if he gain the whole world, and lose his own soul?" Mark 8:36.

This is how serious the warning to those who are in love with the world. We have heard this warning all the time from priests, preachers and teachers but the Words did not sunk in our hearts and souls. Otherwise, the world would have been filled with religious souls seeking the kingdom of God instead of seeking what is in the world. In our external life, the absence of the God's Spirit made us more blinder than ever. We cannot see that God is in our midst because our eyes are severely set on the world. We love what we see, what we hear, what we feel, what we smell and what we touch which block the entry of His Spirit into our mind, heart and soul. This is truly risky to our immortal soul because of such warning from the greatest apostle of Christ.

"For they that are after the flesh do mind the things of the flesh; but they that are after the Spirit the things of the Spirit. For the carnally minded is death; but to be spiritually minded is life and peace." Romans 8:5-6.

Paul was preaching the truth that to live strictly for the flesh is certain death unless we change direction of our thinking. Indeed our journey to God and heaven is very difficult and demanding and Our Lady is teaching Her community to teach and even preach the degree of our difficulties. Certainly, we will encounter stiff resistance and even ridicule from the world and even to those who are close to us but when we are persistent our rewards will be much greater in heaven. There is a warning from the Spirit of Truth that when someone is preaching and the audience feels good, comfortable and enjoying what was preach then there is something very wrong with the message. Go back to Sacred Scriptures and observe if our Lord's preaching made His audience feel good or enjoyable.

In His sermon on the Mount Jesus taught the whole truth and it was filled with admonishment, warnings, instructions and how to be holy and perfect (Matthew Chapter 5, 6 and 7) The people were astonished and stunned for His preaching was so different from the scribes. And with His courage and conviction for the truth, Jesus admonished by exposing the hypocrisy of the Pharisee and the Scribe to the point of cursing them. This is the kind of preaching and teaching that should make souls tremble and shaking with fear that should bring them with tears of repentance unlike those preachers who made their audience love and like them. The preaching of the truth hurts for all of us who are living in this world. Our external life is completely opposite to our spiritual life. And for us who truly wants to spent our life with God then we should be mindful of what Paul warns us.

"So then they that are in the flesh cannot please God." Romans 8:8.

We have heard it many times that we are always an enemy to God because we easily submit to the demands of our flesh instead of denying their sensual desires. And when we let our flesh be our master instead of the other way around then we are really in danger of losing God and heaven.

"For if ye live after the flesh ye shall die: but if ye through the Spirit do mortify the deeds of the body, ye shall live." Romans 8:13.

Thus in our formation as co-worker to our Lady of Unity, we should kept reminding ourselves to live in the spirit for by doing so we are on the way to our reward.

"The Spirit itself beareth witness with our spirit, that we are children of God: And if children, then heirs of God, and joint heirs with Christ; if so be that we suffer with him, that we may be also glorified together." Romans 8:16-17.

We suffer when we deny ourselves with sensual and worldly pleasure but in doing so such sufferings are too little or even negligible to what will be our reward which our Lord promises to those truly follows Him.

Pause five minutes and meditate on what was discuss.
After five minutes, anyone can share whatever their thoughts about living in the flesh and in the spirit. Limit to 25 minutes.
Break 5 to 10 minutes.
Resume Class:

The Exterior Life:
Leader reads the Scripture passage:

"And Jesus came and spake unto them, saying, All power is given unto me in heaven and in earth. Go ye therefore, and teach all nations, baptizing them in the name of the Father, and of the Son, and of the Holy Ghost: Teaching them to observe all things whatsoever I have commanded you: and, lo, I am with you alway, even unto the end of the world. Amen." Matthew 28:18-20.

Our life experiences in the land of our exile brings us to conclude that everything is all struggle. Yet, we have no choice but to go on with our sentencing since this is God's will. We have to continue to strive in an environment that is not conducive to our spiritual life. For those who are not concern about God and heaven to them the world will be their heaven and God. They will do whatever it takes to obtain wealth, power and position knowing by having them they can control their own lives and also the lives of others. Fact is, there was a comment by a famous billionaire whose wealth was in the billions and when interviewed about his faith, he replied that there is no God and religion is created by losers who could not compete and cope in the world. They are hopeless and they seek something that does not exist to create some hope in their miserable lives. Such arrogance surely is an abomination to God and we who are more blest than this powerful wealthy man must continue in our journey to a life of prayer and penances for the world had truly deceived billions with their ambition to have everything they want in this world. Such is the state of our external life and had not the good and loving God intervened we will be like beast and no hope at all to spent eternity in eternal happiness.

Indeed, the coming of our Lord Jesus did drastically changed the condition of our hopeless and miserable world by revealing to us that there is indeed hope to all of humanity. Truly from dust to divinity. This was God's plans for us. But God must heavily involved Himself in the process of our transformation. And the greatest move made by our God was His coming into the land of our imprisonment. His life, death and resurrection from the dead became our hope that what God promises to us will be ours. God already knew that our external life was too hard and too difficult to overcome and for this reason He must enter into our lives and participate in our journey back to our true home. And before Jesus ascended to His Father in heaven, He made sure His church built on solid rock is set and established to help us against our struggles in our external life. And most importantly, He instructed to His apostles and disciples to go everywhere on the earth and baptized everyone in the name of the Father, the Son and the Holy Spirit so they will be incorporated into His Body here on earth while on the right hand of the Father in heaven Jesus brought with Him the Church He built on earth and we have participated in offering ourselves to God as the royal priesthood through our incorporation as His Body on earth. Having done His marvelous works for us and knowing that we need all the help we can get He also give us His Own-self through His Third Persona the Holy Spirit to ensure we are completely equip in our spiritual warfare against our very own corruptible nature made of flesh. And to ensure we get more additional help, God gave us His mother and the Three mystical Body of His Church to guarantee His faithful and loyal follower to get to heaven.

That was the promised He made to His faithful apostles and followers that He will be with us until the end of time. Because God knew that without the establishment of His church here on earth, His absence will be disastrous and we will be lost and like the chosen children of Israel when Moses left them, so we are will also seek the wrong and worthless god.

And as His faithful and loyal soldier here on earth, we no longer be afraid or fear with our external life since we have been gifted with all God's power but most all the

Holy Spirit is roaming on earth renewing the phase of the earth. The presence of His Third Persona made the Church (the baptized) truly invincible and indestructible as God prophesied when He said to Peter, the first pope that on this church the gates of hell will not prevail. Since God is truth then there is no one who can destroy the Catholic Church despite all the enemies who tried to to ruin it. Therefore, we are so much blest now because of what God did for us. Although in ancient times God spoke to his chosen one and performed those awesome miracles, there is no comparison for what God provided for us now. Therefore, there is no need for Him to talk to us nor there is no need for Him to perform awesome miracles for they paled in comparison for what God had given us now. Long to talk and listen to God? Sacred Scripture was given to us and we can talk and listen to our Lord without stopping. In ancient times, God spoke briefly but now He speak unceasingly. Long to see some awesome miracles by God? Just look at yourself. From dust we will be eventually transformed into the image of God after we tame the greatest hindrance of our transformation which is our corruptible flesh. But we need to work out diligently hard with our serious conviction in order to make His works possible. Working together as one guarantee success. And from this corruptible and worthless flesh, we will be transformed into a spiritual being by the involvement of the Holy Spirit which is our God. In ancient times, they were deprived of the Holy Spirit where they can not be transformed like God through the priesthood of our Lord Jesus. In ancient times, they were so remotely far from God and no chance at all to enter the new heavens. Now, there is no need to see any more of God's miracles because we have given much much more than the ancient people of God because the greatest miracle one can ever see or imagine is our transformation from being dust into divinity. Where can we see such awesome and unbelievable miracle? You need proof why there is no more need for God to talk and us and to perform awesome miracles? Do you need proof why we are more bless that the ancient times?

"Jesus saith unto him, Thomas, because thou hast seen me, thou hast believed: blessed are they that have not seen, and yet have believed." St John 20:29.

The gift of faith is our ticket to our blessedness and salvation if we work for it. I am amazed at some unbelievers who said that if only God show Himself and talk to me then I believe. Exactly what Thomas said. But we gathered here have the faith and all we need now is to work with trembling for our salvation. Below are the list of hindrances to our spiritual life and if we do not work hard in getting them, we are certainly at risk of losing our soul.

The love of money. Scripture warns us that money is the root of evil. But we all need money for this is the world's way in exchange for the goods and things we need and want. Thus, it is our resolution to use money for the greater good of society and most importantly for God's greater honor and glory. Therefore, if you desire only your needs and not your wants, money should not be a concerned. Unless of course one could not define need and want. Like the economist said, financial hardship and difficulties were the result of our excessive wants for if we only seek what are our needs then most of us will be free from the financial burden that causes a lot of problems to families all over the world. Our wants is the result from our slavery to covetousness.

The love of honor and fame. We have inherited the curse of pride. Enslaved by our wretchedness and lowliness, we instinctively wants to rise above it. In our external life, we saw how the rich and famous smiled and swayed others of how great their lives were. Thus, seeing their lifestyle corrupted the truth of life. Everybody are drawn to such life that almost everyone will do what they can to make themselves like them. O you can see everybody aspire to be a rock star, a movie star, an entrepreneur, a politician or whatever makes one famous and known. This is our lot. This is pride working in us and the world without the assistance of the devil indeed is doing a great job in deceiving most of us to love what is in the world.

The love of pleasure. We want to see the most beautiful sight in the world. We want to eat the most delicious food. We love to drink alcohol to make us feel good and as drugs makes us high. We love to feel good and will do anything so we can taste, feel, see, touch, hear and smell what is pleasant and pleasurable. There is a limit to our physical needs and to seek excessively is a risk to our spiritual life as mentioned before. In moderation is prudence but better is by minimizing what is pleasurable for by doing so your spiritual life will be much stronger.

There are more things in our external life that we ought to be careful with but the three are the most prominent. But as Jesus conquered the world so does those who truly are serious in advancing to the heights of sanctity. We have everything in our disposal to make us like Him and do not fear the enemies of our salvation for with Jesus and Mary we are also conqueror.

Discussion: Discuss what is the class about. (15 minutes)
Closing Prayer:
Hymn: Salve Regina
Our Lady of Unity pray for us, your community.

Fourth Class: (3 hours or less)

Hymn: Sing together, "I am the Resurrection
Opening Prayer

The Interior Life

Leader reads the Scripture Passage:

"The Pharisee stood and prayed thus with himself, God I thank thee, that I am not as other men are, extortioners, unjust, adulterers, or even as this publican. I fast twice in a week, I give tithes of all that I possess. And the publican, standing afar off, would not lift up so much as his eyes unto heaven, but smote upon his breast, saying, God be merciful to me a sinner. I tell you, this man went down to his house justified rather than the other: for everyone that exalteth himself shall be abased; and he that humbleth himself shall be exalted." Luke 18:11-14.

In our religiosity great care and caution should be practiced because there is so much danger with our spiritual pride. It is so easy to get caught up to this deceptive trap since we all have this thing called pride. It is part of our being. We feel good when we are appreciated for being praised for the good things we do. And during our life, we cannot avoid such circumstances and in this class we focus on how we can control those tendencies. By doing so, and by being vigilant in managing our pride will do so much good to our spiritual advancement.

And so, the Pharisee, well respected Jewish group known to practice perfectly the oral and the written laws saw in himself that there is no one can come close to what he had done by his religious observance of the law unlike those who are with him in the temple who have a way of life that is below his standard. In his mind, seeing some people he knew, immediately passed judgement on them. How easily indeed we are deceived that because we did something good that we put ourselves in the pedestal and there the danger comes. Once we think that we are better than the others surely displeases God. This will be the area as chosen member of our Lady of Unity's community to guard such thoughts and cultivate the virtue that is so pleasing to our Lord, the virtue of humility. Always think of the others better than you and always be ready to serve everyone that truly is in need of your help. By doing both you served God and neighbor.

Thus, anyone that exalts himself will be humbled and those who humbled himself will be exalted. And to be exalted in the eyes of God and to be truly humble is nothing more than to be of service to anyone who needed you.

In the last class, we discuss our external life and our tendency to judge quickly to the things we saw and how quickly we are drawn to the rich and the famous because of their glamor and attraction victimizing most of us into the wrong path leading to our destruction. On the other side of the coin, nobody cares or even looked at the beggar with torn and smelly clothes even condemning them as worthless and useless. Such is and will be our reaction in the external life.

Therefore, the rich and famous are looked up in the external life while the Pharisee is looked up in the spiritual life or the interior life. And the beggar on the street was being looked down much like the publican was being looked down. But in the eyes of God, it is the lowly and the humble of heart that truly pleases Him. As member of our Lady's Order, it is our primary duty and responsibility to focus on the virtue of humility. There is no room for pride and arrogance either in our exterior and interior life. In our prayers keep asking for the virtue of humility and meekness and if pride and arrogance overcome our weak and fragile being which will happen most of the time, do not ever get discouraged nor dismayed for by doing so, the sin of pride had grown in your interior and funny how the devil himself kept telling you that it is impossible to conquer pride. The devil may even kept pounding on our soul (interior) that if he who is pure spirit and with power could not get rid of pride, what more us weak and powerless. But Jesus will always come to our assistance specially in times of temptations and troubles and that is why He gave us the Bible so we can deal how to fight all the enemies of our salvation. When pride and arrogance overwhelms us, remind how the publican prayed:

"And the publican, standing afar off, would not lift up so much as his eyes unto heaven, but smote upon his breast, saying, God be merciful to me a sinner." Luke 18:13.

And our Lord by the publican's act of humility was justified from his sins. When we do the same thing, our sins of pride and arrogance will also be justified.

David, whose heart was like God but fell victimized by the sin of sloth, lust and murder did not get discouraged and dismayed when he realized the gravity and enormity of his sins that he had greatly offended God whom he loves very much quickly fell on his knees and prayed.

"Have mercy on me, God, in your kindness. In your compassion blot out my offense. O wash me more and more from my guilt and cleanse me from my sin. My offenses truly I know them; my sin is always before me. Against you, you alone, have I sinned; what is evil in your sight I have done. That you may be justified when you give sentence and be without reproach when you judge. O see, in guilt I was born, a sinner was I conceived. Indeed you love truth in the heart; then in the secret of my heart teach me wisdom. O purify me, then I shall be clean; O wash me, I shall be whiter than snow." Psalm 51.

This is the greatest and most powerful prayer of confessing one's sin and the Catholic church officially included this Psalm prayer of David in the Liturgy of the hours prayed every Friday as She call and cried out to His Spouse seeking pardon and mercy for all Her members transgression and offenses. For us who strive for holiness and perfection we should pray Psalm 51 when we failed our Lord. Why would God allowed David who was faithful and obedient to Him commit those horrific sin if his heart was like God? This is for all of us to learn that however faithful and devoted one to God there is no guarantee that sin would not corrupt the heart and weakened the soul. This is also a warning for us never trust ourselves. That is why in our formation program we should keep in our mind and heart to keep our soul safe by our strict obedience to the community's rule and to work out our salvation with fear and trembling. As we will continue to struggle with both our external and interior life, we should never lost hope, nor discourage from our frailties and failures because we have God always working and helping us in our journey. Paul, the greatest apostle and teacher of the Christian faith also encourage us by not giving up. He himself struggled with his own infirmities that he could never get rid off even with pleading to Jesus three times. Who knows what was his thorn. Thorns are in each one of us and do not be surprised that we will struggle till our last breathe like Paul. Paul became great not because of his works and teaching but what made him a great saint was that he never give up the race in earning the crown. As we focus on our soul or interior self let us imitate what made St. Paul a great saint. When our Lord did not take away his thorn, Paul remembered His instruction and assurance that freed him from the bondage of guilt.

"And he said unto me, My grace is sufficient for thee: for my strength is made perfect in weakness. Most gladly therefore will I rather glory in my infirmities, that the power of Christ may rest upon me." II Corinthians 12:9.

It was the word grace that made Paul understood that we should never rely on ourselves even though how good things are going. Nor we should be proud of what we have accomplished specially if we are laboring in our Lord's vineyard. What great good we have done is not accomplished without the grace of God. He also understood that his thorn was not taken away from him to remind himself not to be proud and arrogant. Spiritual gifts can make most of us very proud and there is so much danger in our interior life. Paul was mystically taken to heaven and there Jesus revealed to him His sublime teachings and he did shared to us. There are many instances that when someone experience some mystical phenomena he or she could not stop bubbling about the experience. Some even proclaimed they have seen Jesus and most notably they claimed that the Blessed Virgin appeared to them. We all are subject to delusion and that is the main reason why the Catholic church will never believe those numerous claims of visions and apparitions. Back to Paul's experience, he understood that it was God's grace that his thorns remain in him so he will not fall into the spiritual pride trappings. Paul's thorn remind him to never be proud never to boast of himself but only to boast in the Lord. Only and specifically to boast on the Crucified Lord. This is part of our being this thing pride which lead most of us to sin. But as member of Our Lady's Order we must always be vigilant in suppressing pride at all cost. But if this weakness remain in us, then remember it is God's grace that the thorns we have is for our own good and sanctification. When we experience this, we simply follow the example of Paul. By humbly accepting it and by doing so we did the perfect will of God.

Pause and for 20 minutes discuss the issue of humility. Why is it that pride leads to all kinds of sin? Pride made Adam and Eve disobeyed God, in what way. Lucifer's pride caused his eviction from heaven, in what way. Is the publican's humility more admirable than Paul's? How so. David was truly a humble servant. Was pride the cause of his sins?

After the 25 minutes discussion pray:

Heavenly Father, the curses of sin is too heavy for us to bear. We remain stiff neck and our hearts remains cold and harden. The sins of our fathers are our inheritance and our thorns remains in our soul. We give thanks to you always that You give us Jesus Your Son to be our companion in bearing the just punishment of our transgression. By His wounds we were healed and by our baptism we became a part of You. We give thanks to You always for the establishment of Your Church for all the sacraments that shield us from all our enemies. We praise and adore You for giving us the mother of salvation, Our Lady of Unity who will never leave us until we reached into the presence of Your august majesty and glory. O Holy Mother of God, pray for us sinners and at the hour of our death and judgement be there for us pleading for our salvation. Praise, glory and honor to the Holy Trinity now and for eternity. Amen.

Our Father, Hail Mary and Glory Be.
Our Lady of Unity pray for us members of your community.

Leader Continue Reading, The Interior Life.

What is our interior life? As our external can easily be judge, our interior life will be impossible to judge since we can not see the innermost being of a person. Such cliche, never judge a book by its cover holds true in our interior life. Although our visible action and deeds can be seen by everyone, the components of our inner self tells a very different story. For example, we go to church and others saw our piety when we pray and how our behavior and action deserves praise but inside can only be known by God. In the outside, God is pleased by its action but inside could reveal something despicable and displeasing to Him.

What are our innermost being? Interiorly, we are talking about what is in our heart. The heart is the foundation of our interior and exterior life. In the heart is full of desire that if activated can become a positive or negative influence in our spiritual life. As we know, the worldly have an appetite that can never be satisfied. For example, the love for money, one can never be satisfied even though they have more than enough to live on. Because of their strong desire to have more, they could not tell when is enough. For example, as we have seen on the very wealthy that the millionaires are not satisfied with their millions knowing that they have friends and relatives who are also millionaires and in order not to be outdone they strive to make more by doubling their efforts to make even more money. And when they became billionaires, still they knew that there are more billionaires and to keep up with the flow they strive even harder so they can make more money. What they accomplished was nothing else but the accumulation of great wealth but at the cost of neglecting what is the most important, time with family and loved ones but perhaps at the cost of losing God for eternity. As we were warned, what does it profit if we gain the whole world and lose our soul. Or it is much easier for a camel to enter through an eye of a needle than a rich man into heaven. Therefore where your heart is your treasure. Thus, we have to extremely guard what are the desires of our heart and the love of money was the result of covetousness and it was included in the great Ten Commandments of God. Thou shalt not covet thy neighbor's goods. The millionaires desire to become a billionaire was influenced by other billionaires. Thou shalt not steal. By spending all his time and energy, he stole from God that precious time and energy that could have been used in serving God. Thou shalt love God with all your heart, mind, body and soul was another offense to be charged for loving money more than God. Indeed, greed, avarice are categorized as deadly sins. And when the sin is deadly, what will become of our soul?

Break 10 minutes.
After the break, together sing the hymn: Immaculate Mary.
20 minutes discussion about our interior life.

If the heart is the foundation of our external and internal life, what should we do to avoid being drawn away from our desire to advance in our spiritual life? In Sacred Scripture, there was a scene. A very wealthy young man wanted to follow Jesus and he asked Him.

"And, behold, one came and said unto Him, Good Master, what good thing shall I do, that I may have eternal life?" Matthew 19:16.

Remember what our Lord said for it is so applicable to our own lives specially in our world where the goal are world treasure and pleasure.

"And he said unto him, why callest thou me good? there is none good but one, that is, God: but if thou wilt enter into life, keep the commandments." Matthew 19:17.

Observe the humility of Jesus that although He is God in the Second Persona, His humanity though perfect can not be called good since all of humanity (His Church) had not yet been justified by His death on the cross. He not only humbled Himself but also us and giving God greater glory that God alone is good. Remember if we want salvation, remember the Ten Commandments to obey them all. All of it not nine. Perfection.

"The young man saith unto Him, all these things have I kept from my youth up: what lack I yet?" Matthew 19:20.

This is a very admirable young man who wants to follow our Lord and he was perfect by doing all the Ten Commandments. Did he?

"Jesus said unto him, If thou wilt be perfect, go and sell that thou hast, and give to the poor, and thou shalt have treasure in heaven: and come and follow me." Matthew 19:21.

Observe the demands if one truly wants to follow Jesus. The young man claimed he did by obeying all of God's commandments but something was exposed that in reality and in truth the young man lied because he broke a few of His commandments.

Thou shalt love God with all your heart, mind, body and soul and the young rich man lied that he did. Jesus knew he lied because He saw in the young man's heart that material wealth was his greatest love. Thou shalt not covet thy neighbors goods. Did he also broke this command since he possessed abundance and he failed to share to the less needy. He also broke, Thou shalt not steal for the riches he had belongs to God and by not sharing this to the less fortunate he stole something from God Himself. Thus, Jesus exposed that this young wealthy man had the desire to follow Him but his love for his wealth failed him.

"But when the young man heard that saying, he went away sorrowful: for he had great possessions." Matthew 19:22.

Remember the billionaire who spurned God that he did not exist? It was his attachment and his great love for his money that there is no way he could follow God in His perfect teachings.

"Then said Jesus unto his disciples, Verily I say unto you, that a rich man shall hardly enter into the kingdom of heaven. And again I say unto you, It is easier for a camel to go through the eye of a needle, then for a rich man to enter into the kingdom of God." Matthew 19:23-24.

This is clearly the greatest spiritual direction we could ever have. It is not at all really wealth that prevents us to follow our Lord but it could be attachment for pleasure, etc. Clearly, our love is for God alone and when we do we fulfilled also His second greatest commandment.

If we truly prove our love for God then we must work very hard and diligently by doing a heart to heart constant checkup so to speak to see what is truly our love. Is it money? fame? love? praise? etc? Is there a place for God in our heart? If so, is He first, second, third or last? When you go home before you go to bed or whenever you have time please do spent at least 10 minutes and have a heart to heart check up as to who do you love the most, etc.

And if you find that God is not first then rejoice because so very few truly put God as number one. O yes casually we heard so many said that God is their number one but words does not count at all. The love for God can only be measured by how our soul is in the eyes of God. The soul receives what the heart desired. These two entities are the very most important elements of our interior life. The heart and the soul influences our eternal destiny. Of course, we have discussed and knew what is our heart. But it is the soul who will be responsible from what the heart feeds. Let us discuss the soul since it is the greatest treasure we have and also this is the greatest part of the interior life that God gave us.

What is a soul then? A soul is an eternal entity residing in a living person and is responsible for all the physical decisions that can result in either a positive or negative action. Most of us cannot accurately define the human soul. Some think that both the soul and the spirit are the same. They are not. Although both the soul and the spirit live forever, they are distinct from each other.

There are three faculties within the soul: namely the memory, the understanding or intellect and the will and they work as a team in providing our physical being the motivating force in all our actions. Let us observe how the soul influences our decisions and actions with a simple analogy. A destitute beggar, shivering on a winter night, stumbles upon a leather wallet containing two thousand dollars. This beggar, who has not eaten the whole day, is starving and was very excited with his find. Let us carefully follow how our soul operates. The first faculty of the soul is memory, reminding the beggar that the money he found will supply many of his needs and even wants. At this very moment, he could buy all the food he needed to satisfy his hunger. Simultaneously, the second faculty of the soul, which is understanding, drives the beggar to make two immediate choices. He could either keep the money or return it to the owner. The third faculty of the soul is the will, the strongest force that will decide which action to take in collaboration with the other faculties. Therefore, the will of a particular person exposes the condition of his soul. If the beggar chooses to find the owner of the wallet and return all the money on it, then the condition of his soul is considered beautiful because despite his hardships, he opted to make the perfect choice. The beggar's action is a heroic one. In the eyes of God, the soul of this beggar is very precious because what he did was a reflection of His Divine character. Despite his outward or exterior appearance the soul of this beggar sparkled like the biggest and brightest diamond on earth. This is how the human soul works. God is constantly testing our soul every moment of our lives and how we respond to such tests determines wether we are a precious stone or a file of filth.

In conclusion, let us constantly guard first our hearts and its desires and knowing the mechanics of our soul, we should be prudent and careful what choice we should make making sure that what we chose conforms to God's will.

Fifteen minutes discussion about the soul.
Closing Prayer;
Sing together the Hymn, Salve Regina.
Our Lady of Unity pray for us, your community.

Fifth Class: (3 hours or less)

Hymn: Together Sing, Hymn, "Hail Mary"
Opening Prayer

Introducing Our Lady

Leader reads the Scripture Passage:

"And the Word was made flesh, and dwelt among us, (And we beheld his glory as of the only begotten of the Father) Full of grace and truth." 1John1:14

Leader read pages 31 and 32 of the book, "OUR LADY OF UNITY"

After the leader done reading the community silently spent about five minutes slowly reading again pages 31 to 32. After reading, leader discuss pages 31 to 32. Spent 20 minutes discussing what was read.

Why is it that there are billions have no idea how powerful is Our Lady's intercession to the Triune God?

Share to the community how our Lady and mother did help in your life?

Why it is so necessary and essential that our Lady must be pure, perfect and holy?

Of all God's servants our Blessed Virgin Mary did performed thousands and thousands of miracles and apparitions. Name what miracles and apparitions you knew and discuss the purpose and the message. Share your thoughts and opinions.

Why is it that the Muslims revere and honor Mary than our Protestant brothers?

After discussion, leader reads the Scripture passages to the community:

"And the angel answered and said unto her, the Holy Ghost shall come upon thee, therefore, also that holy thing which shall be born to thee shall be called Son of God." Luke 1:35.

Leader reads pages 21 paragraph 6, to 22, 23 and 24.(From the book "OUR LADY OF UNITY) Leader can assign a member to help read vocally. After the vocal reading spent another 10 minutes slowly and silently reading the same pages.

After the silent reading and meditation discuss what was read. Share whatever your thoughts and opinions. Spent at least 25 minutes.

After discussion 10 minutes break.

After the break, together community sings, "Hail Holy Queen."

Leader reads pages 79, 80, 81, 82, 83 and 85 from the book, OUR LADY OF UNITY. Since it is a long reading do take turns so members of the community can participate.

After the vocal reading, community in total silence spent 5 minutes and try to recollect what was read. In your spare time, again read Chapter Twelve of our book, Our Lady of Unity.

Closing Prayer:
Sing together, Hymn, "Salve Regina"
Our Lady of Unity pray for us, your community. Amen.

Sixth Class: (3 hours or less)

Hymn: Together sing, "How Great Art Thou"
Opening Prayer:

Introducing The Saints

Leader reads the Scripture Passage:

"There are they which were not defiled with women; for they are virgins. These are they which follow the Lamb wither ever he goeth. These were redeemed from among men being the first fruit unto God and to the Lamb." Revelation 14:4.

Those who had completed their life's journey and were received in the new heaven crowned with God's glory and honor are called saints. To repeat, the journey to heaven is very demanding and very difficult for us for we are only human burdened with all kinds of weaknesses, struggles, obstacles and worst we are enslaved by our sinful flesh, drawn passionately to the world and deceived by the devil and that is why Our Lady revealed that each day tens of thousands of souls are in hell and there is no improvement at all because we do not set our sight into the eternal life for we are so consumed and we are so concerned with our earthly life as we discussed in the external life. Even the coming of our Lord even with the intercession of our Blessed Virgin Mary and even with the establishment of God's powerful and invincible church, still, not very many answered the call for holiness and perfection. Most of us think of heaven as so far from reality and we forget that we are mortal that any moment in our existence death will claim any of us. Death has no prejudice and she will take any age, any position or simply anybody as she pleased. Thus, when we are not prepared for that terrifying moment the fear of the unknown makes many so anxious that there is no time to say:

"Jesus, remember me when you are in your kingdom."
Or.
"Lord into your hands I commend my spirit."
Or.
"Lord, have mercy on me a sinner and save me from my sins."

When you are facing death, you are in the most horrifying and most terrifying moment that never was experience in your lifetime. The finality of our existence will make any strongest and most powerful of men shook and sweat with the greatest fear that you forget anything. How could anyone think of God and calling and crying out for His mercy when while in good health and strength you never think of Him. With all His blessings and graces, you never give thanks and praise for all the great and marvelous things God had done for us. You do not have any time for Him. If God is not part or center of your life then I guarantee you that you have only avery very small chance of salvation. The saving power of God can save anyone anytime just like the thief on the cross who live his life godless. But, we can not simply just assume that we too can be save just like the thief on the cross. Scripture recorded that scene to remind us the greatness of God's mercy and the greatness of Our Lady's intercessory power. How? Remember at the wedding at Cana how our Lady is always involved in assisting us in our needs. When they were out of wine, she merely hinted to her Son that they needed wine and Jesus even though not his time to perform any miracle did complied. What more when the salvation of soul is involved and indeed our Lady at the foot of the cross did interceded knowing that these two criminals are entrusted to her as her very own children. While filled with sorrow and pain seeing His Crucified Child in agony, she could not just stand doing nothing for her other afflicted children on the brink of losing their soul for eternity. By the inspiration of her Beloved Spouse, the Holy Spirit our Lady of Sorrows pleaded for the salvation of the two thieves.

She was not able to save the other one because of his obstinacy by refusing to follow the lead of the good thief. It was the mother of God that obtain the graces that the good thief was enlightened by the Holy Spirit to call and acknowledge the Savior. The other thief witnessed what was going on but instead chose not to call on our Lord's Name for mercy.

This also showed us why tens of thousands of souls are lost daily. Even with all the promises of our Lord that in His kingdom there are no more tears, pains, afflictions, sadness, wars, diseases, miseries, troubles and all kinds of evils still we insist to follow what is in the world. Even with the promises of eternal joy and happiness and even to reign with God in His splendor, glory and majesty, still, we prefer to seek after the things of this world. If we do not value God then we do not value heaven either. But while we are still alive with all our strength and with all our dreams to have the best in life God was never been prioritized nor or be the center of our lives. O yes everybody loves to go to heaven. O yes we do know and love God but only minimally. We prefer to invest more heavily in the world than the things of God.

In our weakness and blindness we have the wrong notion that once we die we go to heaven and be with God prompting us to live our lives fully in the world enjoying everything offered. By wrongly and blindly embracing such erroneous notion we are putting ourselves in the greatest risk in losing God and heaven for all eternity. By adopting such blind notion in our lives and when we are suddenly confronted to face dreadful death, it would be very difficult for us to remember God since we are not in communion with Him for we were consumed on the lesser and worthless things of the world. The worst scenario for any unprepared or unrepentant soul is that of sudden death. For example, heart attacks, stroke, accidents where death comes like a thief in the night stealing our precious life not expecting such tragedy will come. And when this happens there is no way that you can call or say to our Lord to remember you or mercy on you or commending your soul to Him. Heaven for souls will be lost for eternal damnation for they have lived their lives without God. Logically, our Lady's message that tens of thousands of souls are lost each day makes sense because of our gross negligence to our spiritual life. Our lack of communion to God happens when one neglect to pray and to remember that He is in our midst patiently and lovingly waiting for us to open the door and inviting Him to enter and possess our heart and soul.

On other hand, those who live their lives in constant communion with God need not worry if sudden death happens for they are prepared to face Him with that peaceful confidence graced by their faithfulness in living their lives in the presence of God. Of course, death is always scary simply because we are merely humans and very weak unable to conquer the fear on the unknown. But the main concern is our readiness and preparedness in facing our judgement before the presence of God's justice. To the unprepared and the ungodly once they are in God's presence they simply disappeared from His sight fleeing feebly unable to face the One whom they owed much. They could not face God and even before they hear their judgment one already knew what will be. Thus, it was not really God that sent someone to hell contrary to what theologians believed from Scriptures:

"Depart from me you workers of inequity."

Before they even face their judgment the damned souls knew they have to depart away from Him because in their lives they have already departed from God.

"Depart from me for I do not know you"

The soul of the damn will not go to Him because they too does not know Him.

On the other side, "Well done you who are blest inherit the kingdom that is prepared for you."

Those who are prepared and ready for God will be eager to run to their Maker for they have in their lifetime have waited for such moment when they are now truly in His Presence. They have been faithful and true to their God always obeying His will and never strayed away from Him. Even though how many times they have fallen or failed to live that holy and perfect life they deserved to be with God because they never quit and they never get discouraged with their failures and shortcomings. They have won God because they never give up in seeking, reaching, calling and crying out to Him for his merciful love. By never quitting on God, He who never quits on us rewarded them for their fortitude and holy perseverance. This is the virtue that makes saints. This is our goal as member of our Lady's Order. Fortitude, faithfulness and holy final perseverance meaning to say until our last breathe God will be ours. We want to join the community of our Lady because we want to be prepared and always ready for the Lord when He calls our name. With the help of His grace and with our Lady's most powerful intercession and with our own will, TO BECOME A SAINT AT ALL COST.

After the reading, discuss the following topics: 30 minutes of time.

How strong is your faith that our Lady will be our strongest intercessor at the hour of our death? Do you believe that she can make a great difference in pleading for our salvation?

How about the saints? Do you believe that they too can pray for you? Discuss why most of us think that only those chosen by God will become a saint? Do the religious have a better chance of becoming a saint than the non religious? Explain and discuss.

After discussion take 10 minutes break.
After the break, pray:

"Hail holy mother of God, mother of sorrows, pray for us exiled children of God by obtaining for us the grace of holy final perseverance. As you have dealt with all kinds of sorrows and afflictions keep us always in your maternal care and protection and pray for us to obtain the virtue of patience, endurance and strength to keep on going to our heavenly destination. Stay beside on your helpless and vulnerable children weakened and discouraged by our sinfulness and blindness and obtain for us His graces that we may join all the saints in heaven there to praise and worship the Blessed Trinity and to thank you for being our mother. Amen.

Our Father, Hail Mary and Glory Be.
Our Lady of Unity pray for us, your community.

Introducing The Saints: Continue.

God and heaven saints lived for. They are our inspiration and as member of our Lady's religious Order this too will be our goal. To become a saint. Do not mind those whose thinking that only the chosen ones will become saints. Such excuse is so pathetic and even demonic discouraging others not to try. We have been commanded to be holy and perfect like Him because our good and loving God wants everyone of us to become a saint. It is a foolish theology that only those who are chosen will become a saint.

"For God so loved the world, that he gave his only begotten Son, that whosoever believeth in him should not perish, but to have everlasting life." John 3:16.

It is so clear that everyone of us is called to become a saint. He wants not one nor His chosen ones but for everyone who is in the world and that includes us without exception. Whoever says that only the chosen ones deserves to be judge severely for such sacred scandal.

"For God sent not His Son into the world to condemn the world; but that the world through Him might be saved." John 3:17.

Further emphasis that God wants everyone be saved meaning to say that He wants all of us to be saints. That is why He gave us the Ten Commandments, Holy Mother Church and our Blessed Virgin Mary and even His Presence in our world so we can become a saint. But in reality why so very few became saints was that so very few responded to God's calling to be holy and perfect. They thought that only God can become holy and perfect but those message of holiness and perfection were simply misunderstood what our Lord truly meant. What that meant was, because we are truly unholy and very imperfect and defective Jesus wants us to set a new standard way above our condition because by doing so He Himself will be the One to assist us in all our necessities and by His Spirit working unceasingly in our behalf we will be able to live a new life above our unholiness, our imperfections, our defects and even our sinfulness. What God wants from us is our sincere respond and our sincere effort to give our very best trying for holiness and perfection. Even if we cannot become holy and perfect what matters to God is our respond to such lofty calling. Just say yes and the rest God will do for you so you will become holy and perfect. All Mary had to do was say yes and she became the greatest of all saints. Saints became saints by simply saying always yes to God but our greatest problem was our difficulties in saying yes to Him. O yes, we do say yes to Him but occasionally and that is not very pleasing nor acceptable to His standard which is perfect love and perfect obedience.

Class Discussion about becoming a saint. 30 minutes discussion.

Do you accept the idea that only those who are chosen will become a saint? Are the souls in purgatory saints? Discuss the idea why did the Catholic church established the "Devil's Advocate". Why it is so necessary that before one will be considered candidate for sainthood must produced a miracle in their behalf. Why do saints suffer?

After discussion leader continue by reading.

Why do saints suffer?

Those who answered the call for perfection and holiness suffered more than those who prefer a worldly life. Those who lives in the world suffered less because they make sure that the demand of their flesh be fulfilled and satisfied. When you seek the things of the world one will try to find the greatest pleasure in satisfying themselves. Thus, fornication is very rampant. Pornography had become the most lucrative business because the demand for sexual satisfaction went through the roof. Our lust never stops in inciting us to seek what is so pleasurable that society are flooded with all kinds of seductions from movies, television and even in commercials. Our appetite for delicious food have made us so gluttonous making our bodies susceptible to laziness and illness. The worldly lives fully in the flesh thus they suffered less because they immediately respond to the needs and wants of their sinful flesh.

The saints who won their crown in heaven lives not in the flesh knowing that those who does are in enmity with God as Paul warns us for the flesh is warring against the spirit and the spirit is warring against the flesh. The saints suffer because they do not give in to the wants, the demands and desires of their flesh fearful that its corruptibility also corrupts their immortal treasure which is their precious soul.

Let us give an example why St. Francis of Assisi was so beloved by our Blessed Virgin Mary that of all the great saints of God Francis was the one who closely resembled her Son Jesus. St. Francis was well known for his severe fasting and penances that affected his health contributing to his early death. Was he chosen? Of course, simply He responded just took that greatest opportunity in changing the direction of his life just like you and me. Repeating again that one become a chosen one by simply responding to that call of holiness and perfection. Saint Francis was just like us son of a wealthy merchant and his father groomed him to follow in his footsteps but God had another plan greater than his life. He was chosen to rebuilt the church which was in shambles. When Francis was called he immediately rejected his father's plan that he even return the clothes he wore and they thought that he had got mad. He declared that he had only one Father and that is God. By abandoning everything Francis became a beggar. Then, Francis heard a voice telling him to rebuilt the church. At that time, the Catholic church had lost its luster because the chair of Peter was corrupted and with the Protestant revolt many abandoned the true church. Obeying the call, Francis saw an abandon broken old church at San Damiano and with his bare hands he slowly tried to fix it. And with the help of God's grace some of his friends were drawn to join him and they did finished in rebuilding the old broken church. But God wanted greater things from Francis and that was the formation of the Franciscan Order. He went to Rome, to ask the Pope's permission and blessings to established his community, dressed in their beggarly manner while in the presence of the pompous assembly in their most expensive attire and expensive jewelries, the Pope was humbled and knelt before Francis recognizing the presence of Jesus in him asking pardon for their failures in administering the Papal Office.

Once Francis received the approval and blessings, Francis religious order attracted many followers all over the world and even now, the Franciscan Order is one of the most active religious Order of the Catholic church and they still follow the rules established by St. Francis. The lived in poverty, chastity and obedience and St. Francis never failed in interceding for his Order because so many great saints were member of his religious order. Here are a few famous and powerful Franciscan saints, St. Anthony of Padua, St. Bonaventure, St. Joseph of Cupertino, St. Clare and hundreds more belonging to this blessed religious order. This is indeed an indication that members of religious orders have the advantages over the others simply because their community members are united as one powerful voice in obtaining sanctification of their members. As St. Theresa of Avila taught to members of her community that it is much easier to become a saint by just simply obeying the rules of the community. No need to go all over the world and preached the gospel or become a great missionary or to become a martyr to become a saint but by simply obedience to the rule of the community. Thus St. Therese the little flower become a great saint because she was always obedient to the rule of Carmel by doing the little simple things with great love. She became a doctor of the church and patron saints of missionaries and St. Therese was secluded in the Carmelite convent doing nothing much but obedience to the rule of the community.

The Catholic church produced hundreds of thousands of saints, some were great and famous, some were unknown but they represent every segment of the church population. No church nor any religion can compare to what the Catholic church did in forming, nurturing, guiding and bringing saints to their heavenly home simply because this is the one true church that belongs to Christ. It is not surprising why the Catholic church is God's factory in producing saints in every season and time in our history.

Discussion 30 minutes:

Each member chose their favorite saints and share to the community why? St. Francis, St. Dominic, St. Theresa, St. John of the Cross, St. Augustine and St. Francis Xavier are famous and great saints. What have they in common?

Community Assignment: Read the book, "Lives of the Saints."
Closing Prayer:
Together sing, Hymn, Salve Regina
Our Lady of Unity pray for us, your community. Amen.

Seventh Class: (3 hours or less)

Hymn: Together Sing Hymn, "How Great Thou Art"
Opening Prayer:

Knowing The Father

Leader reads the Scripture Passage:

"And God said, Let us make man in our image, after our likeness: and let them have dominion over the fish of the sea, and over the fowl of the air, and over the cattle, and over all the earth, and over every creeping thing that creepeth upon the earth." Genesis 1:26.

God revealed to His chosen people how creation started. Why did He created us? Adam who was created first could not fathom why. We are more blest for knowing why we are created through the revelation coming from the Word made flesh. But to Adam, he is like a child so innocent that he have no idea at all why he existed. Reading the Old Testament, in Genesis, with all the abundance in the garden of Eden, Adam was not completely happy and knowing the source of his unhappiness, God took a part of him, Adam's rib and made a woman. Eve became Adam's helper and with her companionship improved his condition making him more happier. At that time, Adam had no idea that Eve came from his own body destined to live for eternity free from pain, illness, diseases, fatigued and sorrows. In paradise, all was comfort and ease. It was the perfect place of retirement that we all are seeking. We could have this kind of life for all of eternity had they did not disobeyed God. Instead, we inherited the curse of sin and the world became a place of our exile. What caused their disobedience?

"Now the serpent was more subtil than any beast of the field which the Lord God had made. And he said unto the woman, Yea, hath God said, Ye shall not eat of every tree of the garden?" Genesis 3:1.

Since then, Satan is always present in our midst always staying close to us watching and looking for that small opening so he can enter into our soul inspiring us in doing something that will lead us to our destruction much the same way that happened in the garden of Eden. In our days of technological advances, Satan rejoices knowing the rapid progress we gain had captivated us into the period where our thinking and style of living were affected threatening to erase what was in the past. For example, new survey discovered that most of this new generation hooked on electronics does not believe in the existence of the devil. Those thinking about the devil's existence were on the dark ages where ignorance and superstition were rampant which is great news to the devil. As much as we had advance in all fields, sad to say that such advancement did affected our spiritual life. Latest survey indicates that religiosity had taken a nose dive compared twenty years ago. Most responder laughed when the existence of Satan was mentioned.

Such survey surely made the devil more happy knowing he will have an abundant harvest of soul that will accompany him to hell. This is also a major concern that our Lady is calling and drawing more to her community so more prayers, penances and sacrifices are needed for the conversion and salvation of soul. The progressive society had more time for leisure and more resources in their hands that they are more independent and when this happens they rely on themselves and God is not needed in their lives. The devil indeed rejoices of our great and amazing progress since our desire for God had waned or had gone. But truly like on the old times, Satan had not changed and he existed because he is immortal. And he will do everything in his power so we will become victims like our first parents.

"And the serpent said unto the woman, Ye shall not surely die." Genesis 3:4.

Even though Eve knew that God warned them not to eat the fruit of the tree that was in the middle of the garden because if they do they will surely die. Who did Eve listen and believe?

The greatest deceiver and liar, Satan. Just like on the old days, we do not like to listen to the preachings of God's truth. O yes, during Sundays, we do gathered together and heard the Gospel of truth preached but after attending Holy Mass and religious services we go on living the way that is comfortable and easy weakening our feeble will. We go to our passion and that is to live in the world and enjoy what is in the world. Even Satan himself applauded our efforts in going to Sunday religious services and activities knowing that most of us even though we have ears what was preached and what was taught will not penetrate into our hearts, mind and soul much like God's command to Adam and Eve also did not entered into their mind, heart and soul resulting in destruction. Satan knew we are easy prey just like our mother, Eve. O how we easily listen to the things that are far from the truth. We love to listen what is going on in the world. What is going on with our friends and relatives. Just observed how the social media made themselves a fortune because we prefer to know what is going on the world and our fellow citizens spending too much time on things that really does no good to our spiritual growth and advancement. Truly and really we rather listen to what the world, the flesh and the devil tells us to do rather than listen to God who is the truth.

"And unto Adam he said, Because thou hast hearkened unto the voice of thy wife, and hast eaten of the tree, of which I commanded thee, saying, Thou shall not eat of it: cursed is the ground for thy sake; in sorrow shalt thou eat of it all the days of thy life; Thorns also and thistles shall it bring forth to thee; and thou shalt eat the herb of the field; In the sweat of thy face shalt thou eat bread, till thou return unto the ground; for out of it wast thou taken; for dust thou art, and unto dust shalt thou return." Genesis 3:17-19.

Clearly, the evidence is presented here that even Adam who talk and walk with God chose to listen to his wife Eve instead of listening to what God had commanded them. "Do not eat the fruit of the forbidden tree". Both did clearly heard what God said and His voice was real and instead of listening and obeying Him like our first parents we too prefer to listen and obey those who are lesser than God. Such disobedience became our curse and obviously we too have the tendency not to listen to our good and loving God. Therefore, what our Lady revealed in Her community that tens of thousands of souls are lost everyday make sense because the Word of God had fallen into deaf ears. We have unjustly and ungratefully mistreated our God who only wants our highest and greatest good. By not listening to His Command, Adam and Eve were evicted from God's garden where they could never enter for His angels closed the gate of paradise where they became a wandering sheep knowing not where they are heading but worst of all they have lost their God who gave them the best of everything and such punishment was too much for them to bear. We too, if we follow their lead in choosing not to hear or listen nor obey His Commandments we will in the worst state of our existence. Know that the greatest suffering one will ever experience is losing the good and loving God.

"In sorrow shalt thou eat of it all the days of thy life"

And here we are in this life experiencing all kinds of sorrows, sadness, pains and afflictions until the last days of our lives. Instead of the golden platter and silver spoon, we must work hard for our daily bread even sweating to earn our meal. Not only we lost the friendship and closeness of God, we lost our immortality.

"till thou return unto the ground; for out of it wast thou taken; for dust thou art, and unto dust shalt thou return."

Death indeed is the most terrifying and horrifying moment in our life. Notice how we hated to wake up early in the morning and how we wished we could stay in bed forever and we must asked ourselves why then we are so afraid of death when we do not have to wake up anymore but to enjoy that perfect rest where we no longer to suffer in this forsaken world? The answer is the guilt that we carried in our hearts and souls and the penalties due us for all our offenses and crimes against our loving and good God. Because we knew in our consciences that we will have to face His justice and such terrifying thought clearly affected us that when death overcomes us we can no longer avoid God's judgement. Such is the primary reason why we fear death. For in death we can no longer blame others like what our first parents did when they had to be accounted for.

"And the man said, The woman whom thou gavest to be with me, she gave me of the tree, and I did eat." Genesis 3:12.

Like most of us when we failed we blame others instead of taking responsibility. When we do such things we had inherited from Satan the sin of pride. And like Adam, Eve quickly pointed to Satan as the one to blame.

"And the Lord God said unto the woman, What is this thou hast done? And the woman said, The serpent beguiled me, and I did eat." Genesis 3:13.

Again, this was and is will always be our way out from whatever wrongs and evil we are responsible. We tried to wash our hands from our failings and weaknesses that we tried to find a way who and which to blame.

"Why did God allowed this things to happen to good people?"

This is a familiar complain when something bad and tragic happens in our world. Worst, they even blame the good and loving God for all the problems in our world. The truth is, we can only blame ourselves for all what is and what will happen in our world. If you have a good heart and soul and even a conscience then we should seriously asked ourselves why are we acting and behaving like there is no God. We blamed God simply because we do not have God in our lives and when something bad or terrible happens who else to blame but the One who is not in us. But to those who have God in their lives, they took responsibility that they have not done good enough to change themselves and the world. The godly and the godless is like comparing night and day.

After reading community discuss God and His relation with our first parents. (30 minutes)
Discuss the following:

Adam and Eve walk and talk to God like we talk to each other. Such was the fact of their relationship but discuss if Adam and Eve truly and really knew God intimately?

Do both of them knew the reason why God created them?

Did they love God? If they do, explain how. If not, explain why they did not love God.

How often did Adam and Eve prayed to God or how often they did homage to Him by their praises, worship, adoration and thanksgiving.

What is the primary reason why Adam blamed Eve and she blamed the serpent?

In your opinion, had Adam and Eve did not eat that forbidden fruit, we who are their children could have enjoyed paradise forever. Who should we blamed? Adam, Eve, serpent or even our God.?

After 30 minutes of discussion pray:

"Heavenly Father, you created us for Yourself desiring to make us holy and perfect like You so we can be one with You sharing Your splendor, glory, majesty and to reign in Your Eternal Kingdom where peace, joy, love and happiness will be ours forever but something in our being desired not to cooperate Your will. Eternal Father, in the greatness of Your love and mercy grant us the graces to see the vision of what awaits to those who give all their love to You. Give us the power of the Holy Spirit not to be deceived by the false promises of the world, the devil and our very own sinful flesh for without His Presence in our soul we are bound to go astray. Know Lord that we are Your precious people made in Your Holy Image and fill our soul with faith, hope and love and wash us pure by Your Precious Blood shed in Calvary that we be made worthy of the Indwelling of the Holy Spirit. This we humbly pray in the most Holy Name of Jesus Thy Son who lives and reigns with You and the Holy Spirit, forever and ever. Amen.

Our Father, Hail Mary and Glory Be.
Our Lady of Unity pray for us, your community. Amen.

Break 10 minutes.
After Break, sing the Hymn, "Hail Holy Queen"
Leader reads the Scripture Passage again: Take turns reading the text below.

"And God said, let us make man in our image, after our likeness:" Genesis 2:26.

God created us not for His own toy or recreation. We are the works of His own Hands and it was His desire and plan to make us His greatest masterpiece. A masterpiece can never be duplicated or copied for who could produce a created God. God wanted us to be like Him and when it is accomplished His masterpiece came to fruition. How precious indeed are we!!! Imagine you and I could become God's greatest work. Imagine yourself made of dust becoming a part of God!!!

When we looked towards the skies the sun made us think of how its light gave life to the plants and vegetation. If we study the wonders of science then we should learn that everything in our world works in such orderly and efficient manner that such perfect arrangement could not possibly came by accident. There is someone out there with an awesome power and mind that made all things possible as they are now.

At night, we wondered how the moon, the stars and those planets existed. A scientist did came up with his own theory that the Big bang was responsible. Common sense and logic simply override such theory. Normally, when there is a big big explosion the result is always destruction and chaotic. An accident is always an incident that resulted in destroying what was once functional and operational. There is a supreme scientist who designed and arranged everything in our planets and in our solar system. They are not the product of accident or an explosion. To think that way is out of touch to the supreme truth that everything was created by God.

If you and I are masterpieces by God then we are far more awesome that all of the universe, all the things in this world, far more awesome than the angels of heaven. But, we really must asked ourselves if we truly believe that you and I are His masterpieces.

Despite all the religions that existed in our world everybody struggled with this awesome truth. Despite the coming of our Lord Jesus into our dark world we keep struggling that we are truly God's masterpieces. Even our Lord Jesus taught us to pray, "The Our Father" we are not truly convinced that we are really and truly God's children. We are being upgraded by our Lord Jesus from a masterpiece to children and heirs of the Most High. What an awesome revelation that is by our own God Himself. Still we struggled mightily with our human existence in accepting the truth that we are created so we all have the greatest opportunity to become God in God.

As a member of our Lady's religious Order, your first spiritual direction is as follows:

We all struggle with our humanity ever since sin destroyed the innocence and purity of our being. The curse we carry is overwhelming that we are so prune to commit sin instinctively that we are shackled like a slave. In addition, we are surrounded by sin making it more difficult for us to conquer it. However, do not ever lose hope nor ever despair nor ever get discourage because you are fully equip with a memory, understanding and will so you can fight, resist and even conquer sin. In your memory, remember you are not an animal for God had given you His Spirit far more powerful and far more superior than our lowly flesh. It is His Holy Spirit that will make you like Him but He must dwell in you. You have the knowledge that sin is an abomination to God and to sin you become His enemy. Such knowledge should strengthened us not to sin against our good God. Most importantly, we have a will that is as powerful as His Spirit since our own will cannot be controlled by anyone. Even though He is God, he does not interfere nor intervene with what we will unless God ordains something that supersede our will. Even the devil himself cannot intervene nor interfere with our will unless God allowed it such was the case of Job. Therefore, we are so powerful because we have free will and we can do anything and it is up to us to sin or not to sin. It is up to our powerful will wether we chose or reject God. And to become a saint, really, you have that powerful will to accomplish it.

Together pray the prayer below:

"We call and cry out to you Almighty God and Father knowing we are your children in exile and in distress. We have grievously sinned against You, Lord. And in our distress we need your help. For You alone can help and deliver us from our miseries. Forgive us Lord from all our offenses. Purify and cleanse us so we can become truly your children. Our Lord Jesus Christ, savior of our soul we claim your most precious Blood as the purifier and cleanser of our soiled soul. Send forth Your Holy Spirit into our innermost soul so we can have the power, wisdom, courage and understanding to live our new life according to Your will. We pray in Jesus name who lives and reigns with You and the Holy Spirit now and forever. Amen.

Our Father, Hail Mary and Glory Be.
Our Lady of Unity, pray for us, your community. Amen.

After the prayer, leader slowly read God's voice directing the community:

"I created you with my own Hands and I called you by your name. I know all about you and there is no one like you because you are so very special to me. I breathe my Own Life into your nostril and you will live forever like me. You will encounter all kinds of trials and sufferings just like my chosen children who suffered during their journey to the promised land. But your journey to your eternal destiny will be ever more difficult because the reward is far more greater and glorious for you will be with me. Fear not my faithful ones for I am always with you all the way. Simply be true and faithful to me trusting to my promise that I will never abandon my faithful ones."

After the reading spent 3 minutes in silence and meditate and absorb His voice and keep it in your heart and soul.
Discuss the following topics below for 30 minutes:
Discuss why we failed to possess the strongest faith in God?
Discuss why it is so hard and difficult for us to trust God? We heard so many said, trust in God but most of us failed in trusting Him.
Discuss why most of us cannot really believe that we are truly children of God?
Latest survey that most of us believe in God but why is it that our spiritual life has been deteriorating rapidly?
Most brilliant scientist and academias are not drawn to the spiritual life and to them God seems non existence. Discuss the possible reasons why brilliant minds and thinkers are not serious about God.
Why is it that it is very difficult for us to give God everything when He practically give us His All?
Share yourself to the community how much can you give Him?

After discussion, break 10 minutes.
After the break leader reads the Scripture Passage:

"The earth also was corrupt before God, and the earth was filled with violence." Genesis 6:11.

Nothing had changed as our very own time resembled that time when God's anger was ready to explode. He could not tolerate watching His creation living and acting worst that the beast He created. God was so enraged that they have forgotten that they belong to Him and that His desire was only for their greatest and highest good and now He must decide what to do with this hardheaded and hardhearted people.

"And God said unto Noah, the end of all flesh is come before me; for the earth is filled with violence through them; and behold, I will destroy them with the earth." Genesis 6:13.

Thus, God decided to destroy them all saved Noah. Why only him? What was in Noah that pleased God?

"But Noah found grace in the eyes of God. These are the generations of Noah: Noah was a just man and perfect in his generations, and Noah walked with God." Genesis 6:8-9.

Had Noah joined the others living their evil will, humanity would not have survived. Everything could have ended then. But Noah in a way is a type of the church that his existence preserve mankind and the world. And his family were also preserved. A lesson for us that if we too live a holy and perfect life expect that our family's generation will also be spared from God's wrath.

Thus after instructing Noah to build an ark, he did obeyed to perfection.

"And the Lord said unto Noah, Come thou and all thy house into the ark; for thee have I seen righteous before me in this generation." Genesis 7:1.

As our Lord instructed Peter to build His church we who are members of the true church will be spared from the assaults of her enemies. No flood or fire can destroy the church as was the flood could not destroy the ark.

Obedience, righteousness and reverence to God is the most important thing we should treasure in our hearts, mind, body and soul because this pleases God, our Father. Knowing this, we should then focus in living our lives that pleases our Father.

Another example is Abraham:

"And he said, Lay not thine hand upon the lad, neither do thou any thing unto him; for now I know that thou fearest God, seeing thou hast not withheld thy son, thine only son from me." Genesis 22:12.

From the line of Noah came Abraham who found favor with God. God asked him to offer his one and only beloved son, Isaac to be sacrificed. Sadly and with a bleeding heart, Abraham obeyed God even though it was against his own will. I meant who among us will do such a thing? But God tested Abraham about his faith and with flying colors he passed.

"And in thy seed shall all nations of the earth be blessed; because thou hast obeyed my voice." Genesis 22:18.

Abraham was greatly rewarded by God. He became father of many nations and his seed was blest. In both the Jewish and Islamic religion Abraham was their great patriarch. By sacrificing his only beloved son, he was rewarded with so many children scattered like stars in the sky. What Abraham did was a preview of what God the Father will do in our behalf by sacrificing His only begotten Son, Jesus and by doing so, God the Father will have a multitude of children because of what Jesus did for us and for His

Father in heaven. A great lesson for us that if our Father in heaven wants something from us whatever He wants then we should emulate Abraham sparing nothing even his one and only son.

Lastly, let us study about the relation of God the Father and Moses, the greatest prophet of Israel. What can we emulate with Moses.

"Come now therefore, and I will send thee unto Pharaoh, that thou mayest bring forth the children of Israel our of Egypt?" Exodus 3:10.

Chosen for the greatest mission for His people Israel, Moses answered the call with humility confessing to God that he is not capable of the job because he is not a very good speaker.

Despite of all the hardship and difficulties he had against Pharaoh, Moses then accomplished the mission by freeing Israel from the slavery from Egypt. He also led God's chosen people to the promised land although Moses was not allowed to enter.

In conclusion, we did have a knowledge of God the Father that He who is the first Persona did initiated everything from forming us from the dust but during that time in the Old Covenant we have but a monotheistic God of which the promised of the new heaven was but too far and remote for them. Thus, in the First Person, there will be no new heavens and to console His people, the promised land was merely a preview of the greater things that God the Father did plan for us. We who are in this present time should be extremely grateful and thankful to the Triune God that each one of us will go to the new heavens where before it was not available. Thus, with this knowledge, we therefore must not waste our time and this greatest opportunity to enter the new heavens. We who are formed in our Lady's community will have the greatest opportunity with our formation guided by the mother of God who can truly help us get to the new heavens. And by knowing the Father, we have learned from the example of Noah, Abraham and Moses how we can please our Father in heaven. There are many more servants of God in the Old Testament and we can expand our knowledge of the Father by reading and studying the Old Testament in our spare time. Knowing more our Father in heaven surely increases the fire of our love for Him.

Discuss 20 minutes:
Discuss why Noah's ark is a type of the church?
Do you really think that God will completely wipe out His creation?
Do you think obedience is the greatest virtue pleasing to God? If not, what?

Adam and Eve failed in obeying God in the garden of Eden and suffered the consequences. Noah, Abraham and Moses had some things in common. What are they.

Compare and contrast the consequences and the rewards for those who obeys and disobeys.

In our community, our Lady of Unity promises great rewards to us and we do not have to do great things but simply what?

Closing Prayer:
Together Sing, Hymn, "Salve Regina"
Our Lady of Unity, pray for us, your community. Amen.

Eight Class: (3 hours or less)

Hymn: Together Sing, "Jesus, Remember Me"
Opening Prayer:

Knowing The Son, The Second Persona

Leader reads the Scripture Passage:

"For God so loved the world, that he gave his only begotten Son, that whosoever believeth in Him should not perish, but have everlasting life" John 3:16.

Christians estimated to be more than billion followers of Christ are so familiar with this passage. As Christians, they believed that Jesus Christ is the Son of God who came down for us sinners so we can be redeemed from our sins. The promised of eternal life with Him did drew over a billion followers because of His lofty promise. We Christians do believe because Jesus is the way, the truth and the life. And on the other side of the coin, those who does not believe will not gain eternal happiness.

Why the whole world knew about Jesus and like He prophesied that He Himself will draw everyone. Indeed, He is the truth and because of it, many do believed that He is the only begotten Son of God and He will never renege on His promises. He had been foretold by the prophets of old that He will be the only One who is eligible in taking on the just punishment of our sins. As we have learned from the Old Testament that at that time God the Father was the only Persona known to His chosen people. They were totally focused and consumed with God's First Persona that even though the prophecy was fulfilled before their very eyes, God the Father remained in-gross in their hearts, mind and soul. Kudos to their faithfulness to the Father but they do not know what was and is His plans for all His people.

God will draw all His creation to Himself and what the Father planned was repeated by His Son Jesus so we will pay attention to what God was and is doing for each one of us. Since their insistence of a monotheistic God, the Jewish and the Islam religion could never see nor have the holy vision that God the Father is in need of His Son and His Third Persona the Holy Spirit so all of us will become His greatest work. From dust to divinity. Where can we find a miracle of a worthless dust becoming God? And so, do not be looking for a miracle nor be amazed by it since you yourself is the greatest miracle if only we believe and only if we knew deeply the mystery of our transformation. Therefore as we are more blest than our brothers and sisters in the Jewish and Islamic faith we must pray fervently for their conversion to Christianity under one shepherd so our perfect unity will give God the greatest glory and honor. She called herself our Lady of Unity because she too is working and interceding fervently to the Triune God for the conversion of all to the true faith. But our Lady needs so many who will become her co-workers in accomplishing this unity of God's people. She is our Lady of Unity because she also is calling all those who are devoted and faithful to her. Our Lady of Fatima, our Lady of Lourdes, our Lady of Guadalupe, our Lady of Knock, our Lady of Akita, our Lady of Mt. Carmel, our Lady of Turlock etc etc etc an endless list of our Lady's faithful and devoted followers. Now she wanted that all her faithful and devoted ones join this final revolution before the curtain of our world closes as prophesied by God's prophets. It hurts and grieves our Lord and our Lady of so many souls are lost and if our brothers and sisters in the Jewish and Islam religion will not convert just how many billions will be delivered to the fire in hell completely separated from their loving Maker. Although both offsprings of Abraham, our father in faith, only God knew why they were deprived of knowing our Lord Jesus and the concept of the Triune God. The Jewish religion do believe and expect for the coming of Jesus but they do not believe or see that He was the One presence in their midst preaching, teaching and showing the way, the truth and the life.

Ears did not hear nor eyes see that Jesus had come.

As with the Islam religion, they too were victims of deprivation in knowing our Lord in the flesh. They too are consumed and believed that there is only one God and His named was Allah. Again, kudos to them for believing God the Father for their loyalty and faithfulness. Why did God allowed this? Who can searched the mind of God? Who are we to know? But our Lady does. And she wanted us to pray fervently for their conversion simply that we are one family in God. Remember, the Jewish faith shared to the whole world their God, the Eternal Father and if they did not shared to us we too are in big trouble. And so, in gratitude to God and to our brothers and sisters in the Jewish faith to pray fervently for them for their conversion in gratitude for sharing God to us. Also for the Muslim religion for they too are our family of faith.

Why are so many at risks of losing their soul and God? Why can not God made known to all of us? Such logical questions comes to our mind that if God truly wants to save us all why not pour out all His graces so all will be save.

Good human question but quickly the answer is very simple. God had already did everything for our redemption, sanctification and salvation but we failed Him by simply choosing to exercise the power of our will doing something that are not for our greatest and highest good and that is to become holy and perfect. This is truly our greatest impediment why so many souls are lost to eternal perdition because we have sinned and grieved the Holy Spirit. This is the kind of sin that can never forgiven by our loving and merciful God. God the Father, created us and prepared us for our redemption and when Jesus came and salvation is ours, we merely professed our faith and belief with Him without going to work for our own salvation. If God made Himself Three showing us that the Three Persons of God works so hard for our sake and we who are dust indeed needs to work with fear and trembling for our salvation. God did His part and how about you and me, did we? This is a very serious questions we have to asked ourselves. We need to truly bend and force our will to work very hard in cooperating to God's will. By doing so, even if we keep failing and falling short of our holy goal, our sincere effort to work out our part will always be highly noted by our good and loving God and He will definitely rewards you for doing your part in giving Him glory, honor and praise.

Since most of us claimed to know Jesus, then seriously asked yourself how much and how deep you knew our Lord?

Most of us knew that He is indeed God and man son of the Father conceived by the Holy Spirit and born of the Virgin Mary and He suffered and died for our sins. The cross became the symbol of our salvation and is venerated by all Christians.

Jesus is the way, the truth and the life.
Why is He the way?
Pause and for 15 minutes discuss why Jesus is the way.
After discussion leader continues.
Jesus is the truth?
Pause for 15 minutes discussing why He is the truth.
Jesus is the Life.
Pause and discuss why He is the Life in 15 minutes.
After the discussion take 10 minutes break.

Prayer:

Heavenly Father, behold your children in the land of our exile and in the greatness of your love and mercy grant us the graces to know, love and serve your only begotten Son knowing that without Him there is no hope for us to enter your marvelous kingdom. Our Lady of Unity, holy mother of our Savior, full of grace do intercede for us members of your community for the graces that we will never be separated from Him whom we revered and treasured as our light and salvation. Holy Spirit keep us always in your friendship and make our bodies your holy dwelling place so we can be always united with the most Holy Trinity now and forever. We pray in the most holy Name of Jesus Thy Son who lives and reigns with You and the Holy Spirit forever and ever. Amen.

Our Father, Hail Mary and Glory Be.
Our Lady of Unity, pray for us, your community. Amen.
Together Sing, Hymn, "Immaculate Mary"
Leader resume reading:
"And the Word was made flesh and dwell among us." St. John 1:14.

Read page 9, paragraph 9 to pages 10, 11, 12, 13 and 14. Community take turns in reading the book "Our Lady of Unity"

After reading discuss the contents. Limit time 30 minutes.

Discuss why Mary must be free from sin and that why her immaculacy must be preserved to eternity.

Why is it that the church rightly called the Holy Spirit Mary's Spouse?

Why it is so necessary and essential that Mary should present herself to her heavenly Father in heaven?

Why did Jesus seek baptism from John?

Jesus not only came to justify, redeem and save but established His kingdom on earth and also in heaven.

Discuss why no one can enter the new heaven if one does not belong to His Body which is the Church.

What else did Jesus left us after He ascended to the new heavens.

Seated at the right Hand of God the Father, the glorified Jesus did also took our humanity into the eternal kingdom guaranteeing our entrance to the new heavens. Blessed are those who belong to the Catholic Church for our membership cemented us as the real part of His Body. Discuss our Christian brothers who believe and profess that Christ is their Lord and Savior wether they too are the Body of Christ, are they or not?

The Jewish and Islamic religion does not recognized nor believed that Jesus Christ is the Son of God and Son of man, if they remained to do so, will they be save?

After the 30 minutes discussion leader continue by reading the following text below:

We continue the class so we will be familiar about our Lord Jesus:

We heard so many times that Jesus is the way, the truth and the life. But He had said to us that He is also:

I am the light.

Indeed He is because the world was in completely darkness and there is no light to guide us to the way to our salvation and to the new heaven. Yes, He is the way but we could never find the path to the new heavens without His light. Without our Lord, there is no one who can give us that true light that lit the path to our salvation. Truly, Jesus is the way. Again, He reminded us that no one can come the Father except through Him. He is the way to our heavenly Father. Only Jesus and we must revere Him because without Him there is no hope, there is no heaven, only despair and darkness. He is the light. Our light.

I am the bread of life.

In our human life we need bread to sustain us to nourish and strengthen us in our daily activities. In our spiritual life, we need nourishment to sustain and strengthen us so we can survive the war against our formidable enemies. God's chosen ones ate manna in the desert and they die. Although they reached the promised land, they could never get to the new heavens because the bread from heaven had not come. When Jesus said to His disciples that they must eat His flesh and drink His blood, they were stunned thinking they practiced cannibalism and they were about to left Jesus and abandon Him but Peter, the first pope, stood by his master and said, "Where shall we go, Lord, you have the words of everlasting life."

At that time, Jesus apostles had no idea about the bread of life for the Holy Spirit had yet revealed and taught them the fullness of His truth and teachings.

"Do this in memory of me."

During the Last Supper, the Holy Spirit revealed to His community and the church the necessity of the Holy Mass where ordinary bread and wine will be transformed into His flesh and blood where the faithful will truly eat His flesh and drink His blood in un-bloody manner to fulfill our Lord's prophesy that members of His Body (Church) should eat and drink so they will have eternal life. He is the Life and Jesus will have to feed us with His Own Flesh and Blood to give our soul His very Own Life for Jesus said He is the life.

I am the living water.

Jesus and the Samaria woman was a scene that taught us the essentiality of baptism so we can be enrolled in His Body, the church. Samaria were considered outcast from the Jewish religion and they have no chance or hope for salvation. In our modern days, they were like our Jewish and Islam brothers and sisters who are not members of the Body of Christ considered an outcast since our Lord declared that only through Him salvation is possible. I am the living water that leads to everlasting life. Who else who can take us to heaven but Jesus alone and the water He was talking about was the same water that John poured upon Him during His baptism at the Jordan river. Baptist is so important and necessary for our salvation and even Jesus showed us by having been baptized. And when He accomplished His mission before He ascended to the Father, He was heard clearly to His followers and apostles to go out to the ends of the earth so all will be baptized in the Name of the Father, The Son and The Holy Spirit. This was His last will so to speak to ensure everyone will be baptized. Baptism is the way to eternal life and to the new heavens. This is the truth for Jesus told us. Baptism is the life because we became a part of Him who is Life.

I am the Resurrection.

The greatest title that our Lord give to Himself. For without the resurrection the Christian faith had no foundation just like any religion. The Christian faith would become just like others, just a religion. But His resurrection made the Christian religion the greatest and the most convincing truth because God Himself was truly involved in our redemption and salvation. What religion can you think that God came down from heaven and show Himself just like us so He can share us what is the way, the truth and the life. He inspired us to follow Him back to our God whom we lost by our rebellion and sin. What religion can we find where God united man to Himself by the birth of the God-man so together they can find the way back to our true homeland. God finally giving up His very Own Life for our sake as a ransom for us all. And to make us believe that truly Jesus is God, as promised He came back to life and when His followers saw this incredible miracle they were on fire became great and true witnesses to His resurrection. Witnessed by hundreds of Christians, after His ascension to heaven, the Christian faith became an unstoppable force and from a few hundred turned into billion followers. The Christian faith is the only true faith and as we are so blest to be a Christian then we have a great responsibility in participating by telling the good news to all about our incredible faith.

In conclusion, our way, our truth and our life is Jesus, Our Lord and salvation. Yes, Jesus is our refuge, our helper, our deliver, our breath, our shelter, our rock, our redeemer, our savior, our strength and our all. Jesus is our all. As St. Francis of Assisi called Him, My God, My All. He prayed that all the time. A very short but a powerful prayer but defining the truth of our Lord Jesus Christ who is our all.

In conclusion, discuss what is Jesus for you. If you have anything more to add about Him please do share. 20 minutes discussion.

Closing Prayer:
Sing together, Hymn, Salve Regina
Our Lady of Unity pray for us, your community and lead us to holiness. Amen

Ninth Class: (3 hours or less)

Hymn Together Sing, "Come Holy Ghost"
Opening Prayer

Knowing The Holy Spirit - The Third Persona

Leader reads the Scripture Passage

"The Holy Spirit shall come upon thee, and the power of the Highest shall overshadow thee; therefore also that holy thing which shall be born of thee shall be called Son of God." Luke 1:35.

The Third Persona of God initiated the process in renovating making us acceptable to God the Father. As we all knew, we came from dust and to transform us into His Image and likeness, He personally used His mighty holy Hands and after our formation into visible flesh, God breathe His Life into Adam where he too will live like God for eternity. Notice how truly special we are more than anything He created. Notice that God only used His Words to create everything. Let there be light. He did used the Words. Etc. The whole world and the universe itself God used His Words. But, only in us did God used His Hands and Breathe symbolizing that we are more important than the whole world, the whole universe that even the angels of heaven envied us because we are to be His greatest handiworks. How small we are in this world, or how insignificant we may think of ourselves, in the Eyes of God, we are magnified that in His Sight we are bigger and larger than the whole world and universe. Amazingly unbelievable but this is truth. We cannot believe that this is what we are. If everyone of us truly knew our value then true peace and perfect love could have been established in our world that is completely out of whack. We are like a lost egg that belongs to an eagle but was hatched by a hen adapting the mentality of the chicken. Raised by the mother hen, the baby eagle followed everything the baby chicks did. One day, he saw in the skies a flock of birds flying above admiring and wishing that he too can fly like them. He did not know that he can fly faster and stronger than them for he is an eagle. We too are like that. We are humans surrounded with humans just like that baby eagle and we do follow what humans do, not knowing that they are created to become like God. We are to become heirs of the Most High God where each one of us will reign with Him for all eternity but our humanity had brought us so low that we are chain and condition to be forever in the flesh. We humans are bound to be in-gross in this miserable state and had the good and loving merciful God did not intervene we would have never known the glory, majesty, dignity and honor of our being. Thus, we should always think of God's Third Persona and give Him time to praise and thank Him for He too is really our God.

How did God begin His renovating works? By entering into our miserable and forsaken world for this is the only way we can be raised to the truth of our being. As sin evicted us from the garden of Eden, we entered into this world and the rest of our history was and is a series of destruction and devastation and in the Sight of God, as we continue to fill the earth with all kinds of sin, we became unredeemable and we are in a hopeless situation. It takes God, the most powerful and mighty Being to come to our rescue. And He did and it was the Third Persona of God who made the magical move by entering into Our Lady's holy womb.

But before the Holy Spirit can enter into Mary's holy womb, God the Father, in the greatness of His holiness brought His only chosen child to heaven so Mary be presented making her as God's only chosen daughter and graced unto her the fullness of His divinity making Mary as the only one to have such distinction. Although human like us, God the Father bestowed on Mary His own Being where no sin or evil can penetrate her.

Once Mary received the Eternal Father's direct divine adoption, she was then betrothed to be the holy spouse of His Third Persona so the mystical marriage between man and God can be perpetuated through the Holy Spirit entrance into her holy womb planting the hybrid seed of God and man.

Read page 41, 42, 43 and 2nd paragraph page 44 (Our Lady of Unity book).

After reading, discuss for 30 minutes about what was the message. Discuss the questions below:

Why is it that the Triune God was always united with Mary?

Why is it necessary that Mary was taken up to heaven to be presented to the Father?

Why was it so necessary that Mary was betrothed twice?

Discuss the parents of Mary and their lives.

The Holy Spirit will never depart from Mary. We too can have the Holy Spirit dwells in us but why is it that He will never remain in us?

Mary was troubled about her double betrothal. Why was she troubled?

Jesus, our Lord is also called by the prophets as the Prince of Peace. Why?

After 30 minutes discussion again read page 47 (Our Lady of Unity book)

After reading page 47 discuss the following questions below for 30 minutes.

If we guard our body against sin the Holy Spirit will dwell in us but why is it that the indwelling of the Holy Spirit to our Lady is permanent while we can only have Him temporary?

Why is it that the only sin that can never be forgiven is the sin against the Holy Spirit? Discuss why it can not be forgiven.

St. Paul, the greatest Apostle kept preaching about the corruptibility of our flesh. What are the sins of the flesh?

In our spiritual journey to perfection and holiness, name the three greatest enemy of our salvation. Of the three, which is our worst enemy.

There are seven deadly sin that will grieve the Holy Spirit, name them and discuss each one.

After the discussion pray the prayer below.

Come Holy Spirit, come and let the fire of Your love consumes the impurities of our hearts and renew our hearts to become like Jesus. Make us true lovers of Your Three Persona and never permit us to be separated from You. As Your formed our Lord in the holy womb of Your spouse, transform our soul into the likeness of Jesus. As you made Mary, your spouse holy and perfect, make us also and if we keep failing in our resolution, then grant us the graces of fortitude and holy perseverance so by the intercession of our Lady of Unity we be made worthy of the promises of Christ, our Lord and Redeemer. Amen.

Our Father, Hail Mary, Glory Be.
Our Lady of Unity, pray for us, your community and lead us to holiness.

Break 10 minutes.

After the break leader read below.

As previously discuss, the Holy Spirit is so very active in perfecting the works of the Blessed Trinity. It was the Holy Spirit mission to transform us here on earth by uniting the warring Spirit and flesh forming them into a resolving entity so unity and peace can be achieve creating a new life patterned after God's only begotten Son. After the birth of the Messiah, Jesus went to the Jordan river so He can be baptized. John, his holy cousin could not figure out why our Lord insisted baptizing knowing that God's only begotten Son was sinless, pure and the most holy. John thought that it should be Jesus baptizing him instead. But John knew not that there was a greater purpose in Jesus baptism.

First, Jesus showed the whole world the greatest importance of baptism. Our Lord warns us that if we are not baptized salvation is not possible unless God grant that special grace that He alone can give. But salvation is remote without baptism. That is why Jesus did His baptism so His own humanity and our own humanity can be enrolled in the Book of Life. Jesus was baptized because this is how one can become integrated cementing its membership to His one and only true church. And He who is God is the Head of the church. And to become a member of His Body, then one should be baptized by invoking the Name of the Triune God so the baptized will be united to His Three Persona. Thus, when Jesus was baptized, the Holy Spirit descended upon our Lord conforming the necessity and essentiality of baptism so one will be incorporated to God Himself.

Finally, God the Father ratified the baptismal sacred scene when His voice was heard, "This is my beloved Son whom I am most pleased." If one truly wants to return to God then baptism will make it possible. And when one is baptize specially in the Catholic Church, one will be pleasing to God our Father, as exemplified by our Savior on His Own baptism. Once the Holy Spirit descended on Him, our humanity will also received such sacred privilege once Jesus accomplished His mission on earth.

Again, the Holy Spirit lead Jesus into the wilderness where He was tested and tempted by the devil. As our Lord was about to start His ministry, as preparation for His mission, Jesus fasted forty days and nights and He was starving. Knowing that He was very hungry, the devil challenged Him.

"If thou be the Son of God, command these stones be made bread." Matthew 4:3.

"It is written, man shall not live by bread alone, but by every word that proceedeth out of the mouth of God." Matthew 4:4.

Our Lord conquered the devil by the power of His Word. And we too can also by using Sacred Scriptures as our weapon.

For example, every man is constantly exposed by the presence of beautiful and seductive women and such tempting sight stirs the imagination and passion. If this man has no knowledge of God's words (God's commandments and the Bible), he will lustfully desire to possess this woman in his heart. On the other hand, a virtuous man who is armed with the Words of God understand that it is morally wrong and against God's law to even think of desiring her.

"But I say unto you, that whosoever looketh on a woman to lust after her hath committed adultery with her already in his heart." Matthew 5:29.

And to conquer such temptation, simply remember what Paul's taught how to conquer our lustful inclination.

"This I say then, walk in the spirit, and ye shall not fulfill the lust of the flesh." Galatians 5:16.

The other two temptations that our Lord encountered He easily conquered by using God's Words.

After passing the testing and temptation with ease, our Lord was ready and prime for His ministry by teaching and preaching the way of God, the truth of God and the life of God. With His twelve disciple as witnesses, they then wrote what they have heard and saw about the Word made flesh.

They saw how our Lord was arrested and put on the dark dungeon. He was beaten, spat upon, insulted by blasphemous words, crown with thorns that keeps bleeding on His Sacred Face. He was stripped of His clothes and scourged until His Back was bleeding His Flesh torn.

They made fun and constantly mocked Him and then He had to carry that heavy cross to Calvary with His strength fading where He fell three times. And when they reached Mount Calvary tired and in terrible pain and torment, they laid Him on the cross and nailed Him with large nails that our Lord's Body was in shock. It is humanity's sin and it was His humanity that took all the just punishment and it was His Divinity that sustain Jesus until He gave up His last breathe on the cross.

"Jesus, remember me when you are in Your kingdom" By doing so, the criminal was saved because of the holy Presence of God on the cross and also the presence of Our Lady on the foot of the cross.

Then we, who are truly and really follower of our Lord Jesus should remember Him. What He did for all of us. By doing so, Jesus will remember us that now He is seated at the right Hand of our Father in heaven.

The Holy Spirit was with Jesus all the time strengthening and ministering to Him at His most terrifying and difficult moment accomplishing His mission of our redemption and our salvation.

After His resurrection, Jesus continued to teach His disciples many more lofty things about Him and our heavenly homeland. Some of those teachings are not recorded but what was written in Sacred Scriptures paled in comparison of the many more what Jesus taught them. Some of those lofty teachings His disciples were clueless. But He promised to sent His Third Persona the Holy Spirit to dwell with them so they will be perfectly enlightened with all that He taught them.

"Go all throughout the earth and baptize them in the Name of the Father, the Son and the Holy Spirit."

Again, the emphasis on baptism. As He started His ministry, it was His baptism and after His mission was completed ready to return to His Father our Lord's final instruction to His disciples was to baptize all His people. Then to sweeten and bound the divine deal, He gave us Himself, His Third Persona so He can finally dwell in us. It is the Holy Spirit that will work unceasingly to transform us into His Life making us truly like God.

Therefore we should honor the Holy Spirit by loving Him as our God and by letting Him guide us in life. We should always ask Him for the light and strength we need to live a holy life and to save our soul.

Discussion 30 minutes. Below are to be discuss.
Is it possible that the Holy Spirit dwells on the unbaptized?
What role does the Holy Spirit in the Church?
What role does the Holy Spirit in the Pope, bishops, priest and religious?
Why does the Church described the Holy Spirit as the love of the Father and the Son?
Name the seven gifts of the Holy Spirit.
Discuss each one of them.
After discussion the community pray the consecration prayer to the Holy Spirit so each member will receive His gifts. Pray below.

"Holy Spirit, Divine Spirit of light and love, we consecrate to you our understanding, heart, and will, our whole community, for time and for eternity. May our understanding be always submissive to Your heavenly inspirations and to the teaching of the Catholic

Church, of which You are the infallible Guide. May our hearts be ever inflamed with the love of God and of our neighbor. May our will be ever conformed to the Divine Will. May our whole life be faithful to the imitation of the life and virtues of our Lord and Savior Jesus Christ, to Whom with the Father and You be honor and glory forever. God, Holy Spirit, Infinite Love of the Father and the Son, through the pure hands of Mary, your Immaculate Spouse, we place ourselves this day of our lives, upon Your chosen altar, the Divine Heart of Jesus, as a sacrifice to You, consuming fire, being firmly resolved now more than ever to hear Your voice and to do in all things Your most holy and adorable Will."

Closing Prayer:
Sing together, Hymn, Salve Regina.
Our Lady of Unity, pray for us your community and lead us to holiness.

Tenth Class: (3 hours or less)

Hymn: Together Sing "Amazing Grace"
Opening Prayer

Loving The Father

Leader reads the Scripture passage:

"And God said, let us man in our image, after out likeness; and let them have dominion over the fish of the sea, and over the fowl of the air, and over the cattle and over the earth, and over every creeping thing that creepeth upon the earth." Genesis 2:26.

This is how God loves us. He gave us the whole earth and everything on it is ours. Even the whole magnificent solar system were created for us. The beautiful angels were also created for us. This is how good is our God. He created us so we can share all of Himself His own glory, power, majesty, joy, happiness, beauty and all that is perfectly good. He gave Adam eternal life and the garden of Eden which was paradise on earth. This is God the Father who created us so we can become like Him. So we can have everything that He had and yet we are so cold and so indifference in appreciating for all the marvelous things He had done for us. There must be really something bad and evil in us that prevented us in constantly giving thanks and praises to the One who never failed in taking great care of us even though we keep failing Him. The scripture passage partially tells us the greatness of God's goodness and providence while there awaits something even greater and better than the promised land here on earth. Or the paradise that was on the garden of Eden.

Why does God want us to love Him? If God loves us unconditionally why then He demands our love?

Simply because in loving Him will be for our own highest and greatest good. God is the fullness of love. He is all love. In fact, God is pure and perfect love and being so He really does not want any of ours. Why does God wants our love if He has no need for it? How could a creature give God its love when it does not even know what is all about. O yes indeed we heard so much about the word love and its overused had made love become another worthless word. The love we constantly say every moment of the day has no eternal value at all. Like God, love only exist in our vocabulary, nothing more or less. Just observe our own lives how we mistreated and abused the goodness and God's pure and perfect love for us. Sometimes I am appalled when I heard somebody says O how I love God and I will do anything for Him. Then, when they are with his family seeing his beautiful wife and daughter the tune changes when he said, O how I loved my family. They are the love of my life.

O well, this is us. We do learn from God's chosen one whom our Lord entrusted His church, Peter, our first Pope.

"Peter answered and said unto Him, Though all men shall be offended because of thee, yet will I never be offended. Jesus said unto him, Verily I say unto thee, That this night, before the cock crow, thou shalt deny me thrice. Peter said unto him, Though I should die with thee, yet will I not deny thee. Likewise also said all the disciples." Matthew 26:33-35.

In the real Presence of Jesus, Peter was so courageous in professing his love for his Master and so does the rest of His chosen apostles. Truly we always struggle in our external life. Peter showed his leadership by promising that even if it meant losing his life, he will never betrayed nor denied our Lord. So does the others but when persecution came to our Lord's followers everybody run and hide for fear of their lives. And so, this is what we are made off. Made of dust we easily crumbles when the flesh is threatened with danger. And so, we truly have to be careful in saying what we say. When we says that, I love God and I will do anything for Him then there are some ramifications. God is always in our midst and it is best and prudent to be very careful in what we say specially in our tendency to exaggerate. And even after Jesus asked Peter three times wether he loves Him, he answered he did. Did he?

Even though witnessing our Lord's resurrection from the dead which made Peter courageous in preaching about his Master, he did not measure to what he said to Jesus about giving his own life for Him when during the Christian persecution in Rome, Peter saw the crucifixion and murder of his Christian brothers and sisters and with fear he turned his back from them and fled. Remember Jesus appointed and anointed Peter to be the leader of His church and it does not look good on Peter's resume to abandon his flock when everything was going badly. And so, like us, we should be very careful in professing that we love God when in truth we are not really sure that we do. Perhaps, we even do not have any love for Him.

But, our Lord knew who we are and He knew Peter of his tendency to run and deny what his mouth professes and yes, He understand that we are just like Peter and when we are really getting out of line from Him, God knows how to interfere.

"Peter, where are you going?"

He was shocked hearing the familiar voice of his Master who had already ascended to heaven.

"Quo vadis"

"I am going to Rome where my faithful ones to be crucified again."

Knowing that it was Jesus, Peter knew that He wanted Peter to go back to Rome for he was the leader of Christ flock and he must join them to show the world that persecution and even death will not destroy Christ follower in establishing the church and to expand the kingship of Christ in the whole world. And by hearing Jesus, Peter again regain his strength and courage and successfully lead the church to victory. He did lose his own life and with God's grace he even had the audacity to instruct his persecutors that he not to be crucified like His Master and instead he be crucified in an inverted cross because he is not worthy to be crucified like Jesus Finally, after failing and disappointing our Lord a few times, the great love and mercy of Jesus was shown to us that His grace is enough for us. And when we do say that we love our Lord and God and even though it is only lip service, He will take a note to it and eventually after so many failings, as long as we persevere in trying to love and serve Him, God's grace suffices. Thus, to be religious and to belong to a religious order, we do have the great advantages over those who are not since God is drawing us for our greater good. Like priest and nuns belonging to a religious order one becomes a consecrated soul dedicated to God and He will notice our effort and desire that even though we keep failing His grace will sustain us into reaching our goal much like what happened to Peter.

This class is all about loving God the Father. Yes, keep it in your mind that He demanded and insisted our love purely for our own good. Even all His creation put all its love together does not suffice in return for His love for us. He wants all our love so by doing it, we are on the way in transforming us into like Him. We can be like Him only when we can love Him purely and perfectly, otherwise we fall short of becoming like Him. God knew we are merely dust made of corruptible flesh easily corrupted and easily sway to sin but our sincere and great effort in cultivating and expanding the capacity of our love will make a great difference than not trying to be holy and perfect like Him. When our hearts, mind and soul truly and purely desire to give all its love to Him then God will simply take over and accept our effort and in return He Himself will take the soul into another spiritual heights that are rarely attainable by many. But keep in mind that God will do all He can to help anyone of us to reach such sanctified status and it had been proven by the many canonized saints of the church. Remember, those saints are not angels for they are just like us. What made them saints are their desire to become one and the desire to be holy and perfect that even with so many failings and so many frustration they keep standing up and keep on pushing to their goal - to become a saint. And to become one, only by love we become saints.

How do we love God, the Father? Well, let us get back to where we did begin.

Adam and Eve did walked and talked to God and surely they should have learned from Him what is love. Did they?

They failed by their disobedience. There was no love scene between God and our first parents.

Despite the love of the Father for them, Adam and Eve never did praise, give thanks, adore nor worship Him.

To prove our love the great virtue of obedience should always be exercised when demanded by our God the Father. Obedience at all times exposes one's love has been perfected and purified to the highest level. Obedience clearly makes one lovable and desirable. On the other side, disobedience reveals a rebellious character where its love has not yet been exercise or practice.

After they were evicted from the garden of Eden, having lost their friendship with God and their own immortal status, they produced two offsprings named Cain and Abel. Although conceived in sin and carrying the curses of sin, Cain inheriting the stain of sin did offered to God which was not acceptable because his offering was inferior to what his brother Abel offered. Jealous, he murdered his own brother. Obviously, Cain was full of hatred and there is no love in him. Abel was considered righteous even though he was conceived in sin and also inherited the curses of sin because he did offer to God the best there is. Therefore, Abel did love God the Father by the righteousness of his deeds by offering the best that He deserve. A lesson for us to learn how we can love the Father by emulating Abel in giving our best. Therefore, we offer to God the Father the best in us. And what is our very best but the holiness and the righteousness of a blameless life patterned after our Lord Jesus.

Noah did not particularly said anything such as I love you Lord and I will do anything you wanted me to do. There is no need for him to say anything because during that time he alone live a righteous life pleasing to God while the rest was in total rebellion against God and judgment was enforced to eliminate His creation saved Noah and his family. And to do so, God commanded him to built an ark and obediently Noah did. Everything God told him to do Noah did. Noah spoke no words to prove his love for the Father. Let us emulate him in loving the Father by doing and not by saying. As the cliche, words are cheap but action speak louder than words.

Let us go to Abraham and how he showed his love for the Father. He was tested when Abraham was to sacrifice his only one son and against his will he did thus God rewarded him for his faith and love for the Father. Abraham became the father of many nations. Again, to prove our love for God, obedience surely does.

God the Father needed someone who will be His instrument in freeing His chosen people from the slavery of Pharaoh. As the story goes, Moses was chosen to be His prophet to tell Pharaoh to free His chosen people. After many confrontations, the children of Israel won their freedom from the mighty Egyptian. Again, obedience to God, Moses proved his love although he failed his Lord, still God honored Moses as Israel's greatest prophet. The chosen people of God saw the many miracles that Moses performed through God's power and from what they seen, they did worshipped and revered God. And to make sure that they will continue to be faithful to Him, God gave The Ten Commandments where the love for God and for each other became the standard of God's love. At that time, the law of God must be preserved and obeyed while awaiting for the coming of our salvation.

After the readings, 30 minutes discussion about the question below:

1. The children of Israel did revere and treasure God's Ten Commandments and that they even added more as a token of their devotion and faithfulness to God but salvation for their soul was not possible. Why?
2. As their leader and prophet, Moses was not able to reach the Promised Land. What was the reason why?
3. Why did the children of Israel seek other gods after Moses was gone for forty days?

4. The virtues of chastity, purity, goodness, kindness, humility, piety, faithfulness, poverty and obedience are all pleasing to God. Which of these virtues pleases God the most and why?

Discuss each one of these virtues.

5. In order to be saved from destruction and death, God commanded Noah to built an ark to preserved his life and family, what does the ark represent in the new covenant?
6. Adam and Eve disobeyed God, Lucifer rebelled against God causing their destruction. What do you think will happen to those who disobey or in rebellion against the Catholic Church, the one true church established by Christ? Discuss your thoughts and opinion.

After the discussion take 10 minutes break.
After break, leader reads the following Scripture Passage below:

"And the Lord God called Adam and said unto him, Where art thou?" Genesis 3:9.

To love God the Father, at all cost, we must avoid sin. There was a saint who embraced the motto, "Death before sin." What an admirable advice for us who wants to give God our greatest love. Sin is God's greatest enemy and if we want to love Him, then death before sin.

Sin shames us all. We become so horrible and so ugly in His eyes. Our first father, Adam hid himself from God after he broke His command not to eat the fruit of the tree of knowledge. God who sees and knows everything was not able to find Adam??? Not so. But to us, it had a deeper meaning that when we sin we instinctively separated ourselves from Him that even God could no longer find us. This is the greatest lesson we should remember. Sin shames and separates us totally from our loving God. Lucifer, the prince of the heavenly host by committing the sin of pride swiftly separated himself from God and heaven. He became so ugly that he could not be recognized. The prince of light had separated himself by becoming the prince of darkness. If we sin, we looked worst than Lucifer. Sin is so horrible that even our most pure and holy God became an ugly sight on the cross as He took on all the punishment for the sins of humanity. On the cross, God was disfigured disarranged that the perfect beauty of His divinity was lost. Where is the beauty of my Savior? Where is the splendor and glory of my Redeemer? It was lost and hidden that we will never find it until we see Him again in our final destination.

Pause for 5 minutes and in silence do your own reflection by remembering who you are:

How pure and beautiful you are specially after you went to confession and had been absolved of your sin. How you transformed yourself into His beauty and glory when you received the living resurrected Jesus worthily during Holy Communion. We have become God in God for this heavenly gifts and after communion we should give Him our praises and gratitude for this food from heaven. Do not be so in a hurry after Holy Mass unless you are so badly needed in the service of others. Never in the history of God and us that we have this very special privilege of true and real union with the Most Holy Trinity. And yes, after giving Him your praises and thanksgiving, then you are being challenged in how you sustain the perfect beauty of God in your immortal soul. Do not be disappointed that you looked the same and you do not feel anything because the truth is you are living God's Own Life in yours. Therefore, be vigilant not to sin at all cost. By doing so, you and God found each other in the secrecy of your precious soul.

After 5 minutes of recollection, leader continue reading below:

Spiritual direction for the community:

In our memory, let us always remind ourselves that sin separates us from God and we are no longer His children, the extension of God's Life. With sin, we instinctively run and hide ourselves from Him and God had become our enemy. Enemies do not want to see each other. With sin, we are hidden from God's presence because we have become children of darkness.

In our intellect, let us always possess and kept this knowledge that when we sin we completely lose the light of God and we become so ugly and horrific looking and in darkness we can not see the narrow path leading to heaven and like a blind man not knowing the way the soul is forever lost.

In our will, let us never sin. We have our powerful will and no one can make us sin except ourselves. No use blaming others for your sin. Be honest and truthful to God like David that you and I are responsible for sinning against God. By doing so, we became white as snow. But, the greatest action of your will is that if ever you have fallen into sin quickly and swiftly run and go to confession. This powerful sacrament will make you beautiful again and most importantly being friends with God.

After reading the spiritual direction for this class, together pray below.

"The Lord enthrone in the highest heaven surrounded with His saints
He looks down in all His Creation
The Lord knows everyone and their plans are not hidden
He is pleased to those who walks in the path of life
The righteous and the just touches His heart
But the wicked and the ungodly are repulsive in His Eyes
The Lord guards His faithful servants night and day
No evil would devour them
For God alone is their shelter and refuge

But the wicked seek refuge in the darkness
To hide their evil deeds and their wickedness
The Lord is the King of mercy
He seeks the lost by showing the light of His love
How merciful and good is our God
Forever and ever all creation should sing His praises
For His wondrous deeds
Blessed be God in His Creation
Now and forever. Amen.

Pause and for another 5 minutes in silence and listen to our Lord speaking to your soul:

"SIN CHANGES THE COMPOSITION OF YOUR BEING. MY LIFE IN YOU IS DYING AND DISFIGURED AND DISAPPEARING. I CAN NO LONGER LIVE IN YOU BUT I KEEP ON BREATHING IN YOUR DYING SOUL TO GIVE ALL THE CHANCES FOR YOUR SALVATION FOR YOU BELONG TO ME AND I SHOULD ALSO BE YOURS. I CAME NOT TO CONDEMN SINNERS BUT ALWAYS TO SAVE THEM BUT MOST ARE NOT INTERESTED IN LIVING TO PERFECTION THE LIFE I HAVE GIVEN THEM. YOU ARE IN MY PRESENCE NOW AND I AM ALWAYS PRESENCE BUT MOST MERELY IGNORED ME. BUT I AM ALWAYS TRUE TO MY PROMISE TO BE WITH YOU TILL THE END OF TIME. MY CALLING IS NEVER ENDING THAT ALL OF YOU SEEK PERFECTION AND HOLINESS IN LIFE BUT EARS REMAINED DEAF AND EYES REMAINED CLOSED. AS YOU ARE IN MY PRESENCE, WILL YOU BE WILLING TO LIVE MY LIFE TO PERFECTION SO YOU WILL BECOME LIKE ME? WILL YOU PARTICIPATE IN MY UNENDING MISSION TO SAVE SOULS? TOGETHER WE CAN DO IT. WILL YOU DO IT FOR US? WILL YOU NOT RUN AWAY FROM ME? WILL YOU NOT ABANDON ME WHO LONGS FOR YOUR COMPANY AND LOVE? WILL YOU HIDE FROM ME? DO NOT HIDE FROM ME FOR I CANNOT SAVE YOU. DO REMEMBER MY WORDS AND DO EVERYTHING YOU HEARD AND WE WILL ALWAYS BE ONE."

After the 5 minutes of recollection do pray the Chaplet of Divine Mercy, offering the prayer to our community seeking pardon and mercy for our sins and failings.
After praying take 10 minutes break.
After the break, community sing Hymn, Immaculate Mary.

Leader resumes class by reading below:

It is not so hard or even difficult to love our Father in heaven. To those who truly loves Him, the Ten Commandments are so easy to follow that even the followers of Moses added so many more laws that it is very difficult to remember. However, our

Father merely asked us to follow His Ten Commandments because if we do, we practiced perfection and obedience which surely gain us His favor and mercy. Thus, as a religious community, soon to be consecrated to the Triune God through our Lady of Unity, it is very essential and necessary that we do memorize the Ten Commandments as our very own breath. The true and faithful lover of God meditates His commandments day and night for doing so reveals love for God. Therefore we go back to the basics where our salvation is definitely involved because breaking any one of His commandments hereby breaks all of them. Let us review them and keep them deep in our heart, mind and soul because they are the first step to our salvation.

The First Commandment:
"I am the Lord thy God, thou shalt not have strange gods before me." Exodus 20:2-3.

The main focus of the first commandment was to develop and maintain a personal and real relationship with the living God. We get to know God by practicing His ways and loving others. It commands us to have faith, to have deep respect for holy things and to pray unceasingly and sacrificing everything that is not of God. It forbids idolatry, superstition, spiritualism, occult practices, and the giving up of the faith for wealth or worldly pleasures. To sum it up, God above all things, above everything and never abandon nor separate yourself from Him for God never does.

The Second Commandment:
"Thou shalt not take the name of the Lord thy God in vain." Exodus 20:17.

It commands us to respect Him, and how we show our feelings towards God in the presence of others and to Him. It also forbids the use of God's name in a degrading or disrespectful way or misusing His Name in any way. If we can respect an earthly king or our president, can we not respect God? He wants us to respect Him because true and real lovers respect each other. In a relationship, one can judge true love by how one respects each other. We respect our parents because we love them. Serious sins involving using His Name are those who use God's Name such us pretending to be God's servant gathering and teaching others about God but in reality their motivation was nothing more than their own self interest such us financial or even being honored and revered by his flock. We should only use God's Name in thanking, praising, adoring and worshiping Him.

The Third Commandment is:
"Remember thou keep the Sabbath day." Exodus 20:8.

It is a command for us to go to church on Sundays and days of obligation. It forbids us from missing church through our fault, or from any actions that may hinder us from going to church. Do you still remember when you fell in love with your spouse?

Remember the first date and those magical moments with your future spouse? You wanted to spend most of your time with him or her, and when one was not there, weren't your thoughts and longings always with the beloved? God commands us to spend just one day out of the seven days in the week to be with Him, so we can know Him better, and concentrate on developing our spiritual relationship with Him. On this day we are to develop our time and attention solely to Him. How good is our Lord by giving us six days and only want a day with Him. Actually, by giving all your days to Him imagine what will He gives you in return.

The Fourth Commandment is:
"Honor your father and mother" Exodus 20:12.

This commands us to love and respect our parents and be obedient to them in all things that are not sin. How can anyone not love his or her parents? Our parents sacrificed a very great deal of time, money and energy in raising us and without them, we will not exist nor survive. Honoring our parents does not cease when we become adults. They did God's will with our existence answering the call to multiply for His greater honor and glory. Though there are parents who fail in taking great care of their children, we still owe them our lives. There are parents who were abusive towards their children; parents who inflict so much pain and hurt but if we choose to forget, then we not only honor them but we also give honor and glory to God for our heroic deed. In addition to honoring our parents, it is also a call to care and respect the other members of the family and neighbor. In our spiritual journey, we should always respect and obey our spiritual director and priests for they are our spiritual father.

The Fifth Commandment is:
"Thou shalt not kill." Exodus 20:13.

This is a command for us to live in peace with our neighbor and to respect their rights. We must not hate our neighbor or defame or slander them, as this would kill their reputation and honor. "Ye have heard that it was said of them of old time, thou shalt not kill; and whosoever shall kill shall be in danger of the judgement ; But I say unto you, that whosoever is angry with his brother without a cause shall be in danger of the judgement; and whosoever shall say to his brother, raca, shall be in danger of the council; but whosoever shall say, thou fool, shall be in danger of hell fire." Matthew 5:21-22.

Besides forbidding willful murder, suicide, abortion, and other physical harm, including endangering the life of self or others, it also forbids spiritual murder. One shall never take away from neighbor his faith and love for God.

The Sixth Commandment is:
"Thou shalt not commit adultery." Exodus 20:14.

God condemns all forms of sexual immorality. (Revelation 21:8) It is a command of chastity and modesty and a commandment to avoid occasions of sin. It forbids sex with another's wife or husband, or pornography, masturbation, fornication, homosexuality, incest, bestiality or pedophilia. In our thoughts, in our words and deeds to delete all forms of sexual sins described.

The Seventh Commandment is:
"Thou shalt not steal." Exodus 20:15.

This commandment commands respect for the property and rights of others and forbids theft, the ultimate greed in acquiring things with no regard for the rights and feelings of others. It is selfishness to the highest degree. It forbids damage to properties, fraud and all forms of cheating. Bribery is also cheating by stealing favors from others denying others from receiving it. Corruption demands the great justice from God for denying others what belongs to Him.

There are so many ways to take what is not ours that we could be breaking this commandments against stealing without realizing what we are doing, for example not giving an honest day's work for wages received or giving sub standard work to customers. Even taking long breaks or goofing off at work is definitely stealing. And we stole from God big time if we neglect to take care of our soul and not to work hard for our spiritual growth and well being. By not giving Him time and by not sharing our talents and treasure to the least fortunate.

The Eight Commandment is:
"Thou shalt not bear false witness against thy neighbor." Exodus 20:16.

This demands truthfulness in all things and to respect the good name of others. It forbids lying and causing injury to the good name of neighbor by backbiting and tale bearing. God wants us to be truthful in everything we do. If we keep murdering the reputation of others then we are actually doing it to our God. Remember, we are His children: brothers and sisters we are and to destroy each others divine dignity will surely demand God's justice. Even if their reputation is truly morally unacceptable, we do not have any rights at all to spread them to others because if we do, there is an accounting for such action. As the worldly saying goes, mind your own business. Or best to keep busy working on our bad and imperfect self and God will surely be please.

The Ninth Commandment is:
"Thou shalt not covet thy neighbor's wife." Exodus 20:17.

It is a commandment in purity in thought and desire. It forbids coveting or craving for what is not ours and we should not desire what already belongs to others. We should not have unchaste thoughts or desires of other's spouse. Instead, we should emulate the virtue of Joseph who refused the sexual advances of his master's wife. (Genesis 39:7-9). Unfortunately, in the modern society the virtue of chastity, modesty and purity had taken a deep dive into obscurity. The pollution of pornography, illicit relationships, and sexual permissiveness and freedom had captivated our senses neglecting what is pure, holy and perfect. Our love for sexual pleasures and sexual gratification had downgraded our divine life choking the soul in near death.

The Tenth Commandment is:
"Thou shalt not covet thy neighbor's goods." Exodus 20:17.

This is a call for charity or brotherly love since to envy the gifts of God for others is abominable to Him. This is also a call for generosity. It command us to be content with what we have and to respect the rights of others. This is a reminder to us all that all goods belong to God and are freely given for the good of all. He had already designed everything for us. We are also required to give the best in our vocations. If God planned you to become a priest, then strive to become the best. If God's providence is more towards the other person and you have the lesser, do not be jealous for God had designed it that way. If someone is so blessed with so much wealth, honor and fame, do not be jealous if you are poor, insignificant and always struggling because God's plans are always perfect. It may look like you are deprived in this life but only God can see that your treasure in heaven will be that much more than the one who has much in this world. In this commandment, we should always guard our tendency for desiring the treasures, honors and position that makes us greater than the others.

Discuss for 20 minutes about the Ten Commandments.
Why His commandments is very crucial to our spiritual well being.
Why His commandments is for our own highest and greatest good.
Why is it that disobeying one is disobeying all His commandments.
Why fulfilling His commandments leads to holiness and perfection.
Why is it that most of us could not properly remember all of the Ten Commandments.
Is obedience related to love?
Closing Prayer:
Sing Hymn, "Salve Regina"
Our Lady of Unity pray for us, your community and lead us to holiness.

Eleventh Class: (3 hours or less)

Hymn: Together Sing, "Christ Be Our Light"
Opening Prayer:

Loving The Son

Leader Reads Scripture Passage

"You are the light of the world. A city that is set on an hill cannot be hid." Matthew 5:14.

We remember the eight class about knowing Jesus, the Son of God and Mary. We knew that He entered into our land of exile in our time and executed the mission of our justification and redemption. Jesus Christ alone will salvation be possible. This is universally known. We did studied further so we have more knowledge of Him. Having known Jesus, our hearts should be on fire with love for Him. We should never stop praising Him for what He did for us. We should always give thanks to Him with the greatest gratitude for giving His Life to us so we can be able to enter into the new heavens. All ordinary Christians knew about this. We should have more knowledge than the ordinary Christians about Jesus because of Our Lady's revelation to our community. That our Lord Jesus and our Lady cannot be separated from each other and that we have both of them on our side while our protestant brothers and sisters could never acknowledged His mother as having the greatest part in our redemption.

In this class, we will discuss how we can give the best of our love to Jesus, our Lord and God. Having known how much we owed Him, our hearts should be on fire with love for Him. Let us then focus in this class how we can truly and really love Him. Love is most easiest and common word to say but in loving Jesus is the most difficult and the most hardest thing to do. We are easily deceived with our very own opinionated assessment contradicting what is real and what is truth. We do think that we believe and love Him but sad to say we are so far and remote from the truth and reality. Our love for Jesus is so superficial and to truly love Him takes more than words and even actions. Of course, we will be disappointed about this which may discouraged us with our failures in giving Jesus all our love but cheer and rejoice for despite of our limitation there is always hope that we can succeed in giving Him all our love. Know that our Lord knew that we are merely made of dust and even made of corruptible flesh and our love for Him is truly so limited. But with Him in our midst, we now have the greatest chance and opportunity to expand the capacity of our love beyond ourselves. How? Well, Jesus came and taught us how we can love like Him. And we have a lifetime to work on our mission to make His love our very own.

Now let us learn how we can truly love our Lord. As He is the light of our dark world, Jesus taught that we too have been commissioned to be like Him, the light of the world. To love Him be a light to the world.

The light of God will never be extinguished. The world is filled with darkness drawing many away from the light. The world's treasures and pleasures compensates its darkness attracting many to see a different kind of light than that of God's. Such conflicting lights is a blinding obstacle to our life's journey making it difficult for us to see clearly the way, the truth and the life. The world's light is like the sun pleasant to see making us feel better but deceivingly dark in reality. Many are lead to walk the wide path of perdition because the light they followed was actually darkness. Notice how the blind walks by feeling its way uncertain if he can reach his destination. He cannot. The worldly will experience the same way as the blind unsure if ever they can find the hidden true light of God. However, the children of light despite dwelling in the darkness of the world can enter easily into the narrow path of light because they walk not by sight but by faith. God's grace sufficiently lead them to the way, the truth and the life. How dark is their journey to eternity, the children of light will not get lost since their path is well lighted by the graces of God. The Lord will never abandon nor forsake His Own Body and since God is truth, He will never renege on all of His promises. As children of God we are also children of light. As Jesus, our Lord was sent by the Father to the world to lead us to the way, to the truth and to the life, we need to follow Him always so we can see God's light. Once we embrace His light our mind, heart and soul became illuminated that we can see better the things of God and heaven. Such vision compels us to live the life of God hidden in us. Christ our light made possible for us to see the things that others failed to see. Once we live His life in this world, we in turn become the light of the world and those who lives in darkness will be able to see the light that was given to us by Jesus. To prove our true love for Jesus, we should become the light of the world that all may see the love we practice by our good deeds.

Therefore, in our memory, let us always remind ourselves that we are not children of darkness but of the light. We have been redeemed by our Lord Jesus and we belong to Him alone. We can never repay our redemption and with our greatest gratitude we should strive to give Him all our love. With Him in us, He is our light that will led us to the path of heaven. Without His light, we remain blind and there is no way we can ever find God.

In our intellect, let us always kept this knowledge so we will always follow the light of Christ for He alone will be our guide to find God and His kingdom. The light of Christ will show us how to live the perfect Christian life. Having His light will make us prophets where we can foresee what lies ahead in this life and beyond. Without His light, we are doomed in the darkness of this world that would surely lead us to eternal death.

In our will, let us always do follow our Lord's direction to become His light. Let us always strive to unite our light to that greater Light so its brilliance will be much stronger and greater that the whole world will be drawn to God's marvelous light. By being His light, we have given our love to the Son of God. This is how we prove our love for Him.

Pause for 1 minute and then together pray below:

"The Lord makes day and night so we may know
How His light can make us see the path

The Lord will guide us in how to walk His ways
The way of the just are holy for obeying His commands
But the wicked and rebellious stumbles in the darkness
The Lord made them blind on account of their sins
They had forsaken the laws of the Lord
In their pride, God is beyond their understanding
And the Lord hid the truth in deepest darkness
But the righteous and the just, God filled them with His light
Blessed be the Lord our God and His Eternal Light
For we can see His way, His truth and His life
Leading us to His Eternal kingdom
Where we will live with Him forever and ever. Amen.

After the prayer, remain seated and listen to His Voice: Leader read below slowly His Direction.

"I HAVE SEEN MANY OF MY CHILDREN ARE LOST. THEY CAN NOT SEE THE NARROW PATH I SHOWED THEM. THEY HAVE GROWN ACCUSTOMED TO DARKNESS AND THEY DESIRE NOT TO SEE MY LIGHT. I CREATED THEM AS CHILDREN OF LIGHT BUT THEY ARE DRAWN TO DARKNESS. THEY FIND PLEASURE IN THE DARK BELIEVING NO ONE CAN SEE THE WORKS OF THEIR OWN WILL. MY HOLY WILL IS TO GIVE LIGHT GUIDING YOU TO MY WAY, TO MY TRUTH AND TO MY LIFE. IF YOU LIVE IN DARKNESS YOU WILL NEVER FIND ME WHO IS YOUR LIGHT AND SALVATION. YOU WILL NEVER BE ABLE TO LIVE MY LIFE AND YOU WILL NEVER KNOW THE TRUTH. THOSE IN DARKNESS WILL REMAIN THERE AND IF THEY CONTINUE TO SEEK NOT MY LIGHT THEN FOREVER THEY WILL NEVER SEE ME. MY CHILDREN WHO FOLLOWED MY LIGHT WILL KNOW THE WAY TO MY KINGDOM WHERE THEY WILL REIGN AND LIVE WITH ME FOREVER. THEY WILL LIVE MY LIFE BY FOLLOWING MY WILL AND NOT THEIRS. THEY ARE IN THE LIGHT AND THEY CAN SEE MY WAYS AND THEY EASILY OBEY ALL MY COMMANDMENTS. MY CHILDREN WHO POSSESS MY LIGHT WILL FULLY KNOW THE TRUTH THAT I AM THE ONE WHO IS THE BEGINNING AND THE END. THEY WILL ALWAYS BE DRAWN TO ME FOR I AM ALWAYS DRAWING THEM TO ME. THEY NEVER STOP THINKING OF ME ALWAYS THANKING, PRAISING, ADORING AND WORSHIPPING ME THROUGHOUT THE DAY AND FOR THE REST OF THEIR LIFE. WOULD YOU LIKE TO HAVE MY LIGHT? WOULD YOU MAKE MY LIGHT SHINE SO THOSE IN DARKNESS MAY SEE? ACCEPT MY LIGHT AND YOU WILL NEVER LOSE ME NOW AND FOR ALL ETERNITY.

After hearing His Voice remain seated and in silence. For the next 5 minutes, each re read His Direction and His Voice. Read slowly and absorbed it in your heart and soul.

The leader proceeds and continue by reading the Scripture Passage below:

"Let your light so shine before men, that they see your good works, and glorify your Father which is in heaven." Matthew 5:16.

In our pursuit for God, religion plays a major role teaching and showing us the way in finding Him. There is indeed chaotic competition among religious institution and denomination trying to attract and win members into their fold causing division and even violence. What is happening in Ireland is a bad example to the Christian religion where violence can not be controlled as Catholics and Protestants continued fighting each other. The primary teaching of Christ was and is to love one another as He loves us but by killing each other reduces Christianity's principles of love, peace and joy. The Christian religion emphasized that followers should follow and imitate their Lord and Master, Jesus Christ. However, the life of a true Christian is a very demanding one and those who truly embraces and practiced it are few. There are billions who called themselves Christians but in the final count, the number who really and practices their faith is shockingly low. The life of a real and true Christian can only be done if one possesses the light of God in the heart and soul. Once you possessed the light of Christ you will know and understand everything Jesus had taught. All the darkness in your soul will be enlightened by the light of Christ and the path to God becomes more visible leading us to live a life worthy of Him. As Jesus was sent by the Father to accomplish His mission of salvation, we who possesses His light must also participate in the mission of Christ by showing and teaching those who are in darkness that they may see the light of God so they may be saved.

Therefore, in our soul, in the memory, let us always remind ourselves that the light of Christ will make us see clearly the true path leading us to holiness and perfection. Let us not forget that having the light of Christ makes us His living extension powering the mission of salvation into the end of time.

In our intellect, let us always possess and kept this knowledge that we need the light of Christ in order for us to accomplish the mission of God in redeeming and saving His lost creation. Know that the light of God will make us see that we are all His children and it is also our responsibility to make His light shine on those who dwell in darkness and in the shadow of death. Without God's light, there is no way we can see God in each one of us. We can only see the darkness of sin and hopelessness. The light of God enlightens our soul making us see everything in His very Own Eyes.

In our will, let us always follow our Lord's direction to always seek the light of Christ by doing everything Jesus taught us. Let us always be charitable and kind by doing good works at all times so the world will see and notice our deeds. By doing so the world will see the great works of God through us.

Pray together the prayer below:

"The light of the Lord shines all over His creation
In Him there is no darkness
What is dark to us is light to Him
There is nothing hidden from the Lord's sight
His power and might extend from time to eternity
I am the light of the world and those who dwell in darkness are not my own
Says the Lord
The righteous and the just walk in His light
They will stumble and fall but will rise
We are His children if we follow the Lord's path
But the path of the wicked is always dark
The Lord calls us to become His light
To dispel the darkness of the world
To show sinners the way and the wicked His light
That they may also follow us to become children of Light
Blessed be God in His light shining on us
Blessed be the Triune God who brought us to light
Now and forever. Amen"

After the prayer, the leader slowly read the Voice of God speaking His direction to the community.

"MY CHILDREN CAN SEE ME BECAUSE I AM THE LIGHT OF THEIR SOUL. THEY CAN NOT SEE ME FOR I AM SPIRIT AND LIFE. I GIVE LIGHT TO THEIR SOUL AND THEY CAN SEE ME IN THEIR MEMORY AND THEY WILL NOT FORGET ME. IN THEIR INTELLECT IS FULL OF LIGHT AND THEY WILL UNDERSTAND MY WAY. THEY WILL KNOW THE TRUTH. I AM IN THEIR WILL FOR THEY HAVE ENTRUSTED IT TO ME. THE CHILDREN OF LIGHT ARE MINE. THEY WILL DO WHAT I DID. THEY ARE THE POWERFUL EXTENSION OF MY LIGHT AND THEY WILL SHOW THE WAY TO THOSE WHO ARE LOST IN DARKNESS. THEY WILL LIT THE WORLD WITH MY LIGHT AND SOME WILL FOLLOW IT AND SOME WILL CONTINUE TO DWELL AND LIVE IN THE DARK. NO ONE CAN SEE YOUR LIGHT BECAUSE I AM ON IT. YOU WHO ARE MY CHILDREN WILL LIT THE WORLD BY THE WAY YOU LIVE. YOUR GOOD DEEDS AND YOUR CHARITY TO ALL WILL BE MY LIGHT. YOUR LOVE FOR ME AND FOR YOUR NEIGHBOR GIVES US THE GREATEST GLORY AND HONOR AND THE MOST HOLY TRINITY WILL MAKE YOUR LIGHT EVEN BRIGHTER THAT WILL DRAW MORE TO US. BE OUR LIGHT AND YOU WILL SHINE WITH US FOR ALL OF ETERNITY."

After the Voice, remain in silence for 5 minutes re reading His Voice and absorbing in our hearts and soul.

After silence continue by discussing how we can truly love the Son of God.

Discuss for 30 minutes the following:
Why is it that most if not all of us can not give all of our love to God?
Explain if there are any differences of living in darkness and the godless.
Our Lady revealed to the community that every day tens of thousands of soul are lost to hell. Discuss the causes why so many souls are lost each day.
Why do plants and vegetation need the sun light? Why do we need the light of Christ? There is similarity. Discuss.
There are other religion that does not know Christ as the Messiah. What kind of light they are seeing in their faith?
Why is it that the light of Christ not compatible to the light to the world. How can we His true followers give His light to the world?
In what way can our Lady obtain for us the light of her Son?

After 30 minutes discussion, take 10 minutes break.

Class resume with leader reading Scripture Passage below:

"And he saith unto them, Follow me, and I will make you fishers of men." Matthew 4:19.

This is the calling from God and those who will follow Him certainly proves love for the Son. What does it mean to follow me? The greatest proof that one loves Christ is none other but to carry his or her cross. What are the crosses we have to carry. We can not list or mention them all but generally speaking is that we live a blameless life acceptable to God. A blameless life involves many things in our life. For example, we must avoid sin all the time and at all cost. To follow Christ involves denying ourselves of many things that can make our worldly life more difficult than those who live solely for the pleasures and treasures of the world. To follow Him also involves living a life of servitude not only to God but to those who are in need. We are all called to serve God and others. This is our mission in life. We are to follow our teacher and master to the spiritual path of perfection. As Jesus is holy and perfect we too must become. When we do this, our cross becomes more heavier than those who ignores the calling for perfection and holiness because they can fulfill whatever desires they have in their hearts. The calling from God is not limited for His apostles or evangelist but for all. Do not ever doubt that each one of us had the greatest potential to become another Christ if only we follow Him and truly give all our love for Him. But our own will becomes our greatest hindrance by not conforming to God's will. Most of us are so content to live a mediocre spiritual life depriving us of reaching the heights of divinity. We are called to become His disciples no matter what is our station in life. We are created for God and He expect us to follow Him and give our love to God and serve everyone that needs us. No one is exempt to become fishers of men. We are called to become catchers of souls. We are to participate in the mission of God by contributing our labors in His vineyard. He will make us fishers of men. He will shape and mold us to become like Him so we can participate in saving souls including our very own. To follow Him and to serve Him by becoming fishers of men definitely had proven itself to have loved the Son.

And to our community, to love our Lady's Son, we must definitely love what Jesus loves. And what was and is His love? What else but the salvation of all souls. What else but to sacrifice His Life for the salvation of others. What else but to spent all His time in prayer for our sakes. What else but His eternal servitude to His Body still detained in this world. What else but His continuous prayer to the Father that all will be save. As member of our Lady's community, this is our greatest and highest goal, to strive persistently by never giving up loving Christ with all our hearts, mind, body and soul. And to do what Christ did. This is perfect love.

Therefore, in our memory let us remind ourselves that each one of us had that special role in building the Body of Christ. Let us remember that we do not have to be a priest, ministers, apostles, evangelists or prophets to answer His glorious calling. God had already chosen you to be His Own. We exist simply for the reason that God planned it.

In our intellect, let us always possess and kept this knowledge that we are to participate in God's plan of making us like Him. Know that our station and position in life is never a deterrent in following our Lord. Our wisdom should inspire us to participate laboring in God's vineyards in whatever calling we received from Him. By striving to become holy and perfect surely satisfies God's calling and we became so fruitful in His kingdom.

In our will, let us always follow our Lord's direction to become his devoted and faithful follower. We have the graces of God as our greatest source moving us to become what He wants us to be. Let us always become servants to each other by working and serving to the most needy specially those who are in spiritual darkness.

After reading pray together the prayer below:

"How lovely and pleasant to hear Your Voice O Lord
To come and follow You is a call that energized our soul
Make known your plans for us that we may do what pleases You
Our joy and happiness is to do Your most Holy Will
There is nothing in this world that satisfies us
Only pains and fleeting pleasures trapping us into its darkness
But our soul always longs for You O Lord our God
For with You is fullness of light making us see
The glory, splendor, honor and majesty awaiting for us
As we Your children of light perseveres in walking Your ways
Always following the path prepared for us

Here we are O Lord in Your holy Presence
We are at still always waiting and ready to follow You
We pray in the Holy name of Jesus Your Son
To make us fishers of men. Amen.

After the prayer, leader slowly read His Voice.

"EVERYONE I CREATED IS VERY SPECIAL. BEFORE YOU WERE FORMED IN YOUR MOTHER'S WOMB I HAVE ALREADY MADE MY PLANS FOR YOU. YOU ARE PREDESTINED TO INHERIT MY GLORIOUS KINGDOM. YOU ARE TO BECOME MY CHILDREN AND I WILL BE YOUR HEAVENLY FATHER. I CAME DOWN AS A SLAVE TO TESTIFY TO THE TRUTH THAT YOU WERE CREATED FOR ME. I TAUGHT MY APOSTLES HOW TO BECOME MY FAITHFUL FOLLOWER AND DISCIPLE SO IN RETURN THEY WILL SPREAD THE GOOD NEWS. FOR OVER TWO THOUSAND YEARS MY GOSPEL OF TRUTH HAD BEEN PREACHED AND THOSE WHO BECAME MY FOLLOWERS DID REAP ALL THE REWARDS OF MY PROMISES. BUT FOR EVERY ONE WHO FOLLOWED ME DEVOUTLY THOUSANDS WOULD NOT RESPOND TO THE GLORIOUS CALLING PREFERRING TO ANSWER THE CALLING OF THEIR OWN WILL. YOU HAVE LISTEN AND HEARD MY CALL. WHAT IS YOUR RESPONSE? I HAVE PREPARED FOR YOU THE GREATEST REWARD THAT CAN NOT BE DESCRIBED IN WORDS A PLACE SAINTS SPENT THEIR LIVES PREPARING TO RECEIVE THEIR GLORIOUS CROWN. BUT I CANNOT FORCE MY WILL IN YOURS. YOU MUST EXERCISE YOUR OWN WILL IN CHOOSING ME AND WHEN YOU DO I WILL PROMISE YOU THAT I WILL BE WITH YOU ALWAYS UNTIL YOU WILL BE WITH ME IN PARADISE WHERE NO EYES HAD SEEN NOR WORDS CAN DESCRIBED.

After reading in silence repeat reading His Voice and let it penetrate to your mind, heart and soul. Slowly and absorb. 5 minutes.

After silent meditation community discussion 30 minutes about the following:

We are called to become fishers of men. By doing so, we did prove our love for the Son. How can we become fishers of men? Discuss.

So very few truly and really follow and give all their love for Jesus. Why is it, knowing that there awaits the greatest reward of heaven and God and so few responded?

It is I who chose you. What did our Lord meant? Explain why the grace of God can make the greatest difference in our salvation.

Grace of God is freely given but why so many souls are lost. Others blamed God for sending sinners to hell. What do you think?

In proving our love for Him, what is the best way to show Him?

What are the reasons that the light of God could not enter into the mind, heart and soul of the godless?

Why does not God force Himself on our own will. Why He never intervenes knowing that we have the tendency to do our own will?

After 30 minutes discussion, leader continue by reading the Scripture scene when our Lord and Peter had the conversation.

"Peter, do you love me?" Peter answered: "Yes, Lord."

The Lord said: "Feed my lambs."

Jesus then asked Peter a second time: "Peter, do you love me?"

Again, Peter said, yes.

The Lord said: "Feed my sheep."

And the Lord asked Peter the third time: "Peter, do you love me?"

Peter grieved that the Lord asked him three times, and he answered: "Lord, you know everything and you know that I love you."

Finally Jesus said: "Feed my sheep."

This is also how we must profess our love for Him; We must do what Peter was asked to do. We must feed His sheep. We must take great care of our immortal soul so we can feed others with His love. We must love all souls because by loving and caring for them, we return God's love. We must love what Jesus loved when He was here with us always doing our Father's will. Therefore, in proving our greatest love for Him, we must become servant to all, just as our Lord came to serve and not to be served.

By joining the religious Order of our Lady of Unity, you will become a servant to all. By giving and consecrating yourself to the Triune God, you have made yourself servant to all.

Closing Prayer:

Sing together, Hymn: "Salve Regina"

Our Lady of Unity pray for us, your community and lead us to holiness. Amen.

Twelve Class: (3 hours or less)

Hymn: Together Sing, "Come Holy Ghost"
Opening Prayer:

Loving The Holy Spirit

Leader reads the passage of Scripture below:

"And the spirit of the Lord shall rest upon him, the spirit of wisdom, and understanding, the spirit of counsel and might, the spirit of knowledge and of the fear of the Lord" Isaiah 11:2.

Considered the least known and honored Persona of God, is the Holy Spirit. As member of our Lady of Unity's community, we should make sure we are devoted to Him much like our devotion to the Father and to the Son. We Christians are so close to the Father and of course to our Lord Jesus that it is common usage for Christians to claimed that they have a personal relationship with Him. Of course, words comes easy to say but in reality that personal relationship with Him is truly intimacy. When one claims intimacy with our Lord such statement should be examined if it is really true. Intimacy with Jesus can only be actuated when one had completely made itself one with the Beloved. To claim intimacy, one must have truly known Him and what He truly wants and demands of us. Intimacy with our Lord Jesus involves union of the two hearts, union of two souls and union of two wills. True, everybody seems to say how they love our Lord. They raise their hands, they sing songs for Him, they keep praising and thanking Him but to be intimate with Jesus takes more that those activities we seemed to participate with energy. Unfortunately, when one claims intimacy with our Lord, it is best not to say it loud and clear simply because, we are so far in our personal relationship with our Lord. Much more intimacy. When one is truly intimate with the Lord, He will live life like our Lord and he will do what our Lord did. It cost our Lord the greatest suffering imaginable and it did cost His very Life. Do you really want that intimacy? Grace be with you for the one who truly wants intimacy with our Lord, one has to completely give itself to Him. One has to lose its own life to gain His. This is truly intimacy with the Lord. When you abandon everything including your family, treasure and your life for the sake of Him then you are talking about intimacy with the Lord. Otherwise, let us not brag how we had a very personal relationship with Jesus but simply in the silence of our mind, heart and soul continuously seek Him until such time when His grace makes you truly one with Him. When we talk about true and real intimacy with Jesus, we are talking about the Indwelling of the Triune God in us. This will be our goal as member of our Lady's community that each one of us will be united with the Triune God through our holy consecration during our profession. Faithfulness to our community's rule, our Lady of Unity promises that through her fervent and persistent intercessor that each one of us will obtain the eternal happiness promised by her Son. But the greatest gift we will received through our consecration and profession will be in

Indwelling of the Most Holy Trinity where each one of us will grown into an intimacy with the Triune God.

As mentioned, the Third Persona of God is the least revered and honored although honoring the Father and the Son, being equal with them, the Holy Spirit also is being honored. But as consecrated to the Triune God, we members of her community, much like her, must also cultivate that intimacy with the Holy Spirit. Not so many are aware that of the Three Persona, it is the Holy Spirit who did most of the work to complete God's masterpieces. Of course, each Persona did great works for our transforming process, it is the Holy Spirit that works the hardest. In our work, He was and is the busiest. Let us make some illustration of their works.

The Father started the whole process. He mold us in His Holy Hands, gives His eternal Breathe to us. He was busy observing how His creation was doing and it was so bad that He was about to destroy us except for Noah. The seed of Noah replenished the lost seed of Adam and Eve, justly so because sin could no longer be tolerated by the Father. He called Moses so to continue His marvelous plans for us although quite a ways yet and to make His people happy and appreciative of Him God gave them that promised land filled with milk and honey. A land of their own where they can freely cultivate whatever their heart's desire. Since the new heaven was not yet opened, the promised land was their reward sort of restoring the garden of Eden but once they have their reward, our sinfulness and rebelliousness kept on stirring our poor soul and the Father had to really endure their attitude towards Him. Of course, our Father had to be patience with us knowing that we too had been victimized by the sins of our fathers and that we are suffering unjustly for their own sins. Thus, the great mercy of God and compassion will always be with us knowing our great difficulties in handling the terrible curses of sin that we inherited. And to make up for all we had to endure, God promised us another promised land which is the new heaven. And this is far more greater, far more desirable and far more than anything of us could ever imagine and hoped for. An eternity of joy, happiness, beauty, glory, majesty and possessing everything that is of our God. Like what all the saints in heaven had prophesied, all the sufferings, pains and miseries we suffered in this life is nothing but a temporary inconvenience and irritation knowing the greatness of His reward to those who loves Him.

Thus, the Second Persona, in the form of ourselves came down for our sake. He was the second hardest worker of the Triune God. Worst, God has to become like us with all our weaknesses, our inconstancy, our struggles and burdens made Jesus, the suffering God. He who has everything governs all things possesses everything must reduce Himself into the most miserable creature. Thus, Jesus our God became our slave because He was united to our slavery of sin except He can never sin because of His divine nature. He stayed for thirty three years serving us working hard preaching teaching healing praying and building His church, the new Noah's Ark so it will take us to the new heavens.

Once, He ascended to the new heavens, He then give us His Third Persona the Holy Spirit to finish the greatest work of our God. Us. We are His masterpieces and if all of us truly knew about this truth there should have been no problem here on earth because each one of us will behave and act like true children of God. Everyone of us will love one another perfectly because we are like Him. But sad to say, most of us cannot put into our mind, heart and soul that we are. The truth has been hidden by the extreme darkness of the world and the greatness of the devil's deceptive devices that hid the truth from most of us. But as member of our Lady's community as her co-workers we have that greatest responsibility to make known to others the greatness of our being. As the Three Persona of God works so hard for our sakes, we have that greatest responsibility also to really work hard in our Lord's vineyard. As our Father works hard for us, so we too must work for Him because He is our Father who needs help in the greatest and largest vineyard ever. As His Son, Jesus our Lord works hard for us even losing His life for us, then we too must work hard like our great Brother in helping the least of our brothers and sisters who are lost and could not find that Light. As future Spouse of our soul, who was working from the beginning of time till the end of time, we too who wants to become a faithful and devoted spouse of the Holy Spirit must also work hard inviting others to give their all to the Triune God who gives us Their All.

Returning back to the Holy Spirit let us know more about our Lord in His Third Persona so to enkindle our love and devotion to Him for His greatest role in transforming us to be like Him.

Let us clarify that the Holy Spirit is God, really our God who is the same God as our Father in heaven and also the same God as His Son our Lord Jesus. Let us closely examine His important works pertaining to our transforming process:

The Holy Spirit was involved in the peace process between God and us. He must become the Spouse of Mary to consummate their Plans in uniting the Spirit of God into the flesh of man as the perfect model for creation in order for us to enter the new heavens. In Jesus Christ, peace was made where we can be back to Him not only in this life but forever with Christ as our guide and light. The union of Spirit and flesh became our model in how we too can conquer our sinfulness by having the Spirit of God in our lives (the corruptible flesh). This model of our salvation was never made available during the time of Moses and God's people in the Old covenant. We are more blest and more fortunate to have and to know this great and perfect model for our salvation. Most important that the new heaven is available now for us. Unlike the Old covenant they have to wait for thousands of years before they can enter into the new heavens courtesy to the redemptive works of our Lord Jesus.

The next important work of the Third Persona was proclaiming to the whole world that the Holy One baptized in the Jordan River was truly the Son of God recorded by John's testimony where John saw the Third Persona descended on Jesus. He then heard the Father's voice that He was most pleased with His beloved Son's act of being baptized. Of course, They all know Their Plans that through baptism the Third Persona will also come down on the baptized person much like what happened to Jesus. The baptism was necessary to our Lord for our benefits, both spirit and flesh whom He represented as the perfect Model for creation. As previously discussed, baptism is so important for in doing so, one will be truly integrated to the Body of Christ.

After our Lord's baptism, the Holy Spirit then lead Him to the mountain to be tempted and tested. Quite shocking but the purpose for Him was also to test the enemies of our salvation. We all know that Jesus is both God and man or spirit and flesh. The devil did his best to tempt our Lord by offering the world, the devil and of course the flesh. Our Lord saw the devil's lie when he offer the whole world to Him knowing that the world belongs to Him for God created it. Refusing the bite the devil's bait he continued to tempt Him knowing His flesh was hungry but He rejected him by teaching us to live in the Spirit and not on the flesh. Finally the devil flee knowing he was badly defeated. It was also a great example for us true follower how we though made of flesh and spirit can also win our battles against all enemies.

We all should know that the Holy Spirit was always present in His humanity. Of course, He was always present in Jesus Divine nature. The Holy Spirit gives the humanity of Jesus all the seven gifts to draw and attract followers of His lofty teachings. They were both working as One for our sakes and we should know that they were working hard and to invalidate Their great works one will put itself in the greatest risk of losing God and heaven.

After doing all Their great works here on earth, time for our Lord Jesus to offer His Life for our sake on the cross and after His mission was completed He gave up the Holy Spirit back to the Eternal Father. It is not His divinity that gave the Holy Spirit but His humanity.

During the resurrection, both His divine and human Persona became permanently cemented into One as our preview that with Him in us, we too will be resurrected having the genetic makeup modeled to our Lord. When we are raise up it is the Holy Spirit doing the work in making us like our Lord Jesus.

Indeed, before He went back to the Father, Jesus promises His followers that He will sent the Third Persona knowing that without Him, we will be in great trouble much like what happened to God's chosen people when Moses left them behind. Knowing our feebleness and our affinity with our flesh and our infidelities, at this time God made sure we have all the necessary help so we can safely reach our heavenly home.

Christ promised that this Spirit of Truth would come and would remain within us.

"I will ask the Father and He will give you another Paraclete-to be with you always: The Spirit of truth, whom the world cannot accept, since it neither sees Him nor recognizes Him; but you can recognize Him because He remains with you and will be within you." John 14:16-17.

The Holy Spirit came at Pentecost, never to depart. Fifty days after Easter, on Pentecost Sunday, He changed the Apostles from weak and fearful men to brave men of faith that Christ needed to spread His Gospel to the nations.

The Holy Spirit is present in a special way in the Church, the community of those who believe in Christ as Lord. He helps the Church to continue the work of Christ in the world. By His presence people are moved by His grace to unite themselves with God and men in sincere love and to fulfill their duties to God and man. He makes the Church pleasing to God because of the Divine life of grace which He gives. By the power of the Gospel He makes the Church grow. He renews it with His gifts, and leads it to perfect union with Jesus.

The Holy Spirit guides the Pope, bishops, and priests of the Church in their work of teaching Christ's doctrine, guiding souls, and giving God's grace to the people through the Sacraments. He directs all the work of Christ in the Church — the care of the sick, the teaching of children, the guidance of youth, the comforting of the sorrowful, the support of the needy.

We should honor the Holy Spirit by loving Him as our God and by letting Him guide us in life. St. Paul reminds us to do so.

"Are you not aware that you are the temple of God, and that the Spirit of God dwells in you?" 1 Corinthian 3:16.

Since the Holy Spirit is always with us if we are in the state of grace, we should often ask Him for the light and strength we need to live a holy life and to save our soul.

Discussion of the Holy Spirit's role in us. 30 minutes. Discuss the question below:

The Holy Spirit was given to us as the most powerful weapon against the enemies of our salvation. Why is He the most powerful weapon?

Who will transform the bread and wine into the real Body and Blood of our Lord Jesus? Discuss the methodology of its transformation.

What sacraments that the Holy Spirit is heavily involved?

The Holy Spirit dwells in us only if we are in the state of grace. Why He does not dwell on those who are not?

Share to the community your experiences about the Holy Spirit.

Why is it that the only sin that can never forgiven is that sin against the Holy Spirit?

During the Pentecost, our Lady was with the Apostles waiting for His coming. Was it necessary also for her to receive the Holy Spirit or not? Discuss.

After 30 minutes of discussion take 10 minutes break.

Class resume by singing, "Immaculate Mary"

Then together community prays, below.

"Come, Holy Spirit, Creator blest!
And in our souls take up Your rest;
Come, with Your grace and heavenly aid,
"To fill the hearts which You have made.
O Comforter, to You do we cry,
O heavenly Gift of God Most High;
O Fount of life and Fire of love,
And sweet Anointing from above!
You in Your sevenfold Gifts are known;
You, Finger of God's hand, we own;
You, Promise of the Father, You,
Who do the tongue with power imbue.
Kindle our senses from above
And make our hearts overflow with love.
With patience firm and virtue high,
The weakness of our flesh supply.
Far from us drive the foe we dread,
And grant us Your true peace instead;
So shall we not, with You for Guide,
Turn from the path of life aside.
Oh, may Your grace on us bestow
The Father and the Son to know;
And You, through endless times confessed
Of both the eternal Spirit blest.
Now to the Father and the Son,
Who rose from death, be glory given,
With You, O holy Comforter,
Henceforth by all in earth and heaven. Amen
Pause 15 seconds
Leader:
Send forth Your Spirit and they shall be created;
Together Community respond;
And You shall renew the face of the earth.

Let us pray. God, You have taught the hearts of Your faithful people by sending them the light of Your Holy Spirit. Grant us by the same Spirit to have a right judgment in all things and evermore to rejoice in His holy comfort. Through Christ our Lord. Amen."

Leader reads the Scripture passage below:

"I solemnly assure you, no one can enter into God's kingdom without begotten of water and Spirit. Flesh begets flesh, Spirit begets spirit." John 3:5-6.

Clearly, the Church was established by our Lord Jesus Christ to gather those who were baptized into His Body. As He ascended to the Father in heaven, He brought with Him, us, His Body assuring that if we remain with Him while we are still detained on earth, our entrance to God's everlasting kingdom in the new heavens. However, having us already in heaven, we have that greatest responsibility that once integrated to God's Body must be very vigilant in how we live His Life here on the land of exile. As Christ easily took on our sinful flesh and perfectly consolidated into His Spirit, we, however will encounter some difficulties and hardship in receiving His Spirit into our corruptible flesh. Thus, the Third Persona of God must actively involved in us knowing that without Him in our midst, it will be so very difficult for us to perfectly consolidate His Spirit into our rebellious flesh. And so, we are so blest with His Presence in the world for He will be the One who will teach and show us how we can perfectly consolidate His Spirit to our sinful flesh.

"This much I have told you while I was still with you; the Paraclete, the Holy Spirit Whom the Father will send in My Name, will instruct you in everything, and remind you of all that I told you." John 14:25-26.

There are skeptics that claimed that Sacred Scriptures were written by men and not by God. It is simply their ignorance and the lack of comprehension about the things of God. Of course, it was written by men but what they have written was inspired by the Holy Spirit. Who could have written such lofty ideas about the divine things except from the One coming from the highest heaven. The Bible was written some time after our Lord went back to heaven. How could they remember or recall everything Jesus said unless the Holy Spirit came into their assistance instructing them everything that was written in Sacred Scriptures. Thus, Jesus told them that everything will be set since the Holy Spirit will do everything for them. It was Him who reminded them of what they have seen, heard and witness about the Son of God. Had the Holy Spirit not come, the Bible would not have existed except the Old Testament. As Jesus followers waited for His coming….

"When the day of Pentecost came it found them gathered in one place. Suddenly from up in the sky there came a noise like a strong, driving wind which was heard all through the house where they were seated. Tongues of fire appeared, which parted and came to rest on each of them. All were filled with the Holy Spirit. They began to express themselves in foreign tongues and make bold proclamation as the Spirit prompted them." Acts 2:1-4.

Although the news of our Lord's resurrection rapidly increases the Christian community, it was after the coming of the Holy Spirit that produces powerful spiritual forces that energized not only the Apostles and disciples but also the newly converted Christians. They were bold and brave in witnessing for their faith unseen before. It was like a large forrest fire assisted with the strongest wind making the wild fire unstoppable and uncontrollable and it spread to the ends of the earth. Thus, the old earth had been replaced with the new one as the world was renewed and recreated by the Holy Spirit. Most importantly, God distributed all kinds of graces to His Body by providing them with all kinds of gifts that would benefits the whole

Church so they will be able to fight and defeat the enemies of our salvation.

"To each person the manifestation of the Spirit is given for the common good. To one the Spirit gives wisdom in discourse, to another the power to express knowledge. Through the Spirit one receives faith; by the same Spirit another is given the gifts of healing, and still another miraculous powers. Prophecy is given to one; to another power to distinguish one spirit from another. One receives the gift of tongues, another that of interpreting the tongues. But it is one and the same Spirit Who produces all these gifts, distributing them to each as He wills."

With the Holy Spirit always with His Church, what Jesus told to Peter became reality that on this rock where His Church is built nothing can destroy it even the power of hell. This is why it is truly very important to be baptized in the Catholic Church because it is the new ark an invincible ark that will bring all its member home. Also, with all the powers given to its members, the Church member shared everything in its treasury making the member fully equip in its journey to the heights of divinity.

Pause briefly 2 minutes in silence then leader leads the Consecration Prayer to the Holy Spirit so its member will be guided and directed by its prompting.

"Holy Spirit, Divine Spirit of light and love, we consecrate to You our understanding, our hearts and wills, our whole being, for time and for eternity. May our understanding be always submissive to Your heavenly inspirations and to the teaching of the Catholic Church, of which You are the infallible Guide. May our hearts be ever inflamed with the love of God and of our neighbor. May our will be ever conformed to the Divine Will. May our whole life be faithful to the imitation of the life and virtues of our Lord and Savior Jesus Christ, to Whom with the Father and You be honor and glory forever. God, Holy Spirit, Infinite Love of the Father and the Son, through the pure hands of Mary, Your Immaculate Spouse, we place ourselves this day, and all the days of our lives, upon Your chosen altar, the Divine Heart of Jesus, as a sacrifice to You, consuming fire, being firmly resolved now more than ever to hear Your voice and to do in all things Your most holy and adorable Will."

Our Father, Hail Mary and Glory Be.

Discussion 30 minutes.

Scripture says that baptism is so necessary if we want to get to heaven. In what other way that one can enter the new heavens? Share your thoughts to the community.

If a child dies before receiving baptism, what will happen to their soul? Are they in heaven, hell or purgatory. Share your thought and opinions.

Is it possible that the Holy Spirit is also present in other churches or religion. Share your opinions and thoughts.

In the farthest and remotest places on earth where the Gospel was not preached and the people living there have no idea or knowledge about God and His saving mission, can their soul be save? Share your thoughts and opinions.

How can we discern that what we do comes from the Holy Spirit? Share your thoughts and opinions.

Break 10 minutes.

The Holy Spirit was the One who united God and man. The Holy Spirit never stops working for our sanctification and salvation. He will be the One who finishes the work of the Father and the Son. He will dwell in us to transform our hearts, mind, soul and spirit so we can become like God. Therefore, with sincerity slowly the community prays together that each one will receive His seven gifts necessary for our goal to become holy and perfect.

"Blessed Spirit of Wisdom, help me to seek God. Make Him the center of my life and order my life to Him, so that love and harmony may reign in my soul.

Blessed Spirit of Understanding, enlighten my mind, that I may know and love the truths of faith and make them truly my own.

Blessed Spirit of Counsel, enlighten and guide me in all my ways, that I may always know and do Your holy Will. Make me prudent and courageous.

Blessed Spirit of Fortitude, uphold my soul in every time of trouble or adversity. make me loyal and confident.

Blessed Spirit of Knowledge, help me to know good from evil. Teach me to do what is right in the sight of God. Give me clear vision and firmness in decision.

Blessed Spirit of Piety, possess my heart, incline it to a true faith in You, to a holy love of You, my God, that with my whole soul I may seek You, Who are my Father, and find You, my best and truest joy.

Blessed Spirit of Holy Fear, penetrate my inmost heart that I may ever mindful of Your presence. Make fly from sin, and give me intense reverence for God and for my fellow men who are made in God's image.

Grant, we beg of You, Almighty God, that we may so please Your Holy Spirit by our earnest prayers, that we may, by His grace, be freed from all temptations and merit to receive the forgiveness of our sins. Through Christ our Lord. Amen."

Our Father, Hail Mary and Glory Be.
Closing Prayer:
Sing Hymn, "Salve Regina"
Our Lady of Unity pray for us, your community and lead us to holiness.

Thirteenth Class: (3 hours or less)

Hymn: Sing together, "How Great Thou Art"
Opening Prayer:

Serving God

Leader read the passage below:

The second greatest aspect of our intimate relation with God is to serve Him. In reality though, to serve God is nothing but a facade for it is God always serving us. Why is God is so great? As our Lord Jesus instructed His apostles and disciples that anyone who wants to become great in the kingdom of God one must become a servant or even a slave to all. How great is God indeed for He is the greatest servant of all. He kept serving us wether we are good or evil in His Sight. He sustain the sun giving light for all the vegetation and fruit trees for our benefits. Therefore, let us not be so proud if we were able to serve others in their needs because in reality it was God's bounty that move us into His servitude. It is our God doing all the serving using us for His greater glory and honor. What then will we do to serve Him? Truthfully, nothing. He reminded us to be at still knowing that we are nothing and He is God. We can truly serve God by simply waiting for Him. Like a faithful slave, we shall always be waiting for our master voice, his words. In serving the Almighty God, we like a faithful servant always wait for His command. And we did received all His commands. Holy Scriptures were written as our greatest gift so we all know what He wants from us. Be still, should not be confused that we don't do nothing but to wait and wait for the Lord had already given us everything and to be at still meant to contemplate His Words. This is the greatest service we give to our Lord, reading, listening, absorbing and contemplating His Words. Be still as in contemplation, and we will know Him through Sacred Scriptures. Like our Lady, her greatness was Her total absorption and contemplation of God by keeping everything about Him into Her immaculate heart. The secret of how one can get most closest to God was through contemplation. If one desire to be united with the Holy Trinity one must become a contemplatives focusing only on the things of heaven and eternity. Thus, the great Carmelite Order, are known for their charism as contemplatives. Thus, three great doctors of the church were three great Carmelite saints. Saint Teresa Avila reformed the Carmelite Order and through her deep contemplation of God she was able to write great spiritual books on how we can enter into the most intimate union with God. She taught members of the Carmelite Order that only through contemplation that one can quickly come to know God. The way to perfection, the seven mansion and other spiritual books written by Saint Teresa became great model for the serious soul who wants to become not only saints but great saints. Saint John of the Cross, another great Carmelite saint wrote great books influencing many to seek the highest spiritual life. As doctor of the church, Saint John of the Cross formulated the "Nada Doctrine" that if perfected one becomes one with God. And thirdly, Saint Therese of the Child Jesus became a doctor of the church by teaching us the spirituality of the little way. She wrote the book, Story of the soul where she inspired millions how one little weak soul can become a great saint by doing the little things but by doing it with the greatest of love. These three great saints and doctors of the church became great because they serve God through their contemplative life discovering how one can become closest to God. And so, we who belongs to the Order of our Lady of Unity will both serve the Most High through contemplation and also through our active participation in serving the needs of the church. Recalling the scene in Scriptures where Jesus dropped by to see His friends, Martha and Mary how we can also learned how we can perfectly served God by being active and contemplative. As Martha was so busy preparing food for our Lord she was a little upset she could not get any help from Mary who was so busy and engrossed looking and listening to Jesus enjoying the great joy of His company. Hearing Martha's complain our Lord gently rebuke her that Mary did the greatest thing by choosing to listen and learn from Him. Thus, it validates that the greatest way in serving God is through contemplation. Of course, Martha was also serving God by all the works she did by preparing food for their Divine Guests. And we who aspires to become Co-Founder with our Lady must strive not only to become great contemplatives but also very active in participating in the mission of the Church. Thus, we who belongs to Her Order does satisfy what James preached, that faith without works is dead. As contemplatives we should possessed the greatest faith in God and as active participant in the works of salvation we showed our works.

Pause for 10 minutes and silently and individually recollect what was read. Asked yourself if you have live a contemplative life where you read Sacred Scripture and meditate on what you were reading. As Catholics, we not only have faith but also works. Asked yourself how active you are in the mission of the Church. In the parish you attended, have you been active in serving what was needed? Have you been generous to your parish in contributing your talent, treasure and time? As member of our Lady's Order, we are both active and contemplative. What we contemplate we bring into action benefiting not only the Church but also the whole world. Our membership to Her final mission involves dedication and commitment for the reward cannot be described for what we are sowing should result in the harvesting of billions of lost souls. Help me help you. This is what our Lady is asking everyone of us so we can participate in our Mother's last mission. And as proven from the past our Lady had harvested millions of souls and in the future with the help of Her dedicated and committed community billions more will be converted and save.

After ten minutes of silence and reflection, leader proceeds by discussing the following: Spend 20 to 30 minutes.

As contemplatives, what Scripture Passages that you kept in your mind and heart. As a Third Order Carmelite, "Be holy and be perfect for the heavenly Father is." This passage will always remind me of His calling to become like Him. For some twenty five years, it remain with me. And I know why, He revealed to my wretched soul that I am the most unholy and the most imperfect of all His creation and because He pitied me of my wretched condition I must respond to His calling to be holy and perfect. Please share what scripture passage that you heard and if 30 minutes is not enough time please do make it an hour. When Scripture passages are embedded in the heart, mind and soul then truly it is God calling the soul to answer the call.

After discussion, do take a 10 minutes break.
After the break sing the Hymn, Immaculate Mary.
Leader proceeds by reading the following passages below.

In our servitude to God, let us do it by serving His Three Persona. By doing so, we cultivate a very special relationship not only to a monotheistic God whom the Jewish and Islam religion embraced but to the other Two Persona, Christ Jesus the Son of God and man and the Holy Spirit the Third Persona. Thus, we recall what we learned on the seventh to the twelfth classes where we knew the Father, Son and the Holy Spirit and we knew how to love the Father, the Son and the Holy Spirit. This is our mission for the rest of our lives to serve the Triune God with all of our hearts, mind, soul and with all of our strength because by serving the Three Persona one truly becomes a servant of the new covenant where the monotheistic religion spiritual stagnancy had been replaced by a dynamic or transforming religion where the impossible of transforming dust into divinity is now possible. This is why God became Three Person otherwise we will never become like God. Or sad to say, we remain worthless as dust. But with the new covenant and with the appearance of God's other Personas we are now certain and guaranteed to be transformed into God. Now, just think what kind of wondrous things our God had done for us? Think seriously about our nothingness. Think of what our God had planned for us? Think how awesome is our future. What a great injustices we did to God by refusing to believe His awesome plans for each one of us. What great ingratitude if we ignore our glorious destiny. Yes, indeed, we deserve the greatest punishment possible because God work the longest the hardest in making sure we will become like Him. As God continues to serve us, is not so grave injustices that we give our servitude to the One who deserves our service. If we serve our bosses or our employers well, should we not serve the One who gives us all that belongs to Him? If we serve our spouses, our children, our friends and strangers well, should we not serve Him well? Thus, in gratitude to God, our Maker, our Redeemer and Great Server, we then should serve Him by giving our all since He gave us His All.

In serving His First Persona, Our knowledge and love for Him should inspires us to serve Him by giving all of ourselves by always obeying the great Ten Commandments for this is the greatest desire of our Father in heaven. The Jewish religion did had the greatest intimate relationship with the First Persona because they were chosen to be the witness and promoter that God truly exists and His only concern was for our highest and greatest good. In justice and in righteousness was His desire for each one of us. He wants us to walk in His path to live and walk humbly with Him and this is the greatest reason why He gave us the Ten Commandments as an initial installment so to speak that we may win His favor and blessings. Although so remote from our greatest destination to be transformed into God, The First Persona initiated the first move so all of His creation will be swayed back to Him. Although not His fault but ours, the great good God in the greatness of His humility kept on serving us by taking great care of our needs in the land of our exile. As the most kind and generous Warden, He never abandon nor fail us by His generous Bounty in the land of our imprisonment. Remember, in this world we live in, we are prisoners sentenced to serve justly what was owed. Although it is much easier to blame our parents for our existence and for their sins, we must also remember that we born in the flesh fashioned in darkness are conceived in sin and in truth we are worthless as dust and we have no future or even hope to live in eternal happiness sharing the glory of God. But, in His great love and mercy, God is doing all He can although worthless we are to make us something greater that we can ever hope or imagine. This one greatest opportunity to be transformed by the Holy Trinity into His likeness and into His Being.

Let us therefore learn how we can please God the Father and serve Him by responding more than what Jonah did when God called him to preach in Nineveh. Though chosen by God, Jonah tried to evade his mission but was shipwrecked and even swallowed by the whale where he was taken to the place assigned for him to preach. Jonah's attitude is familiar because it is our attitude to try to run away from our calling. But once you are chosen for a serious mission there is no escape. Jonah did preached in Nineveh and they repented and were spared from God's wrath. Jonah was unhappy that they repented because he wants them punished severely. If you love God, when you are called to do something for Him, rejoice and be glad for you are given such opportunity to earned His reward. For the love of the Father, go to Nineveh without hesitation and get excited that you are chosen to do so. Be the greatest witness and preach with your greatest passion and fire to ignite souls to repent and be converted. And when they do, do rejoice and give thanks and praise to God for His mercy that they were spared saved. Unlike Jonah, jump with joy and be happy that they turn back to God. This is the kind of love we should do to our Father in heaven.

Let us imitate the following prominent prophets of God in how they serve Him well.

Noah was instructed by God to build an ark to save His creation and without hesitation the righteous man did despite the ridicule from the people. When we answer God's call, our deeds and actions are different from the world and they think we are fanatic and like Noah persevere in doing what are your inner calling. This is how to serve God well - always obedient to Him at all cost.

Abraham was asked to sacrifice his only one beloved and although it is against his will, He willingly did and He was rewarded greatly by God. This is how we serve our Father well, always obeying what He ask us to do. No hesitation but do it promptly and with no excuse. Abraham could have made an excellent excuse by refusing God that to kill someone special like your very own child is not right and it is certainly against Your commandment. Abraham despite the most difficult demand of God did obeyed. This is a great example for us to always be obedient to God in all His words and Commands and it is a guarantee you will be greatly rewarded.

Moses was called to lead Israel out from the slavery of mighty Egypt and knowing the degree of difficulty of his mission, he reasoned to God that who is he to tell the powerful Pharaoh to set the people free? He tried to tell God that he is not a good speaker to convey God's message to Pharaoh but He immediately give Moses his own brother Aaron to be his voice. Again, the obedience of Moses is what we should imitate with our own calling.

Joshua, Jeremiah, Isaiah, Elijah, Ezekiel and all God's prophet shared the same trait by telling God's people what God wants of them. Again, obedience to what God's words and commandments.

We received the greatest treasure from God and that is the Ten Commandments and this is our calling to obey all of them and to teach them to others and when we do we will gain much treasure in heaven. God's promise is not like our own. He fulfills it.

And remember, we have no excuse that we are not chosen nor called by God because all of us with no exception are called to become like Him. To make an excuse not to answer His call will be our greatest regret and sorrow because we refused and rejected God's greatest gift to us - Himself.

Break for silence 5 minutes recalling what was read pondering how we can follow those great examples so we can serve the Father well. Keep in your heart, mind and soul that the virtue of obedience is most pleasing to God. By this great virtue one will certainly gain God's favor. Before the coming of Jesus, the Ten Commandments of God was the standard where one can obtain His favor by perfectly obeying all not nine. As member of Her Order, we will surely gain what was promised if we obey perfectly all the rules of the community. This will be our greatest goal and mission as professed and consecrated members to obey perfectly.

Leader resume reading the passage below:

In the extreme opposite, we should always learned greatly from the following examples so we can avoided them.

God commanded Adam and Eve not to take and eat the fruit of the forbidden tree and they did. Lucifer was commanded to serve us but refused to do so. Instead, he started a revolution believing he can replace God so he will possess heaven. Cain was not pleasing to God because of his offering. His own chosen people despite all the favors they received from God was always complaining and keep displeasing Him by their wicked ways and by serving other worthless gods.

Clearly, disobedience, rebellion, distrust of His Providence, ingratitude, irreverence are abomination in God's Sight and at all cost we should avoid them. Let us become pleasing to God by serving Him perfectly like His Son and like His chosen daughter.

How do we serve the Second Persona of God perfectly?

A very wealthy young man came to Jesus and asked Him how can he inherit the kingdom of God and our Lord told Him to obey all His commandments and he replied that He did. Knowing he lied, Jesus commanded the young rich man to sell all his possession and give all to the poor. Like most of us, we are so attach not only to material wealth but other things in the world that most of us had difficulties detaching from them. The rich young man simply cannot do what our Lord commanded him to do and he was so sad that he could not give all that he have. He was divided. The young rich man was leaning to follow Jesus but he made a mistake by telling our Lord that he did obeyed all God's Ten Commandments when the truth was he broke most of it. If he truly obeyed them perfectly, he could have easily dispose them all and he could have become one of His disciples. Indeed, for the very rich and to the very wealthy would find it difficult to follow our Lord. Of course, there are so many wealthy and charitable people who did give and share what they have to the least fortunate but what they have given does not guarantee entrance to heaven. For our Lord did said that it would be very difficult for the rich to enter His kingdom that it is much easier for the camel to enter into the eye of the needle. Again, this is truly a validation to all of us that the salvation of our soul is not that easy. Rich or poor, we have to work for it. We have to cooperate with God's graces and His assistance in order for us to get to heaven. And so when they asked Him how could we enter His kingdom He replied for us it is impossible but with Him it is now possible. Thus again, this particular passage should clearly lead us to make possible our salvation was to become a part of His Body. By becoming a legitimate member of His Church, then we are now a part of Him making possible what was not. By becoming His Body, to pass the eye of the needle is no longer impossible and it is no longer impossible for us to enter to heaven since after His ascension He carried with Him us where in mystical theology we are already in heaven but had to pass the processing and this can only be done with our perfect servitude to our Lord and Redeemer, Christ Jesus, the Second Persona of the Triune God.

Let us then serve Him perfectly by imitating His twelve disciples. We can serve Him perfectly by this simple message to carry our own cross to deny ourselves and that can only be done by giving our all to Him. Peter, John, James, Thomas, Jude, Matthew and the rest became His perfect follower by leaving everything and went out spreading the Gospel. What Jesus loves to do, they did also. As Jesus became the Savior of mankind, they followed Him by making known what He did so souls will be saved. By giving their all to the One who gives its All, they became great in His kingdom because they served their Master well. They did not count what it cost even the cost of their very own precious lives. But losing their earthly lives clearly does not compensate what was gain. Sharing the glory, honor and splendor of God and to reign with Him for all eternity where no words can describe what awaits to those who serve God well. As servants and Co-Founder of Her Order, we applied what we learned from His disciples by spreading the charism of the Order so souls will be save. Just like what the apostles did, we have such great opportunity in serving the Triune God in expanding His kingdom that all may know why the Most Holy Trinity must be known loved adored and glorified. To make known our Lady of Unity and to help her help us in our journey to become God in God.

Take 10 minutes break.

Resume. Sing the Hymn: Jesus, Remember me.

Ten minutes discussion in how to serve our Lord Jesus perfectly. In what way did the rich young man lied to Jesus that he did obeyed all God's Ten Commandments? How could anyone be saved without God's Second Persona? Or how could we have Jesus, without the Blessed Virgin Mary?

After discussion, leader reads the following passage.

"Be ye therefore perfect as your Father which is in heaven is perfect." Matthew 5:48.

To serve God perfectly, let us then keep this passage in our mind heart and soul into our last breathe.

By the spirit of adoption through Jesus Christ our Lord, we have become truly children of God. It is only through our baptism to the Catholic church that we became member of Christ Body. This is our greatest gift becoming a Catholic. The world can never give us such highest honor and dignity. Children of the Supreme God. Like God!!! This is our dignity. Our title. Our greatest inheritance and treasure. We should always remind ourselves who we truly we are. We are not ordinary. We belong to the One who honors us. Can the world give you such great honor or such incredible inheritance? Can your neighbor or even your own family can give you such dignity? There is no honor or accolades nor any crown in the world that can surpass this greatest gift our God had given us. Yet, we are not up to it. We are dragged down so low by the darkness and blindness of our humanity. We are living miserably scrambling, scratching and stepping on each other for the things and honor of the world. We are fighting relentlessly for the garbage of the world while reluctantly refusing to respond and claiming the honor and dignity of our adoption as His very Own children. Why is this? Simply because we are so limited in our vision blocking the truth of our being preferring to embrace the inferior lives we inherited as human flesh stunted by our spiritual stagnancy. We have difficulties believing that we belong to divine royalty. Just observe how we behave. Observe how we treat each other. Seeing how we live and act it is hard to believe about our divine destiny. We simply can not accept such divine honor and dignity because of our limitation that simply we are merely humans trapped in the world so full of evil, sufferings and miseries. When we see the wretchedness of our existence, the tragedies, the oppression, the calamities and all the evils experienced made it so very difficult to believe that we are children of the most powerful God. When we see how the poor and the lowly are treated, abused and looked down it is so difficult to believe of who we are. We are blinded by the darkness of the world and in our very own soul depriving the vision to see that we are truly God's children.

Our Soul's spiritual direction:

In our memory, let us always remind ourselves that God wants us to strive for perfection even though it is so difficult and demanding. Keep in your mind that if we do not strive to be holy and perfect, God can not help us much because we do not give an effort to do so. Remind yourself that it makes tremendous difference if we do try to become holy and perfect.

In our intellect, let us always possess and kept this knowledge that the reason why God wants us to strive for perfection is because of our gross imperfections. We are so filthy and gross in His Sight that He is setting a standard that high so we can climb to His Heights. We are humans but if we set our goals as humans then reaching the heights of divinity is remote and impossible but when we try and try to become like Him, we acquired that determined habit of perseverance which will bring us closer to Him. By trying to do so, God will definitely will come to our assistance through grace and He will do the rest in transforming us like Him. Without trying, we remain static and stagnant grounded on earth with no possible hope in reaching God and heaven.

In our will, let us always follow our Lord's direction by reaching the highest standard of spirituality so the life of God can be manifested in our lowly nature. Let us do it by the power of our will otherwise we will never be like God. Our true destiny is to become like God in God but if we are content and comfortable with our lowliness then we will never fulfill the will of God. We have a lifetime to accomplish the will of God but in delaying to answer the call of perfection and holiness as it always does, procrastination kills the cat so to speak. Procrastination was and is always the perfect tool used by the devil killing so many innocent and ignorant souls. You have known the dangers of delaying to answer His call and to be safe today is the perfect time to strive for perfection and holiness.

Pause for 5 minutes meditating on His calling about holiness and perfection. Remember that tomorrow is never a guarantee that it will come. Think what is holding you in responding to His call to be like Him. Truthfully, there should be no reason not to do so. Learned how sad was the rich young man when he could not follow what Jesus told him to do.

After 5 minutes leader lead the prayer below:

The Lord is great and all His works are perfect
When I see the stars, the moon and the universe
The beauty of the sun as it rises and as it rested
Those colorful flowers that adorns the earth

Such marvelous works can only be design by the Perfect One
The Lord is holy and perfect and there is no god like Him
No one can restrain Him in doing what He wills
He created me by His will and with His Own holy Hands
The breathe of God is my life and I will live forever
How sinful and imperfect I am my God created me perfectly
The Lord wills that I am what I am in His Sight
What God wills what He ordains is all perfection
Let us now give thanks and praise to the One who is holy and perfect
For through Him, in Him and with Him
I will be perfect.
Amen.
Our Father, Hail Mary and Glory Be.

After the prayer do the 15 minutes spiritual retreat exercising the three faculties of our soul recollecting and receiving God's Voice.

In the silence, Listen to Him.

"There are so many good souls who gave up striving for holiness and perfection because they think it is not possible. I know how difficult it is even impossible to become like me but if I do not set a standard of sanctity most will fail in reaching the heights of heaven. I desire that everyone should be inspired in climbing the highest summit of sanctity because I will be there waiting and I will be the one to bring you to perfection. If I do not set the highest standard of your spiritual life then it is not possible that you can be with me in my kingdom. I commanded you to be like me and all you have to do is try and give your very best sincere effort to be holy and perfect. By doing so you have began that climb and I will not fail in meeting you in the summit of perfection where your humanity and my divinity will merge transforming you into my likeness. You have to try to reach for my standard for the reward can never compensate all the efforts expended. So many times my faithful servants did preached to set your sight on the things of heaven and eternity but like the olden times, ears remained so deaf and eyes remained so blind and your presence here with the community is graced by your desire in answering my call."

Silently asked yourself what other goals you have. Family, friends and careers does influence us in answering God's call. True they are important in our lives but think how important they truly are compared to what God is calling you. Think of what they can do and help you in fulfilling your greatest and highest good. Think of your own judgment before the Throne of God. Did you truly chose Him over the others? In truth, there is only you and God when the accounting begins. Which one do we serve?

After the 15 minutes silent retreat and exercise pray below.

"O Holy Spirit, Spirit of Fire and Holiness, surpassing Strength, always bringing me hope, today fill my heart and prepare it to love You always. O Purifying Fire, consuming my soul, come into my life with Your Courage, surround my being with Your Presence, and make me holy, as You are Holy. O Holy Spirit, Pure Love and Light, move me to love and serve You always; calm me and give me patience and lead me to experience Your wonderful peace and tranquility; fill my life with Your Joy. O Holy Spirit of Awe, and Wonder, come, enter and dwell within my life forever. Come and let my heart be a sanctuary of Your sanctifying rest. Keep and sustain me in the mystery of Your Divine Presence; protect me from the power of the evil one and deliver me from all danger of falling into sin. Sanctify me with the same Spirit of Jesus, and lead me to the created purpose intended by the Father. O Refreshing Spirit, in Your Love, Truth, Goodness, and Beauty, make me holy and constantly lead me to be with You forever. O Holy Spirit, Come and make me Holy. Amen."

Our Father, Hail Mary and Glory Be.

After the prayer, leader read the passage below.

Knowing how to serve the Father and the Son, let us learn how we can perfectly serve the Third Persona of God. Scripture repeatedly warns us that flesh and spirit is always in enmity with each other. They could not get along. They are always at war never at peace. The are not compatible because what the flesh desires or wants is not the spirit wants. Simply, flesh and spirit does not like each other or they hated each other so to speak. Theologians agreed in principle that such incompatibility of two diverse entity made it so difficult for us to be holy and perfect. This is why God and man is always in enmity because God is Spirit and man is flesh. Indeed, we are facing extreme difficulties in saving our soul and thanks to God that we have the Catholic Church providing remedies and solutions through the seven powerful sacraments. For example, when the flesh failed the spirit, the sacrament of reconciliation became that saving tool granting absolution to the sinner restoring that state of grace in the failed soul. To strengthened the flesh and soul, the real flesh and blood of our Lord became a powerful instrument in subjecting the craving of the flesh restoring order and peace in the two warring entities. Without the Church powerful and potent seven sacraments salvation is so remote and we who are baptized in the true church indeed had the greatest advantages over the other religion or faith simply because they are deprived of those sacraments. Most of us Catholics simply took for granted what we have in our disposal so we can become not only saints but great saints. The book, YBA a Catholic simply reveal why this is the only one true church that we all should become members to ensure our soul isn safe and secure.

How do we serve the Holy Spirit then?

Here are the few important points to ponder and remember in how we can serve Him perfectly.

Most important is to be very vigilant by not committing a sin. Even venial sin should be avoided at all cost. What happens when we start accumulating those little venial sins the soul will start to drag down making it lethargic and if it continues to do so it exposes itself to the danger of falling into mortal sin. To serve the Holy Spirit perfectly, frequent confession cleanses and wipes out the stains of sins in our soul and it pleases the Holy Spirit making it desirable for Him to dwell in it. An unstained soul lessen the powerful desires of the flesh and the spirit does have control of it and even bring it to His subjection. When this is done when flesh and spirit becomes one the Holy Trinity dwells in the soul. Again, as consecrated religious this will be our every moment challenge not to commit a single sin. And do not ever get discouraged if sin can not be conquered because eventually by frequent confession and daily reception of Holy Communion one will triumphed over it. It was my own experienced that I had this terrible weakness that I could never conquer but I keep going to confession and going to daily Mass and after twenty six years by the grace of God I was able to do so. True what Sacred Scripture taught that through perseverance one will be save.

We can serve the Holy Spirit perfectly by living in the Presence of God. Would you commit serious or even venial sin when you put yourself always in His Presence? Do you dare to do something evil or wicked in His Presence? I do not think so. Brother Lawrence a simple Carmelite saint wrote that if one will only live its life in the Holy Presence of God it is impossible to commit sin. What a powerful witness and declaration by this truly humble saint. As a professed Carmelite, I can supplement what Brother Lawrence wrote for I did practice it constantly and when I forgot to live in His Holy Presence that is when I failed Him. Thus to serve the Holy Spirit well, do practice living in the Holy presence of God. I guarantee that if you do, seldom and rarely you will commit a sin.

Lastly but also most importantly, never neglect a life of prayer. Prayer is the fuel that powers our spiritual life. Without prayer, the life of the spirit staled and one's advancement to holiness and perfection stagnate. Prayers draw the attention of God and one becomes pleasing to Him. Yes, all prayers are heard contrary to what others say. All prayers are noted by God and He will not forget every words or sighs one had expressed. How awesome and powerful God is, only by praying that conquers God. By constant prayers, one exhibited love for God humility is exercised and patience is practiced and to persevere holiness is obtained.

By perfectly serving the Holy Spirit, one is guaranteed salvation because with the soul's servitude He dwelt on the soul never stop working for its sanctification since He is the Finisher of God's greatest works. Remember, this is the same Holy Spirit that overshadowed our Lady giving birth to both God and man. As we are enslaved by the flesh, the in dwelling of the Holy Spirt in our soul is that powerful force that will bring subjection to the flesh making its union peaceful and amiable where the two becomes one in harmonious merger. This is the same Holy Spirit transforming ordinary bread into His Own Flesh and ordinary wine into His Own Blood. This is the same Holy Spirit that will transform and that will make perfect His Church.

In conclusion, endear His Third Persona for this is the key to our salvation. Jesus made good on His promise that He will be sending His Third Persona to make sure His Body will be transformed into the perfection and holiness of the Triune God.

Discuss for 15 minutes about what was read about the Holy Spirit. Share whatever your experience with the Third Persona of God.

Closing Prayer:
Hymn: Sing Salve Regina
Our Lady of Unity pray for us.

Fourteenth Class: (3 hours or less)

Hymn: Sing together, "Servant Song"
Opening Prayer:

Serving Neighbor

Leader read the passage below:

Because of the greatness of our being, we all have this selfish tendency to become great. We see how athletes spend long hours in the gym perfecting their wares working on their weaknesses so they will become great. In every field of human endeavor, we tried to do our best to become great in whatever we do. Unfortunately, greatness are rarely achieved and the majority can only become very good, good, average, below average and those who failed in what they do. There is only one Shakespeare, one Mozart, one Einstein, one Michelangelo, one Babe Ruth and one Enrico Caruso. How did they became great? Talent? Treasure? Perspiration? Perseverance? Perhaps destiny? Obviously, a combination of these things. But one thing is certain why they became great was their servitude to their passion. Kobe Bryant spent most of his days in the gym even neglecting his family and friends because of his commitment to become the greatest. Michelangelo ignored food and rest by giving his all for perfecting his art. The same thing with Einstein whose mind and energy were consumed in trying to figure out the things of energy and mass so he could understand the mechanics of science. Shakespeare was drawn to writing and he spent his life doing it creating classic story that taught humanity what we all must face in life. All the great men and women in this world past, present and the future did something to our history but in the final analysis, the truth is what they did was great for the world but has no value in the realm of eternity. Once greatness is achieve in this life the coming generation will simply forget them. We only remember their names because history made a record of their achievement. Yes, they were so great but once its gone, reality sets in and their greatness was only a faded glory that will be remembered but never sustained. One thing that certainly taught us is that greatness can only be achieve if one is willing to do what must be done in order to achieve it. One must have that burning passion and fire to achieve it. In our world and in our very own lives though, we can try but most of us will failed. We can see from experienced and from the facts that most of us did not achieve greatness in what we do. Of course, we may be a great wife or a great husband or father or mother or even a great friend but such greatness does not count that much for it is our moral duty and obligation to become a great human being. What inspire us to do great thing was the accolades and honor received from others. Being recognize by the many eyes in our world made us work hard and strive for greatness. This is the condition of our humanity. We all strive for greatness in this world but sadly in vain.

However, there is that kind of greatness that trampled what was and is the greatest in the world but so very few of us work and strive for. The kingdom of heaven. The greatness we all have a chance to achieve for all of eternity unlike the greatness we hope for in the world where its gone suddenly and quickly. What greatness one can be when we will be like God. What greatness that will be when one is transform into God? Let us be awake from the slumber in the darkness of our soul. Know who you are. You are bound for greatness not in this world but in the kingdom of God. The enemies of our greatness is Satan. He will kept you in darkness. He will put you down keep you down by polluting and clouding your thoughts that we are merely nothing made of flesh and soon will die with nothing else to hope for. There are so many desperate and deceived souls that had fallen to this miserable trap set up by God's greatest enemy. Lucifer had completely lost God and heaven. He knew what is in stored for us. He knew we are destined to become like God. He wanted so much to become like God that he even deceived himself that he can replace God. Now, he and his co workers are working very hard in deceiving and discouraging God's children that our greatness lies in this life and that we all must give our all in achieving it. This of course is contraries to God's holy will. We all can see Satan's deceit as each day the world is in a great hurry to do something in achieving great things for their own selfish motives. Exception are those working very hard for the city of God. But we who are called and responded to the calling of our Lady of Unity are blest knowing that indeed we are all called to be great in His kingdom.

In Sacred Scripture, let us see and hear this scenery.

"I want my son to sit on your right hand."

The others who heard were somewhat upset and jealous knowing that they too desired to be seated at the right Hand of God. Again it showed us our desire to be great. It even extend not only in worldly greatness but in eternity.

"Not for me to decide which one will sit on His Right but only my Father."

Jesus responded that only those who does the will of the Father will have the privilege in sitting on His Right. Thus our Lady enlightened the "boy" that only those who belongs to the legitimate Body of Christ will be seated on His Right. Again, this is our Lady's message of the greatness of the true Church and how anyone can be integrated and incorporated into His very Own Body. Baptize them in the name of the Father, the Son and the Holy Spirit was a very important message to His workers so salvation is possible. When one is baptize invoking the Father's Name one become His child, and by invoking the Son's Name one's justification, redemption and salvation accomplished and by invoking the Name of the Holy Spirit, one will have the privilege to receive His seven powerful gifts of wisdom, understanding, knowledge, fortitude, piety and the fear of the Lord equipping them to do what is good, holy and perfect in the Sight of God. When we remain faithful to our baptismal vow into our final breath, as a legitimate member of Christ Body, then the Triune God's work is completed and perfected. As to our Christian brothers and sisters baptized in the name of the Holy Trinity salvation is possible but they do not sit on His Right but there is a place reserved for them in heaven for in the

Father's House are many mansions prepared to those who truly loves and serve Him. The "boy" was also informed that in the new heavens each reward received will be different from each other. He was reminded that what we sowed here on earth will be our harvest in heaven. Like in life, one who works sparingly receives little than those who works hard. Thus, our Lady reminded the community to keep it in our mind not to waste our time, talent and treasure for the things that brings nothing in return but rather to spend them wisely for the greater things of heaven. And for those who wants to be great in the kingdom of God then she said echoing Her Son's direction and example to become servant of all. This is our goal, to serve everyone that needs us.

Therefore, to do the holy will of God, then we must be servant to each other. This is our standard in serving our neighbor. We are one in the Lord member of His Body one for each other and this is our greatest good to have our neighbor as our companion to eternity.

And as member of our Lady's community let us spend 15 minutes by listening and following our Lord's direction for our community.

"And the Lord God said, it is not good that the man should be alone; I will make him an help meet for him." Genesis 2:18.

Although God the Father was referencing to His intention of giving Eve to Adam, it is also applicable to our lives and specially in our community where our calling was to become servant to each other. It was God's designed that we have each other knowing how helpless and hopeless we are by ourselves. There is that saying that no man is an island. We need each other in order to live and survive. In our earthly life, we need our parents to start and support us. Without them, we will surely die. As we grow and mature becoming more independent we still need someone to provide us jobs for our daily sustenance so we can also support our own family. In our community, in our country and in our world we need each other so we can live and survive. For example, the country of Saudi Arabia is providing us oil so we can use to operate our economy. We need our army to defend our country. We need each other!! And for our spiritual life, we are in great need of God, otherwise, we will never be able to reach the heights of divinity. In our spiritual life, it is God alone who will lead and guide us to Him. It is good to have each other so we can truly live and survive. We need each other so we can execute the love of God to others through serving.

Spiritual Direction:

In our memory, let us always remind ourselves that we can not live and survive in our own. We need each other and we need our God to be our all. An isolated soul is an unproven entity untested in charity unable to show its fruits. By our integration and interaction to each other is the greatest measuring stick of how we love and serve. Thus, our exile in this world although not pleasant and desirable can be our greatest blessings with how we accomplish God's will through our love and servitude to each other.

In our intellect, let us always possess and kept this precious knowledge, to value and treasure humanity's existence and with our very own participation because it trains and molds us how to become the most profitable servant. What we have met and known in our lives are part of His awesome Providence in our own formation and sanctification. How we treat each of them will be recorded in the ledger of our life. How we looked down on them can become our greatest opportunity to correct ourselves of our defective nature and to install in our understanding that everyone existed is indeed very important regardless of status for He had ordained our existence for His very Own purpose. Make no mistake the president of a country and the garbage collector are equally ordained by God to do His works in them. Thus, we are ruled by God in the power of the president and we are served by God by the cleaning and sanitizing work of the garbage collector. How each performed their works are noted and recorded by God where at the end accountability and responsibility are demanded by the Just Judge.

In our will, let us do everything in our power to treasure and value each other as precious knowing each one of us had a role to play in building and expanding His kingdom here on earth. Although most of us had difficulty in believing our importance, it is up to our will to strengthened such believe of how each one of us is so important. Therefore, to please God, be very vigilant and be very careful to never invalidate one's importance. For the holy God will resist the proud and the arrogance.

Together, the community prays the following prayer below:

"The Lord God created the moon and the sun
The sun gives life to the plants and all vegetations
Blessed be the Lord for the bountiful fruits and harvest
I am filled and my stomach is satisfied
At night the moon and the stars brings beauty to mine eyes
The universe and the galaxies are His reminder of His Greatness
Wherever I go there is not a place or a time
That my yearning soul longs for Him
How rich and abundant is the Lord's bounty
My heart and soul remains restless
For the void unfulfilled by all the earth's richness
I keep living and looking and even with all my find
I am still alone unconsolable by the grief I carried
Who can satisfy my heart and soul
There is nothing I can find in this life
Who can give me rest and contentment
There is no one but the Lord my God alone
Can bring me His greatest gift

Being united to His Life and Love
Blessed be God now and forever
For He had bring me to the fullness of His Truth
Amen
Our Father, Hail Mary, Glory Be
Our Lady of Unity pray for us, your community

Do the silence spiritual retreat for 10 minutes

Spiritual Exercise: In silence, listen intently and apply what you heard contemplating everything absorb into your soul His Voice.

Listen to our Lord:

EVERYONE HAD DIFFICULTIES EMBRACING EACH OTHER. IT IS YOUR WEAKNESSES BEING HUMAN MADE IN THE FLESH. WHAT YOU SAW IN EACH OTHER DEFINES WHAT IS IN YOUR SOUL. WHAT IS SEEN IN THE EYES REVEALS A SMALL SAMPLE OF THAT PERSON BUT THE BEAUTY OF THE SOUL CAN ONLY BE SEEN BY ME. WHAT YOU SEE IN THE FLESH BRINGS CORRUPTION FOR WHATEVER BEAUTIFUL OR UGLY THE PERSON SEEMS TO BE ITS APPEARANCE OR PRESENCE SUPPRESSES THE SPIRIT TO SOAR ABOVE WHAT IS TRANSITORY. SET ALWAYS YOUR SIGHT ON THE ETERNAL WITH YOUR UNWAVERING FAITH THAT ALL MY PROMISES WILL ALWAYS BE FULFILLED TO THOSE WHO LISTEN AND FOLLOW ME TO WHAT IS TRUTH AND TO WALK IN MY WAY SO MY LIFE IN YOU WILL SHINE SALTING THE EARTH PRESERVING MY BODY THE CHURCH AS IT CONTINUES TO GROW AND ADVANCE TO HOLINESS AND PERFECTION. ALL MEMBERS OF MY BODY HAVE A ROLE IN MAKING A CONTRIBUTION HOW SMALL OR LARGE THE CALLING TO ENSURE THAT EACH ONE STRIVE FOR HOLINESS AND PERFECTION. THERE IS NO COMPROMISING IN REGARDS TO IN WORKING AND SEEKING YOUR GREATEST AND HIGHEST GOOD AND YOU CAN OBTAIN ONLY THROUGH HOLINESS AND TO BE PERFECT AS WE ARE. THIS IS THE ONLY WAY ONE WILL BE SAVE AND THE ONLY WAY YOU CAN BECOME ONE WITH US. THEREFORE, TREAT EACH OTHER AS PRECIOUS AS I TREATED YOU BECAUSE IN MY EYES THERE IS NO SLAVE AND MASTER NOR RICH OR POOR FOR YOU ARE EQUAL IN MY EYES. ANYONE WILL HAVE THE ONE AND ONLY OPPORTUNITY TO BECOME HEIR OF THE KINGDOM OF HEAVEN. AS I GREATLY NEEDED THE CHOSEN TWELVE APOSTLE IN MY MINISTRY SO YOU WILL NEED EACH OTHER IN YOUR MINISTRY AS CO WORKER WITH THE LADY OF UNITY FOR THE ABUNDANT HARVEST OF SOUL. WE ARE ONE BODY. WORKING FOR

ONE SOLITARY GOAL THE CONVERSION AND SALVATION OF SOULS. AS I AM ONE WITH THE FATHER AND WITH THE HOLY SPIRIT AND AS THEY ARE IN ME SO WE ARE IN YOUR MOTHER AND YOU ARE WITH US. THEREFORE, DO NOT SEPARATE YOURSELF FROM THIS BODY. AS YOU ARE UNITED WITH US ALWAYS EXERCISE KINDNESS AND LOVE FOR ALL WHATEVER YOU SAW IN THEM."

Break 10 minutes:

After the break sing the Hymn, Hail Holy Queen
Thirty minutes discussion on serving our neighbor: Leader reads the passage below:

"Then the lord of that servant was moved by compassion, and loosed him, and forgive him the debt." Matthew 18:27.

The master knew that his servant having owed him a large sum of money felt sorry and pity on him that he erase his debts. Such act of mercy and kindness by the master is a great example for each one of us to follow if ever we encounter such situation. The servant was filled with joy knowing he is no longer bound by his debts. This is the kind of service we do to our neighbor that earned great merits in the eyes of God. Blest with power and wealth, this master became a great servant to his very own servant by how he serve him through his kindness and compassion. In every moment of our lives, we have all kinds of opportunity to serve others whatever may be the position or status we have.

"But the same servant went out, and found one of his fellow servants, which owed him an hundred pence; and he laid hands on him, and took him by the throat, saying, Pay me that thou owest. And his fellow servant fell down at his feet, and besought him, saying, Have patience with me, and I will pay thee all." Matthew 19:28-29.

The servant's joy turned to hostility once he saw a fellow servant who owed him money. By his reaction and attitude he exposed himself as a wicked one. He had no more obligation to pay a huge sum of debt to his master but he was so greedy by demanding the little sum of money owed by his fellow servant and worst when he could not pay he committed a despicable act by.

"And he would not; but went and cast him into prison, till he should pay the debt." Matthew 18:30.

This is our struggle in this land of our exile. The servant having received great blessings lost that great opportunity by greatly serving his fellow servant. He could not share his joy of being debt free to other servant but instead instigated the judgment due to him. Instead, upon hearing the wickedness of this servant, the master summoned him and pointed his sin.

"Shouldest not thou also have compassion on thy fellow servant, even as I had pity on thee? And his lord was wroth and delivered him to the tormentors, till he should pay all that was due to him." Matthew 18:33-34.

Therefore, to serve our neighbor well and perfectly let us never forget that this is the second greatest commandment of God, to love our neighbor as self. Had that wicked servant exercised love of neighbor he could have easily forgiven his small debts having made a profit by the kindness of his master. It is so easy for us to make a judgment that this selfish and greedy servant deserved punishment for his wicked and unjust ways of dealing to his neighbor.

To become pleasing to God each one of us should always exercise kindness, justice and above all mercy to our fellow brothers and sisters specially the afflicted and those who are in the greatest need of our help.

In Sacred Scripture, our Lord clearly defines who is our neighbor when he told the story of the man left on the road badly beaten and robbed where nobody extend help. There was even a priest that merely passed by ignoring the helpless man lying on the ground. Then, came someone who assisted him and brought him to the inn where he gave money to the innkeeper so he could take care of his need. He even made a promise to give him more once he came back. Who of us would have like to be in that badly beaten man's shoes left on the road? How do we feel if nobody came and help us? Thus, our Lord set that standard of serving our neighbor to the highest degree. Even though the man does know the badly beaten stranger he did not hesitate in extending all the help he can to make sure he was well taken care of. This is the kind of service we should do to each other. We give great service to those who are in the greatest need of our help just like that badly beaten man. In our love of God and neighbor there is no stranger for everyone is our neighbor. When we set the highest standard in helping our neighbor we have imitated God's way and most importantly the will of God was accomplished through us. We also showed that we do love God by our charitable deeds to the most helpless and needy.

Therefore, as member of our Lady's religious Order we must always strive to serve everyone specially those who needed our help the most regardless of race, religion, gender for we are all God's children.

As sons and daughters of the Church we therefore follow Her teachings how each one of us can perfectly serve our neighbor. Most of us should know the following works of mercy.

We can serve our neighbor by feeding the hungry. When we saw someone that has no food we then tried to extend our help by providing them something to eat.

When someone is thirsty, we should give them something to drink.

When we saw someone is naked we should give them clothes.

When we saw someone who is homeless we should provide them shelter. However, prudence should be exercise with regard to this matter since such responsibility exceed the scope of true charity where it may compromise the stability of the family unit. For example, a family of five living in a three bedroom house had no business in bringing in a homeless for by doing so it may create a stressful situation thus by being charitable to one the four member of the family may suffer some stressed because of taking such unnecessary act of mercy.

Never neglect in taking care of the sick specially in our own family or friends who had no one to take care of themselves. Again, prudence should be exercise in providing service to the sick specially when there is a time restraint. For example you work full time and you have your own family to serve then it is not prudent to extend yourself unless you have super energy in serving them.

To visit the prisoner. Also, prudence should be exercise when doing so. For a family member or close friends, we must set a special time to do so knowing that the prisoners are in need of close personal contact specially members of family relatives and friends.

To bury the dead is another way to serve our neighbor. Family and friends who passed away one must attend its funeral service so one's presence bring some consolation to the family who lost its loved ones.

The seven corporal works of mercy taught by the Church should always be in our mind for by exercising them we have gain merits in God's eyes. In addition, great merits are accumulated by how we serve our neighbor by our spiritual works of mercy. They have more weighed in the day of our judgment because our servitude was for the highest good of one's soul. As our Lord Jesus came to save souls our spiritual works of mercy brings great rewards. Therefore, let us pay close attention of the following spiritual works of mercy.

As member of our Lady's Order, we must take advantage when there is an opportunity to evangelized by helping and guiding someone who is lost. Specially the godless and those who are outside of the Church. We can do this by doing the following spiritual works of mercy.

The conversion of sinners. Although we could not judge the state of someone's soul, one way of life usually reveals the state of their soul. For example, living together without the sacrament of marriage showed that both are risking their souls to perdition. One should be bold by gently telling them about the risks they are taking with their soul. Such boldness could jeopardized yourself to lose their friendship or even harsh negative reaction but in the eyes of God you have gain merits with your concern of your neighbor's eternal welfare. In your daily prayers, unite them to all the Holy Masses being said that day for the conversion of sinners.

Instructing the ignorant. The poor, the uneducated and the innocent are deprived of knowledge about God and in what way they are lacking in regards to their spiritual life and for their advancement certainly needs our greatest assistance by teaching and helping them to grow and advance in their spiritual life. Again, you are risking resentment and even ridicule but you did gain merits by your spiritual work of mercy for your neighbor. You may become their enemy but certainly you gain the friendship of God.

Advising the doubtful. Either you have the strongest of faith or the weakest, doubt will never stop entering into our mind. Thomas the doubting apostle was with our Lord all the time. He saw everything He did. The raising of the dead, the driving of the demons, the miracles of healing and all His works Thomas did saw but when the news of Jesus resurrection from the dead, Thomas doubted it. He only believed when our Lord showed him His wound and He even let Thomas touched them. Simply we are doubting humans and we are all subject to it. Thus, we can also erase our doubtful nature by making those doubters believers by teaching them the three cardinal virtues of faith, hope and charity. That in God alone we have our being and our mission in life was always to know, love and serve Him. By inspiring each other specially those struggling with doubts will certainly earned us merits.

Comforting the sorrowful. In our life's journey, everyone of us will experience all kinds of tragedies that brought sorrows in our lives. Divorce, financial losses, death, accidents, physical and emotion pains bring sorrows in our lives. God gave us each other and this is another avenue in exercising love to our neighbor by giving them comfort and consolation by our sincere involvement with their well being. Your presence and your availability can certainly make a difference in their well being.

Bearing all the wrongs patiently. Since each one of us inherited the affliction of our sinful and rebellious nature each day we live we do encounter all kinds of wrongs and injustices. This is and it will be our lot until our last breathe. And because we are in this world, we cannot escape such situation and to show God how really we love Him, we should always strive to be patient with our neighbor's fault and whatever wrong they had done to us. This was commanded by God to love them as we love ourselves. For example, an insult wrongfully thrown at us, by restraining anger and not returning back harsh or offensive words one gain great merits for exercising the great virtue of patient. This is what our Lord meant that if someone threw stone at you throw back bread. Or someone slap you in the face then turn the other cheek. Of course, what this truly meant was to bear whatever wrong done to us. Of course, in reality if someone threw stone or slap you in the face, they could face some serious charges in the court of justice. But if it actually happens, you did the just and right thing to have the perpetuator arrested and charged with the crime of assault. To become like Christ, we should meditate in how He did bear all the wrongs done to Him.

Forgiving all injuries done to us. If someone did threw stone and slap your face, you have the responsibility to file charges and after justice was served, you exercised forgiveness by praying for that person who did harm you. To have the heart of Jesus, forgive and forget the injuries since this was His final pleading to the Father to forgive us for we do not know what we were doing. Most of them that does injuries to others are either godless or simply mentally ill. A normal person just do not threw stone or slap somebody's face. Therefore, if that was their case then they indeed did not knew what they were doing. There is also that special circumstances that passion can overwhelmed the most patient and disciplined person that he will act beyond reason. Again, as His follower, always forgive. This is how we showed our love for God in how we exercise mercy to all. Even to our worst enemy. Remember, we are all God's enemy and yet He forgive us even though we viciously, cruelly and wickedly murdered Him. To become pleasing to Him, we should at all times forgive those who have hurt or harm us. By doing so, we did what He did and we gain much merits by living His life in us.

Praying for the living and the dead. As co founder with our Lady, and as professed member of Her Order, our prayerful life focuses on the conversion of our brothers and sisters who belongs to the Jewish and Islamic faith because this is the primary reason why our Lady established Her community. They are offsprings of Abraham father of our faith and we as member of Her Order who prayed for them will definitely gain much merits. Remember that no one can come to the Father except through His Son and by praying for their conversion to the true Church they will then know our Lord Jesus and also know the Mother of God. They would also rejoice in knowing the Three Persona of God and this was made possible by the active and contemplative participation of our Lady's religious Order. We then give the Most Holy Trinity the highest honor and glory with their conversion to the true Church. And the most acceptable to God was and is the prayers for the dead or for the holy souls in purgatory. We showed how we greatly love God by how we prayed to the souls in purgatory for they are our neighbors who truly needed our help since their sufferings cannot be measured in worldly ways. Those who are negligent in praying for their brothers and sisters in purgatory loses a lot of merits and we who belong to the Catholic Church had the greatest opportunity by offering Holy Mss for our neighbor in the most need of help and mercy.

Break 10 minutes.
After the break, sing the Hymn, Immaculate Mary.
Thirty minutes discussion of how we can perfectly serve our neighbor.

The teachings of the Church about the corporal and spiritual works of mercy definitely showed us the way how we can served our neighbor perfectly.

Of the seven corporal works of mercy which one earns the highest merits?

1. feed the hungry 2. give drink to the thirsty 3. clothe the naked 4. shelter the homeless 5. visit the sick 6. visit the prisoner 7. bury the dead.

Of the seven spiritual work of mercy which one earns the highest merits?

1. Converting sinner 2.instructing the ignorant 3. advising the doubtful 4.comforting the sorrowful 5. bearing all wrong patiently 6. forgiving injuries 7. praying for the living and the dead

The Catholic Church teaching that faith without works is dead and that faith should be accompanied by works and to become a great saint one must show how much he or she works in serving others.

In closing, sing the Hymn, Whatsoever you do to the least of my people.
Closing Prayer:
Sing the Hymn, Salve Regina.
Fifteen Class: (3 hours or less).
Hymn: Together Sing the Hymn, "Open My Eyes".

Fifteenth Class
Serving Self

Leader reads the Scripture Passage (slowly and clearly)

"And God said, let us make man in our image, after our likeness." Genesis 2:26.

This is the self. This is us. After serving our neighbor, our greatest responsibility is ourselves. It may sound selfish but it is not if what we do is solely for God's greatest honor and glory. We owed to Him this greatest privilege that we are to become like Him. He worked very hard for our transformation and we too must work very hard that His Holy Will be done and will be accomplish through our servitude to God and self. Also, we were commanded to love ourselves and as we do our neighbor and for doing so God is most pleased. We need to love ourselves first not in a very selfish worldly or pleasurable ways but in doing the Holy Will of God. Therefore in this class, we study and learn how we can serve our own selves. There is that saying that before you preach or teach other make sure that you have preached and taught yourselves the way to holiness and perfection.

Going back to the Scripture passage let us remind ourselves that God created us not for His own toy or recreation. We are the greatest work of His Hands and it was His desire and plan to make us His greatest masterpiece. A masterpiece can never be duplicated or copied for who can produce a created God? God wanted us to be like Him and when it is accomplished His greatest masterpiece will come to fruition. How precious indeed is our existence!!! How precious indeed we are!!! Imagine, you and I could become God's greatest work. Imagine yourself being God!!!

When we looked towards the skies the sun made us think of how its light gave life to the plants and vegetation. If we study the wonders of science then we should learn that everything in our world works in such orderly and efficient manner that such perfect arrangement could not possibly came by accident. There is someone out there with an awesome power and mind that made all things possible as they are now. When we looked at the sky during the night we wandered how the moon, the stars and those planets existed. We can not conclude they are there by an accident or some imagined big explosion. Common sense and logic simply override such ridiculous theory. Normally when there is a big big explosion the result is always destruction and chaos. An accident is always an incident that resulted in destroying what was once functional and operational. There is a Supreme Scientist who designed and arranged everything in our planets and in the solar system. They are not the product of accident. To think that way is out of line out of touch to the absolute truth that everything was created by God.

If you and I are masterpieces of God, then we are indeed far more awesome than all of the universe all of the things in this world far more awesome than the angels in heaven. But we must asked ourselves if we truly believe that we are His masterpieces?

Despite all the religions that existed in our world everybody struggled with this awesome truth. Despite the coming of our Lord Jesus into our dark world we keep struggling that we are truly God's masterpieces. Even our Lord Jesus taught us to pray "The Our Father" we are not truly convinced that we are really and truly God's children. We are being upgraded by our Lord Jesus from a masterpiece to become children of the Most High. What an awesome revelation that is by our God Himself. Still we struggled mightily with our human existence in accepting the truth that we are all created so we all have the greatest opportunity to become God in God.

This is who we are. This is the reality of what is in store for us and we will all find out once our lives ends. If we ignore or neglect this truth then we all have all of eternity of unbearable grief and inconsolable sorrow and it so late that even God can not fix it. As member of Her religious Order we have been enlightened by this absolute truth and knowing such grace should inspire us to never compromised what we have been taught.

Spiritual Direction:

We all struggle with our humanity ever since sin destroyed the innocence and purity of our being. The curse we carry is overwhelming that we are so prune to commit sin instinctively that we are shackled like a slave. In addition, we are surrounded by an environment of sin making it more difficult to conquer or avoid it. However, do not ever lose hope nor ever despair nor ever get discourage because you are fully equip with a memory, understanding and a powerful will so you can fight, reject, resist and even conquer sin. In your memory remember you are not an animal for God has given you His Spirit who has the power to conquer sin. You also have the knowledge that sin is an abomination to God and to live in sin you have become His enemy and such situation should made us tremble with fear. Most importantly, you are made to become like Him and because God hated sin we too must hate sin like it is our worst hated enemy. And what is God's greatest powerful gift to us? Yes, the third faculty of our soul and that is our will. Our will is powerful that we can practically do everything we wanted to do. Do you know you have the power to destroy the whole world if you truly exercise your will to its utmost limit. How so? By studying and developing a deadly strain of virus and spreading them to the ends of the earth. Or developing a system where you can hack the secret code of all the world's missile system and unleashed them all over which will surely destroy the whole world. Indeed your will is so powerful that it can even transform you into God by simply conforming it to His. But the greatest problem we have is that we misused such great gift and power entrusted to us by God. Instead of choosing to become like Him we chose the other things that have no eternal value nor merits.

Prayer:

We call and cry out to You Almighty God and Father that Your Will be done into us. Your Second Persona, Jesus Christ Your Son taught us to call you Father for He made us Your children through adoption. Our Father, we have grievously sinned against You. And in our distress, we need Your help. For You alone can help and deliver us from our miseries. Forgive us Lord from all our offenses. Purify and cleanse us so we can become truly Your children. Lord Jesus Christ, Savior of my soul, I claim Your Precious Blood as the most powerful purifier and cleanser of my soiled soul. Send forth Your Holy Spirit into our whole being so we can have the power, the wisdom, courage and understanding to live Your Life as our very own which was and is in conformity of Your Holy Will. We pray in Jesus Name who lives and reigns with You and the Holy Spirit. Amen. Our Lady of Unity pray for your community.

15 minutes do the silent spiritual retreat recalling the reading of the passage. Know who you are. You are not what you think, nor feel who you are because our thoughts is not the thoughts of God. We have been broken, beaten and destroyed by the consequences of our sins but glory and praise to our Lord Jesus who justified, redeemed and restored us to a new creation where we are to be His priest, prophet and king. This is unbelievable!!! Truly unbelievable. This is our thoughts and this will be our thoughts if we remain in darkness but it was Jesus Christ who change us into Himself by our integration to His Church becoming His own Body thus the truth is now if we belong to Him we are indeed are priest, prophet and king. As member of Her Order, you are formed into the Body of Her Son through Her powerful help and intercession. Listen to our Lord:

I CREATED YOU WITH MY OWN HANDS AND I CALLED YOU BY YOUR NAME. I KNOW ALL ABOUT YOU AND THERE IS NO ONE LIKE YOU BECAUSE YOU ARE SO VERY SPECIAL TO ME BUT BEING IN DARKNESS YOU ARE DEPRIVED OF THIS TRUTH. I BREATHED MY OWN LIFE INTO YOUR NOSTRIL AND YOU WILL LIVE FOREVER LIKE ME. YOU WILL ENCOUNTER ALL KINDS OF TRIALS AND SUFFERINGS LIKE MY CHOSEN CHILDREN WHO SEVERELY SUFFERED DURING THEIR JOURNEY TO THE PROMISED LAND. BUT YOUR JOURNEY TO YOUR ETERNAL DESTINY WILL BE EVEN MORE DIFFICULT BECAUSE THE REWARD IS FAR MORE GREATER AND GLORIOUS THAN THEIRS. BUT I ASSURED YOU THAT I WILL ALWAYS BE WITH YOU ALL THE WAY. DO PLACE ALL YOUR TRUST, HOPE AND LOVE IN ME AND FOREVER WE WILL BE ONE.

Fifteen minutes discussion:

Why is it so necessary that before we serve others we should serve ourselves first.
In what ways we can serve ourselves?
Since we have a dual life which is physical and spiritual, discuss how we can best serve our physical and spiritual needs.
In serving ourselves, how can we discern that we are being selfish?
Share your own thoughts in how we can best serve ourselves.

Leader reads the following passage:

As our model is both God and man, made of spirit and flesh, we too are made of flesh and spirit. What separates us from our Lord and God is He does not sin while we are so susceptible to commit sin. In every moment of our lives we are so prone to sin and we called it our nature to do so. In other words or truth, there is no hope for us. Thus, the world we live in became the darkest place and in order to go living we do whatever we can to sustain the survivability of our being. God no longer has a place in our being. We are consumed in our very own being. We participated unjustly the punishment ordained to our first parents. We have no other choice but to accept whatever lot we received in this life and by doing so God's will was done. Such acceptance of our fate by living our wretched and hopeless lives God was touched by our extreme miseries and hardship specially His chosen children of Israel who wandered in the desert without knowing they will reach their destination. As cursed creature we simply have to survive and live what was ordained without even knowing that God was always in our midst for we could not discern nor felt His Presence. Being the Just God He is, He pitied us when we carry the sentence supposedly reserved to our first parents. Looks like God contradicted Himself being known as perfectly just and yet why we have to carry the sentence and pay the penalty of the sins of our fathers. No, God is always perfectly just and what we suffered from the sins of our fathers He will greatly compensate us by sending His One and Only begotten Son Jesus Christ which will be the One who in turn paid and rewarded us by accepting unjustly the punishment which we do not deserve. Obviously, look and behold the Holy and sinless One on the cross who willingly took on all the punishment reserve for all of humanity. Thus, what we did in accepting unjustly the punishment reserved for others you can see clearly the picture that in doing so we acted like Jesus. And as our Lord Jesus was greatly honored and glorified by God the Father we who imitated Him by accepting God's will we too will be greatly honored and glorified not only by the Father but also by the Son and by the Holy Spirit. Thus great saints became because of their willingness to take on whatever sufferings, injustices done knowing by doing so our Father in heaven will be greatly pleased and glorified seeing them living the Life of His Son into perfection. Having known the ways of God, the saints rejoices when they encountered whatever severe suffering they unjustly received knowing that they will be greatly compensated and awesomely rewarded for following their Lord to the cross where the tree of life became their reward by losing their lives but gaining the greatest and supreme Life that is of God. More than amazing was the punishment of our parents definitely were worst than what we receive. Can any theologian see why it is so? Do sit still in silence and do a reflection why we should never complain much if we are gifted with so much suffering. Also try to think why our first parents who were responsible for the curses of sin received severe punishment than we who have been justified and redeemed by God Himself? Spend at least five 5 minutes.

After silent meditation and reflection do share to the community your thoughts and opinions.

After the fall, humanity paid severely for their sins against the good and loving God. Compare what we have now and what they have. Remember, in the Old Covenant, they have no idea at all when God will come to their assistance. Remember how hard they prayed, fasted and endless offerings to God yet their prayers were heard but no answer. They prayed without knowing what they prayed for. They did realized their wretchedness and their sufferings were too much for them to bear but despite of their stiff neck ness and rebelliousness by His grace they continued to pray, fast and offerings though unpleasant and unacceptable to God. But His greatness and goodness God was always with them watching and protecting invisibly which made their sufferings more intense than ever. Truly their faith was tested beyond what was acceptable and even prudent. Case in point was when the Lord commanded Abraham to sacrifice his one and only beloved son and you can just feel what intense suffering Abraham must endure. Yet, by passing the test, Abraham was rewarded greatly but as I pointed out his reward can not be compared for the reward and compensation available to us. And again, when those faithful and loyal followers of God have to wait for their rewards thousands and thousands of years while we can have them immediately (of course this takes the complete giving of our lives and will to God and to truly love God perfectly and purely and when it is done heaven and God will be ours without waiting for thousands of years). And so, having clearly saw what awaits us should enflame our hearts and soul to take advantage of such opportunity never found in any time or place. How stiff neck are we? Are we worst than our fathers who serve God to the best of their ways? Or do we prefer to do our ill will spending our lives in seeking the things that gives our physical senses the greatest pleasure? Recall our Lord Jesus who wept bitterly over Jerusalem. If we were in His place after doing everything for our greatest and highest good but giving no value of the free gift of our salvation then we understood why our Lord wept bitterly over our ingratitude. As Co Founder with our Lady, we should treasure everything our Lord Jesus did for us by cooperating in His mission in saving humanity. As previously taught in our formation classes we should be equip in working out our salvation by the simple methodology of living the life of the spirit instead of living the flesh. Recognizing the problems of our humanity and our severe attachment to the flesh St. Paul kept pounding in teaching the new convert not to seek the things of this world but to seek the things of God and heaven. To live fully in the spirit and not on the flesh.

Thus, in this formation class, to be able to serve self perfectly we should always remind Paul's warnings and admonition about our wretched condition when our spirit and flesh never stops fighting for attention and care. We then discuss how we can take great care of ourselves so we will have the energy and power to be conqueror of the enemies of our salvation. In serving self perfectly there are two main areas of our concern.

The first and most important one is our soul. If we lose our soul then it will be forever gone with no more hope of obtaining heaven and most importantly possessing God. It was written what does it profit if we gain the whole world and lose our immortal soul? Even if I would rule the whole world or even the whole galaxy never would I trade my soul. For it was written that what can you exchange for your soul? None. Now we knew that our immortal soul is God's greatest gift to us and our infinite treasure and it would be absolutely foolish if we neglect to take great care of it. Don't we carefully count our purchases because we value money? Do we not work so hard and long even until in our old age so we can preserve whatever wealth we have accumulated? In each one's heart possesses a different kind of treasure and we were warned that we should be careful what are they? Is our most prized possession is in our heart? Or not. As Co Founder's we should know that God alone should be the sole possessor of our heart. God alone and nothing else should be enthrone in our heart, mind, soul, spirit and in our whole being. But, as each one of us knew, we are torn apart between God and others. Thus, if we are not able to make Him as our all then we will have great difficulties in possessing God and heaven because our free will chose not to make God our all. Still salvation is always possible by our sincere effort in trying and striving to make God our everything. If our attachment remains then we can still have God and heaven but we would be in the same boat to our brothers and sisters who have to wait thousands and thousands of years to be in the new heavens and to be one with God. Though, in our case we will be waiting in that prison of love called purgatory and depending on the gravity of our attachments to other things than God determines the length of time and the intensity of our pains and sufferings ordained by His perfect justice. It was written clearly that in order to avoid such lengthy separation from our loving God we were given a choice either to lose our life here on earth by gaining God's Life. Put simply, we live God's Life to perfection or simply said to live in the spirit not on the flesh. How we detached ourselves from the things that are not of God and heaven simply determines how long our detention in purgatory. Our brothers and sisters in Christ who does not believe in purgatory have committed that grave sin of presumption by ignoring God's perfect justice when they taught and believe greatly that once they have believe in Christ and committed their lives for Him will go to heaven. Not so simply because it takes more than believing but a lot of hard and long works in achieving our salvation and even if we do so still holiness and perfection we all fell short. And if those ancient theologians did not make the cut to God's sacred standard should be also our reminder to greatly step up in working hard for the sake of our salvation. It was written and warned that we have to exceed the righteousness of the Scribes and Pharisee that this free gift of our salvation should never be taken lightly but with all of our strength, energy, endless effort in living a righteous and holy life making us acceptable to God's standard. We have studied in the formation classes the methodology in stepping our spiritual life to the highest level because our calling to be holy and perfect is not a joke and should taken seriously otherwise we will terribly fail. But, again, reminding us do not get discourage by the great obstacles, difficulties and demands of our journey simply because our transformation into God is not that easy. Think of where we came from? Do you truly think and believe that all we have to do and believe and accept our Lord Jesus as Lord and Savior will do? Absolutely not. When we do, such serious sin of presumption will derail us and our detention will be purgatory for thousands and thousands of years. Glory honor and praise that our Jesus established His Church with Its Three Bodies to make it easier for us in our transforming journey. With the Holy Mass being offered every moment of our day those who are supposed to spent thousands of years in purgatory can actually be shortened drastically by members who constantly offer Holy Mass for them. And to unbelievers and heretics the neglect of not offering Holy Mass for the souls in purgatory will definitely reap what they sowed. By doing so, their stay in that prison of love can not be shortened. Again, if we are truly serious to get to heaven and be with God then we should place the safety of our soul as our highest priority in this life. After the break discussion about how to make our soul safe and how we can get to heaven and be with God without spending long years of detention.

Break 10 minutes.

Community Together Sings, The Magnificat

My Soul Proclaims the Greatness of the Lord

In the song, Mary's soul expressed her perfect union with God and with no perfect and proper words to described such inseparable intimacy, Greatness was the appropriate one to chose. But if we were in her place probably no words can come when we are perfectly united with God for such experience will make us dumbfounded for our spirit soared to the highest level and to be bounded in God surely our rejoicing can not be contained since His greatness we too have become. For our Lady's Co-Founder, each professed and consecrated member are to be formed through the construction of Her Formation and Mission Handbook so one can experience the inseparable intimacy so we too can experience what our Great Lady experienced. This is the priceless gift to the responder for their commitment and desire in joining the Order participating our Lady's last mission. A very simple and precious book for the SOS Missionaries, "How Safe Is Your Soul" if religiously practice will surely bring the greatest benefits to the one who followed what was taught. A few serious souls did experienced those benefits and as professed Co Founders it is highly recommended we make it as part of our formation program. One who wished to have this book please inform your leader of your interest so we can give you one. In the book is laid the perfect methodology in how to take great care of our immortal soul. This book will help us to know and understand that our greatest purpose in this life was and is to answer the calling of God to be like Him. Believe not the cliche, "Nobody is perfect" for such pathetic excuse will either reap us the reward of eternal death or ten thousands years in purgatory. True that nobody is perfect but we can not live our imperfection till our last breathe because if we do the stagnancy of our soul remains and will never grow or advance to that level prescribed and even demanded by our loving God, TO BE HOLY AND PERFECT AS THE FATHER IS. I have known many good priest and pastors who are truly dedicated to God who constantly failed in inspiring others to seek perfection and holiness and instead relying only in God's love and mercy and to simply embrace our humanity. A truly good and great shepherd's primary and sole concern was to inspire and encourage his flock to become holy and perfect and when this is done, God will be greatly honored and glorified and such servant deserves the greatest reward as it was written that they will shine brightly like the stars of heaven of which they will undoubtedly received the Triple Crown reserved only to those who truly and really love Him. A saint reminded us we are solitary and social souls. In serving others we pleased God but before we do so be reminded that we have the greatest responsibility in ourselves by serving what is and what will be our greatest need. Taking great care of our immortal treasure which is our soul. If we served others and neglecting in taking care of our immortal soul then we failed God by not taking great care of His gifted Life that needs to be nurture and nourish. Remember, our bodies are His temple and God the Holy Spirit desires to dwell in us and if we failed to take care of our soul then the corruptibility of our bodies will make us so repulsive that God simply can not live in us depriving the soul and the spirit of His Life. Since we are both solitary and social beings, the saint taught that we have to be solitary soul so we can gain wisdom and profound understanding of how we can gain our salvation. A solitary soul is in essence a contemplative soul that thinks deeply and seriously about its being. A social soul seeks not the innermost of his being but rather seeks others like itself finding pleasure and comfort of their company. Such bonding can either be good spiritually if its goal was the things of God and heaven otherwise social activities though desirable and good for our physical, mental and psychological being spiritual growth and advancement could be stunted. The truth of the matter is the solitary soul has the advantages over the social soul in terms of one's spiritual development simply because of the fact that contemplatives hears the silent Voice of God while the presence of many or even another soul creates a noise restricting or drowning silence. We are constantly taught or reminded that only in silence we can hear everything even God's Voice. On the other side, noise drown or deafened everything including God's Voice. The saint also reminded us that during our judgement day which all of us must face we stood alone and how many friends or what is our position or accomplishment in this world can not help us unless what we did in our lives perfectly conforms God's will. And God's will was and is that we become holy and perfect like Him. Thus in this class, serving self involves the taking great care of our soul before we do embark in any other endeavors how noble or good they are since God's most Holy Will was to make us holy and perfect like Him. And our greatest move is to make sure our soul is safe.

As Co-Founder, it is of utmost importance that we know what is a soul. Many devout religious and even theologians can not properly define or explain what is a soul and how it functions and operates in our daily activities. It shocked me that a professor in theology said that soul and spirit are the same which they are not. What is a soul then? A soul is an eternal entity residing in a living person and is responsible for all its physical actions in thoughts, words and deeds. Both the soul and spirit will never die nor be destroyed because both are an eternal entity. We heard preachers, pastors and priests constantly preached about our soul but most of them can not properly explain its operation and function. In our soul, there are three faculties namely the memory, understanding or intellect and will. Logically, each faculty definitely can not be deleted nor destroyed and they will remain forever. As one theologian wrongly said that both soul and spirit is the same in essence he was partially correct because what he said about the spirit is that third faculty of the soul which is the will. In the Psychology of the soul, the will is the most powerful of the three for its action applied is what the spirit is all about. For example, God's will through His Words became a powerful Spiritual Force which resulted in the creation of the world and the solar and universal system. Hitler's evil will unleashed a powerful force (spirit) which killed millions of God's chosen people. Thus, it was written that there is constant warfare between flesh and spirit which comes to the conclusion that only by the power of our will we can subject the corruption of the flesh. Simply put, it is the war between our will and sinful flesh. Thus, in our struggle to be holy and perfect, our will determines how we can advance to such sublime standard set by God. We are taught about how fasting and detachment from the world and self train our will into becoming a powerful force which will make us conqueror over all the enemies of our salvation. This should be always our reminder that our own will or spirit determines our eternal destiny.

Knowing the power of the third faculty of our soul let us then proceed and study and discuss the other two faculties which is also very important and crucial in our spiritual growth and advancement to the prescribed level demanded by God.

The memory:

We all know what is the memory. They are the things and events that happened in our lives stored where it can be recollected or recalled as very useful in our present or in the future. Memory can be our greatest teacher in how we can effectively prepare ourselves when facing the same situation experienced in the past. Memory can also be detrimental in our physical, emotional, psychological and spiritual formation because of the negative and harmful experiences in our lives. We heard of the term, wounded souls. We all are wounded souls because of all the bad, undesirable and negative things that happened to us. It could be verbal, physical or sexual abuse by the one we trusted. It could be a tragic event which deeply affected our lives such as the loss of loved ones, financial disaster or failing health or devastating accident. And there are still many many more that wounds us which will remain in our memory.

Whatever what was stored in our memory wether they are good or bad, as part of the soul which we have to take great care of, it is very important that whatever wounds inflicted we should work diligently in healing them. Such process involves difficult and hard work but it was written that we do work hard for our salvation. In each one of us had different kinds of wounds and if left untreated will be an incurable infection which will eventually cause severe sickness to our immortal soul that may led to its demise. For example, someone did horrific things to you which you could never forgive and if it remains unresolved will be detrimental to our soul's salvation. It will not be easy and it is not always that easy to forgive but then again you have the power to do so by the strength of your will (spirit). Thus, this is how our soul operates that although there are three faculties they operate as one entity. For example, the memory is having difficulties in erasing its wounds but by itself it has no power to heal but with the will with its power to forgive and forget the injuries brings healing which makes the soul healthy again.

Finally, the understanding or intellect. This faculty of the soul if properly schooled or graced with wisdom will be the governing faculty which will instruct the memory and the will to the right path where God's will alone should be the only deciding factor in making or choosing what moves or action be taken in our lives. This faculty will be very influential to the memory by its enlightenment that through its knowledge of God's ways to always forgive the greatest of our enemies knowing that as God did forgive us all so must we. The understanding and intellect is the soul's fortification against erroneous and false teachings about the things of God and heaven. This faculty is the fountain of divine discernment where the Words of God can be easily understood and dictated to the will bringing spiritual fruits to the Church. In conclusion, we are introduced to our soul and how it operates which determines what will be our final destiny. Again, the book, "How Safe is Your Soul" can truly make the greatest difference in our spiritual growth and advancement for its proven methodology.

Having taken care of the most important aspect of the self which is our soul we then discuss the lesser one although it is important in our existence so we can properly and efficiently live our lives in the service of God and neighbor. Our physical being which included the flesh.

After the soul we then take care of our emotional and psychological health by avoiding situation that may severely affects our well being. Although stress can never be avoided do try to spend time in peaceful and quite meditation. Prayers works wonder in controlling stressful situation. Then in serving self make sure to take great care of your body not indulging in too much eating, smoking or drinking which are destructive to our health. To be active by exercising regularly to keep the body healthy and strong.

Spent twenty 20 minutes or more discussing how we can serve self to our greatest benefits.

Spent more time in the three faculties of our soul. Learn its mechanics and how our soul operates.

Closing Prayer:

Community Together Sing, "Salve Regina"

Sixteenth Class

Hymn: Abba Father (Community sings together).
The Opening Prayer:

Our Transformation

"And be not conformed to this world: but be ye transformed by the renewing of your mind, that ye may prove what is that good, and acceptable, and perfect, will of God." Romans 12:2.

Fifteen minutes of silent reflection on this passage. Each one write your thoughts invoking the Holy Spirit for enlightenment and after fifteen minutes community shared what was this passage about.

Thirty minutes of community sharing.

After the community sharing, leader reads the following passage:

There is no story like ours. The greatest book ever written was Sacred Scriptures and such masterpiece can never be duplicated for this is our story and how God is greatly involved to make sure that our will conforms to His. There is no other way that we can be transform into the likeness of our God unless our will is perfected into His. Thus the entrance song we shared together is an inspiring melody that should be constantly sung in our hearts, minds and soul as a constant reminder that we are bound to become His greatest Masterpiece, transforming dust to divinity. Have anyone ever read such story? Perhaps there are great fantasy stories that makes us feel good but our story is reality and truth. We are created by God so He will be greatly glorified much like us when we did created something beyond our ordinary capabilities. We are God's greatest project and what He created such as the beauty of the universe or the cosmos are nothing to Him when compared to what He is doing to us. Indeed our story and God's story can never be replicated for who can surpass the genius of our God?

As we all journey to our final destination, it was God's plan that each one of us will be transform into like Him. And this is indeed impossible for the simple reason that we can not do it by ourselves but only with God can we be transformed. Abba, Father, Your are the Potter and we are the clay the works of Your Hands. Thus, if God is not working in us then we remain a clay worthless as the dust that we came from.

Let there be light and came light and also darkness. Everything existed by merely using God's word but we are the only created beings that God used His Hands and Lungs by breathing into our nostril His Breathe of eternity. From the dust we were formed into our flesh reflecting His Own Image. Once we were formed in His Image did God stop working? No. He has a very long way to go before we can be perfected just Him. At the first stage of our creation He was pleased with the works of His Hands but the ultimate plan was He has a very long way to go. And He knew the greatness of the task in transforming us into like Him. Most of us is not aware how God works so hard and unceasingly to accomplished His greatest work. O how easy for others to preach that all we have to do is believe in our Lord Jesus Christ and we will go to heaven. Such preaching is very dangerous to the ignorant soul for if God works so hard for our transformation, we too must also thus we must work out our salvation in fear and trembling. We must exceed the righteousness of the scribes and Pharisees who dedicate their lives strictly observing the religiosity of their faith. And our greatest deprivation is that our lacked in knowledge that it takes the Three Powerful Persona of God to transform us and completing His works into perfection. When everything is said and done our transformation into God will give Him the greatest glory, splendor, honor, power and majesty that losing His Life here on earth was worth it. And we who works so hard with trembling and fear striving for holiness and perfection for the sake of love and for the sake of His greater glory and honor will also be greatly rewarded by the share He allotted to those who give its all to Him. For God can never be outdone in His generosity. Those who gives its all definitely will also receive His All.

As Co Founder with our Lady, we all should ponder this truth and cement it in our hearts that giving our all to the Triune God we too will receive His All. What do you think why our Lady received the fullness of God? She did simply because she gave her all to Him. This should be always in our hearts, mind and soul and by doing so it will greatly enhance our spiritual advancement to a step higher than before. Although our transformation is too far away do not lose heart nor ever be discouraged for our constant failures for God knew who we are and that it takes His full participation to make it possible. Thus, being a member of Her community we are so privilege of Her formation program not available to anyone for she alone knew how we can be transform into His likeness and that can only be done by the indwelling of the Holy Trinity in our soul. She alone knew how to be intimately united to the Father, to the Son and to the Holy Spirit. She knew well that God is the Father and that she was the only choice to make possible the impossible plans of God. By the intimate involvement of the Third Person, humanity was infinitely integrated to the Triune God and such permanency can never be broken benefiting us to climb the highest heights of the divine. The virgin flesh of our Lady became the Holy Spirit's permanent dwelling place because of its immaculacy and purity that He will never depart from her. Thus our Lady became the holy spouse of God a great privilege reserve only to the truly pure and holy and such union of flesh and spirit born the Messiah, our Lord and Redeemer, Jesus Christ. When we truly strive for holiness and perfection like what happened to our Lady's spirituality, we too can become the spouse of God. In the history of the lives of the saints some of them were wedded spouse of God. Example was Saint Rose of Lima was wedded to our Lord. We members of Her Order if we are truly serious to become the bride of Christ nothing is impossible specially how our Mother will intercede for us. But even if we failed short to our desires, we will not be disappointed nor dismayed for in the end on our side is our Lady of Unity pleading for us and you know it is very hard for the Triune God to refuse Her.

From what she experience our Lady's transformation taught us some valuable lesson in advancing our spiritual life and that is we can advance quickly if we are intimately united to the Most Holy Trinity. On the first year of the formation classes we were taught how to build such intimate relationship with the Triune God. Review the seventh to the twelve classes and cultivate that special relationship with the Triune God. Great indeed when one proclaimed he or she had that great and close personal relationship with Jesus but greatest will it be when one had that great and close personal relationship with the Triune God. One will received that triple crown if one had that intimacy with the Holy Trinity. The triple crown mentioned should not be taken literally but symbolically but the reality of it is that one receives a reward three times than those who did not cultivate that intimacy. For example, both the Jewish and the Islamic faith professed their intimate relationship with the Father and for those who made it can have that singular reward. Same with those who had that great intimacy with our Lord Jesus will receive its singular reward. That is why to maximize our rewards our community were inspired to cultivate intimacy with the Three Persona of God much like those saints who are now enjoying the vision of the Most Holy Trinity. They enjoyed their rewards tripled than those who were not intimately united with His Three Persona. Our Lady enjoyed the greatest reward ever for a creature because of such intimacy with the Triune God. Don't get me wrong that the greatest challenge for us in our most difficult journey to God is always been the salvation of our soul. Those who love our Lord Jesus surely will gain its salvation. And those who does love the Father greatly will also be saved. The same with those who loves the Third Persona of God will also be saved. Again, those who have the greatest intimacy with the Three Persona of God will have the greatest enjoyment gaining that triple crown or merit deservingly earned by its love for the Triune God. Saint Elizabeth of the Blessed Trinity testified that the in dwelling of the Holy Trinity in one's soul is indeed very possible specially to those whose burning desire was to become one with the Triune God. And such sublime possibility is greatly enhanced with the powerful pleading of our Lady of Unity. Thus, Her order to establish the community is to form and prepare its co-founder so it can be consecrated and dedicated to the Triune God. Once the co-founder made its profession and its commitment to Her Order, our Lady will present to the Holy Trinity her co founders and it will greatly obtain powerful graces that it will bring tremendous transformation and conversion to all heretics and blasphemers. What joy it will bring to our God when all His children will come and join the Body of His Son specially the chosen children of Abraham, the Jewish people who shared us their God but are deprived of knowing the concept of the Trinitarian God. Also, our Moslem, Hindu and Buddhist brothers and sisters who could not accept such saving and transforming concept of becoming real and true children of God. Again, reminding us that the transformation to become like God is His greatest work ever.

As co-founder with our Lady, she will treat us specially because of our yes to Her in helping our Lady in her last mission. We all marvel how we honor the twelve apostles for their works being called and chosen to spread the good news of our salvation to the ends of the earth. How the Catholic Church honored them having their own feast days as a tribute for answering and following the Son of Man and the Son of God's calling in helping Him spread the Gospel of our salvation. And you know what? Those who responded to become a co founder of Her Order will have the same merits or even more than those twelve faithful apostles of our Lord Jesus because their participation in our Lady's last mission is indeed a continuance and an extension of their labor of love in saving all souls. As our Lady open the drama of our salvation story she will also close the story and indeed she needed all the help she can get from all of her children. As the twelve failed in their missions in bringing the good news of our salvation to the ends of the earth and the failure of the Catholic Church in its mission to bring all God's children to salvation the last hope in bringing all of God's beloved children rest solely on the Mother of salvation and those who are Her co founders becomes the great participants and will definitely earn that triple crown reserved for those who truly give their all to the Triune God through our Lady of Unity. Serious to answer such sublime calling will have the benefit in transforming themselves through the formation program instituted by the Apostolic Administrator by the help of Her intercession and the community's intercession for the graces provided by the Most Holy Trinity.

As this class is about our transformation, let us examine and study how we can be transform into the likeness of our Lady and to our Lord.

Mold us and fashion us into the image of Jesus Your Son.

This is the absolute truth in our transformation that only He the Most High have the power to transform us into like Him. But, everything or anyone can be a powerful instrument in our transformation. In every living soul, each and every moment of our natural lives is a transforming process just like the hands of the potter using every moment of its labor in making the finished form of product desired. Thus, contrary to our thinking and opinion that we wasted so much time in our lives is not true. Every single moment of our lives is not wasted though we thought they were because perhaps of inactivity, laziness or under achieving to what our talents and capabilities we have. In God's moment, nothing is wasted because His Three Persona is always at work in our lives. But because we are so blind and so deprived of His Wisdom and Knowledge we simply can not get it. But the absolute truth is God never takes a break in His works in making us holy and perfect.

How do God transform us into His likeness?

The establishment of the Catholic Church is the greatest transformer of our nothingness into His greatness. Great and ordinary saints were formed and transformed by this magnificent and true Church. There is no other church that can do such sublime works of God than the one true Church established by the Most Trinity. O yes, those brilliant theologians would definitely say that Jesus Christ was the founder and the only

One who appointed and anointed Peter to build His Church. But, let us remember that it was the First Persona of God, the Father who revealed to Peter that Jesus was His Son. Such revelation by the Father was made possible by the Third Persona, the Holy Spirit. Thus, the true Church was founded by Jesus but by the active participation of the other Two Persona of the Holy Trinity.

Can we be possibly transform without the Catholic Church?

No. Despite the mighty and incredible powers of the Most High, we can not be. Once we separated ourselves because of our sin, God can not unites Himself to us. In the land of our exile we encountered and faced all kind of trials and tribulations that truly transformed us into an ugly and deformed creature become a beast of burden. In our exiled, having lost God we became worst than an animal merely concern of ourselves for our own survival. Thus, our selfish tendencies remain in us even today with the establishment of His saving and transforming Church. Even though our miserable experiences in this land of our exile be aware that in every single moment is but the grace of God working in our behalf despite our separation from Him. Yes, our sufferings how great or little it maybe is great grace because it is a powerful tonic to our soul and to our salvation. Those single moment of our exile is more of a preview how our sufferings will also be the suffering of our God when He came to our rescue. The Messiah while on earth also went through a transformation process just like us. How could this be? It begins in the womb of our Blessed Virgin Mary where God was transformed to man and man will be transformed into God. Non Catholics or even some Catholics could not see the greatness of our Lady's role not only for our salvation but most importantly our transformation. Theologians would say that once saved we are transformed into Him. In the process of our transformation to God takes tremendous processing methodology unfathomable to us limited creature but revealed to the true church by the existence of the Three mystical Body of His Church. Such sacred doctrines can not be found in any religion or any churches created by man except in the Catholic Church. These three powerful Bodies operates much like the Three Persona of God to achieved its desired design. The first Body was the Pilgrim Church where all baptized Catholics became members of the Body of Christ but is not guaranteed for salvation unless one is in the state of God's grace at the time of death. Once saved, there is no guarantee that one can be transformed into God unless while in the land of our exile one achieved perfection and holiness where no speck of sin or stain of sin remained in the soul. Out of 10,000 saved soul only one went directly to God and such estimate is done generously for the simple logic that it is almost impossible to be transformed into God at the point of death. Thus, the Second mystical Body of the Church, called the Church Suffering or Purgatory is God's greatest invention and grace for our transformation and perfect union with God. This is the final checkpoint before we enter into His glorious and majestic Presence. This is where we all willingly plunge into the furnace of fiery flames where all our filths, stains, impurities, attachments melting anything that is not of God. Frankly, it is not God who sent us to purgatory but simply His Third Persona inspiring us to go into the furnace of love for perfect cleansing and purification making us very presentable and very worthy of such sacred union. Once done, then enter into the Church Triumphant where we joined all God's saints who made it triumphant over sin and death. And as members of the Body of Christ, we are united with our Lord and Savior and guess what? We will be seated on God's Right Hand. The mother of Jesus' apostle was asking the Lord that her son sit on the Right not knowing that those who belongs to His Body will be seated with Jesus on the Right Hand of God the Father. But Jesus did not revealed to her that her wishes had already been granted if we truly become His disciple and follower. They all did by losing their lives for the sake of His Kingdom. They did drink the cup and salvation was theirs now sharing the glory and splendor of their Master and Lord.

Thus, the Catholic Church must exist and established for this church is truly the new ark where all God's children will be brought safely back home. Wether one is baptized in the Catholic church or wether what religion one belongs their salvation was made possible because of this Church, the Bride of Christ where its worthy member becomes His spouse.

Ten minutes break:
Begin by singing "Immaculate Mary"

Reading of today's Gospel:

Please listen carefully and take notes of what was the reading about. Spent ten minutes in silence and write whatever the Holy Spirit reveals to you. Share to the community what you have written. Twenty minutes time discussing today's Gospel.

After the discussion reader reads the passage below:

When we thought that our exile was our greatest fall the truth is, it is not. Some theologians I knew mentioned that Adam and Eve messed everything for us. We could have been enjoying paradise where there is no war, diseases, illness, sorrow, pains and death. Everything were handed to them and we could have the greatest retirement ever where there is abundance of everything. However, such theological thinking was merely baseness for God had already planned that our first parents must fall for they were not perfected contrary to some theologian that they were created perfect. What we perceive as perfect is not for God's eyes they were so imperfect. They were so far from what is perfect that their transformation has not yet began. Once they were evicted from paradise and once they have lost their friendship and favor from God and once they have lost their immortality and all the abundant privileges, begins the process of our transformation. Once death became a part of life also starts our transformation process.

The first stage of our transformation is the physical or our flesh. Since the punishment of sin is death, God also included in the transformation package pains, trials, tribulations, sufferings, hunger, thirst, diseases, illness, fatigued, discomfort and all kinds of disagreeable to our five senses. For our first parents it was a tremendous shocking experience specially when they have to struggle and find food, shelter and comfort. Like an executive having all the wealth, conveniences and security in life, now was transform to an unemployed beggar with nothing left. A brilliant theologian then term such shocking sufferings we encountered in life is the purgative stage where each one of us must participate as an initial way of reparation from our sins. This is like purgatory here on earth. Real purgatory is purgation of the soul and spirit. Our purgation here on earth is merely for our flesh. However, one could evade the real purgatory if what he or she suffered here in this life satisfies God's justice.

"I am a man that hath seen affliction by the rod of his wrath" (Lamentation 3:1).

In the purgative stage of our transformation, God is involved by using His Rod disguised as all kinds of affliction so to get our attention so we can advance to this next stage of our transformation but we have to call and cry out to Him. But some of us could not see His Rod working on us until such time when one is brought down to the lowest point where one has no more choice but to call and cry to Him.

"My tears have been my meat day and night, while they continually say unto me, Where is thy God?" Psalm 42:3.

This will be the time that the Holy Spirit enters into the equation where the loving and forgiving God exercises His mercy where the most miserable and wretched sinner shared the Psalmist prayer in trying to be healed and restored to His friendship and grace.

"Wash me throughly from mine iniquity, and cleanse me from my sin. For I acknowledge my transgressions: and my sin is ever before me." Psalm 51:2-3.

God saw our broken heart and spirit and once we truly humbled ourselves before Him will God start to lead us to the next stage of our transformation that will lead to our exaltation if we follow His ways. And this next stage is the illuminative stage where the tears of repentance begins to wash away the guilt and the Holy Spirit begins its transformative works on the convert. The Holy Spirit is the One who inspire and taught us to pray rightly.

"Create in me a clean heart, O God; and renew a right spirit within me. Cast me not away from thy presence; and take not thy holy spirit from me. Restore to me the joy of thy salvation; and uphold me with thy free spirit." Psalm 51: 10-12.

When we ask something from God He can immediately answer by either yes, no or wait. Most of us ask the wrong things but if it is truly good for us God quickly answer the prayer. When asking Him to have His Life in our lives then the Holy Spirit quickly entered into our lives constantly leading and guiding us to the path of righteousness and justice. In the illuminative stage of our transformation, the Holy Spirit which is now very actively involved in its formation bestows on the soul His gifts of wisdom, understanding, knowledge, counsel, fortitude, piety and the fear of the Lord and if it persevere in faith, hope and love then it is prime to be transformed into the unitive stage where God and man practically became one. This is the final stage of our transformation where we have reached the summit of union with God.

"Truly my soul waiteth upon God; from Him cometh my salvation. He only is my rock and my salvation; he is my defence ; I shall not be greatly moved." Psalm 62: 1-2.

Once we reached that unitive stage of our transformation, we will always wait for God to lead and guide us so we can be save. And when we are truly united with Him, who can separate us from His love and protection? No one for we are on solid rock where God is our All.

Spiritual Exercise:
At least fifteen minutes:
In silence, focus on NOT TO CONFORM

Slowly read and absorb its words and plant it in your heart.

I WARN YOU NOT TO CONFORM TO THE THINGS OF THE WORLD BECAUSE OF THE DANGER AND RISK INVOLVED WHEN YOUR WHOLE BEING IS CONSUME TO WORLDLY PLEASURE AND TREASURE. WORLDLY SOULS WOULD FIND GREAT DIFFICULTIES IN TAKING CARE OF THEIR ONE AND ONLY IMMORTAL TREASURE - YOUR SOUL. YOU CAN BE IN THE WORLD BUT DO NOT LET THE WORLD BE YOUR MASTER BUT BE ITS OWN MASTER. (Slowly and silently repeat twice then think about your self and your view of how the world did deceive you. Also think of your own family and friends and their difficulties of the world's trappings. Wide indeed is the path leading to our eternal ruin with so few were able to walk the narrow path leading to our salvation. How true and real are the warnings that our salvation should never be taken lightly or for granted because of the difficulties in transforming ourselves into God's likeness.

In silence, focus on BUT TO CONFORM TO GOD

Slowly read and absorb its words and sowed it to your soul.

ONCE YOU WERE EVICTED FROM PARADISE THE SEPARATION IS FOREVER BUT BECAUSE OF MY LOVE AND COMPASSION I WAS GREATLY INVOLVED DEVISING WAYS WHERE I CAN CLAIM YOU BACK TO ME. ONCE YOU HAVE LOST ME YOU BECAME WORTHLESS AS THE DUST WHERE YOU CAME FROM. I BECAME THREE IN ORDER TO RECONCILE YOU MY PRECIOUS CREATION AND SHOWING YOU HOW YOU CAN BE RESTORED TO ME. BUT ALL MY GREAT EFFORTS AND ALL MY GRACES WILL BE WASTED

IF YOU DO NOT CONFORM TO MY WORDS AND WAYS. (Slowly and meditatively repeat it twice. Think of how you value or treasure your redemption and salvation. How do you showed to God and others that you do treasure your salvation. Examine deeply and seriously that you truly treasure God and His ways by always conforming your will to His.

Sowing them into the three faculties of your soul, do this spiritual exercise for thirty days and no doubt you will advance spiritually.

Closing Prayer:
Sing, Salve Regina.

Seventeenth Class

Hymn: O God You Search Me
The Opening Prayer:

Recollection Of One's Life

"For He knoweth our frame; he remembered that we are dust. As for man, his days are as grass: as a flower of the field, so he flourisheth. For the wind passeth over it, and it is gone; and the place thereof shall know it no more." Psalm 103:14-16.

Spend 15 minutes in silence listening to what the Words mean in your own thinking. Write your thoughts. Before you do pray and invoke the Holy Spirit for His Light and then write so it will be shared to the community.

Thirty minutes of community sharing about Psalm 103: 14-16.
After the thirty minutes of community sharing, leader reads the below passage.

In our history million of books were written about all kinds of biographies by various author sharing their lives revealing whatever accomplishment or whatever failures they have. Each one of us have an amazing story although the majority of us are not famous than the great ones be it known that each life had an incredible story. We may not know that even though we do not write our own autobiography, the Author of our life is filing the pages of all the things we do, every words we spoke, every good and bad things we did and every single moment of our lives are recorded in His Book. Theologians called it the Book of Life. Thus, all those biographies written by authors simply fell short compared to what was on the Book written by the Great Writer and the Greatest Author and that is, God. God's Infinity have the capacity to store and record every thing that is happening in each one of His creation. He even knows the number of our hairs and such revelation clearly supports how each one of us are intimately connected to His Infinity that nothing can escape Him. O where can I hide from Your Presence? No darkness, nor heights nor depths can we escape from Him. For in the palms of His Hands God hold us closest and He alone knew us perfectly. All our thoughts is ever before Him that no single moment is not known to Him.

Unfortunately to most of us never give it a thought of God's real Presence in each of our lives. When we are fully occupied with the things of our world and its surroundings God is not in our thoughts. He is left behind and such attitude clearly identifies us as ingrates and when there are bad things happened to our lives we then blamed God. Truly we have not changed at all from the time God's chosen people despite all the great and marvelous things He had done for them they treated Him with ingratitude and even with great insults. But God understood who we are and indeed He is very patient and understanding of our ways.

He who created us knew we are made of dust and how could He expect greatness from us when we are worth nothing like that we came from. Unlike the angelic spirit expected to be perfect and pure, God does not expect us to be like them. Thus when Lucifer the prince of angelic host committed one sin of disobedience God quickly cast him and his followers to hell where they never have the chance to return to their Maker. When Adam and Eve committed a sin of disobedience, God simply cast them away from paradise but He had already made plans for us so we can return back to Him. This then the great mission of our formation as Co Founders with our Lady of Unity how we can turn back to Him and how we will be united with Him for the rest of our lives ensuring our eternal salvation. To do so needs our great resolution to focus on our mission to imitate our Lord's and our Lady's ways in living the Life of God entrusted to each one of us as the only way we can be transform into Him. Thus, Co Founders were given the community rules as our guide to our transformation. Every member's growth will not be the same. It is up to our Lady's dispensation in obtaining grace to each professed and consecrated member of Her Order in helping us to grow and mature into the likeness of our Divine Model. Thus, each member should constantly review and learn the twenty four formation classes so it will be in our hearts, minds and soul. The formation classes will be instrumental in one's spiritual growth and advancement along with constant review of the rules as the foundation of our spiritual life.

Class seventeen will help us in how recollecting the past will make a great difference in our advancement. Most of us have experienced all kinds of hurts, pains, tragedies and sufferings of all kinds either it be mental, physical, emotional, psychological, spiritual and infirmities that wounds us. All of us are wounded souls and no one is exempt from this tremendous gift from God. Shocking statement but it is true which we will expound later. Our wounds are essential and so necessary for our salvation. Our wounds healed or not is a constant reminder of our brokenness of the sickness of our soul. We all are very sick souls even though we look or even behave normally because our sickness can not be seen by human eyes. But in the eyes of God, He saw our sickness and for this reason He is so merciful to us that He is always involved in each one of us through His consolation, encouragement and strength. My grace is sufficient for you. Everything is all but God's grace. Due to our intense infirmities and the darkness of sin have deprived most of us to see the vision of how intense is the involvement of our God in our lives. Some in total desperation have totally abandon the idea of how our good God is intensely involve in trying to draw us and lead us to our highest and greatest good. We all know many who have lost their faith in the good and great God because of the extreme wounding they have received from His loving Hands. These desperate souls have no idea at all that our wounding is but God's greatest grace that will lead them closer even closest to God. These deceived souls thought that if God is good why is it that these bad and terrible things happen to them. They have no idea at all that in this world nothing is permanent and every moment here changes like the ocean tide. In our lives there are times of happiness but there are times of sadness and sorrows. There are times of abundance and there are times of shortages. There are times of war and times of peace. There are times we are in good health and times we will be sick. Like the Scripture taught us that for time is a season and since we are here temporarily we all are subject to changes of seasons. But to those who have faith and who truly believes that God is with us then all the sufferings and trials experienced will be accepted though against its will. But to those whose faith is weak or to those who are not exposed to God and to His ways have no tolerance in accepting what is tragic or bad things in their lives. They do not have the Words of God in their lives depriving them of knowledge and understanding how God works in us.

"And, behold, there came a great wind from the wilderness, and smote the four corners of the house, and it fell upon the young men, and they are dead; and I only am escaped alone to tell thee." Job 1:19.

Job's servant gave the tragic message of the death of his sons. This is the kind of tragedy that tested our faith in God. How many abandon God and have lost their faith upon hearing that their only son who is so good with a lot of potential was taken away in an accident. He was only 22 years old and had just graduated Cum Laude from Harvard Business School ready and willing to make a great contribution to the world but just like a blink of an eye is forever gone. We all have experienced all kinds of tragedies in our lives and our faith determines how strong or weak we are. This very prominent wealthy business man who lost his only son cursed God and became an atheist abandoning completely his faith in God. Contrast this tragic event when their eldest daughter was raped and murdered and when the news came to them they were shocked and crying loudly why this happened to them. After a few minutes, the man hugged his wife and together they fall down on their knees broken hearted with tears flowing in their faces and prayed, "Blessed be God for giving us beautiful and good daughter and we give thanks to you Father knowing that your will will always be done in us. We are saddened but we offer to you everything that happens in our lives for this is your will."

Such prayer simply comes from the Holy Spirit for who can pray like that when such terrible tragedy took place. Certainly this blessed couple possessed the strongest faith by their acceptance even though against their natural wills. Not surprised of their strong faith because these couple were devout Catholics and were professed members of the Dominican Order.

"And said, Naked came I out of my mother's womb, and naked shall I return thither: the Lord gave, and the Lord hath taken away; blessed be the name of the Lord." Job 1:21.

Equipped with the words of God, they imitated the faith of Job realizing and knowing that God had given them those precious time and moments with their daughter providing them with love and tender affection giving God glory and honor for their servitude to Him by taking great and good care of their daughter. Most of us surely will be overcome with emotional distress when confronted to such a tragic situation but to those who knew God's way and those most closest to Him will not hesitate to accept and embrace them with love. Prime example, on the foot of the cross, our Mother saw the most terrifying and most tormenting sight of Her crucified Son and took all the pains and sorrows even though against her natural will. Indeed, she was wounded beyond any imaginable pains and sorrows one will ever experienced saved her Son. As Her Co Founders, we must embraced our wounds for this salve brings us closer or even closest to God. Yes, truly the greatest our wounds be, the most closest we will be to God.

"Faithful are the wounds of a friend; but the kisses of an enemy is deceitful." Proverbs 27:6.

In this land of our exile, careful discernment should be exercise always when confronted with prosperity and adversity. In our lives we will encounter those times when we are so prosperous and everything is just perfectly right. Recall the saying that it was so better in the old days but in the past actually was similar to the present for what is going on our lives in this world remain the same. Our great grandparents worked very hard so they can provide well to the family and their own parents did the same. There are never been a change to our desires in having and possessing what is good or pleasant in our lives. Thousand of years did past and today we have the same mode of operation and that is to work and strive hard for the betterment of ourselves and to those we love and care. Scriptures reminds us that in times of adversity we should remember those times of prosperity and it is best to refrain in enjoying too much during the times of abundance because those adverse times will certainly come without any warning. Great teaching from the great Apostle Paul that he learn well in how to live during the time of plenty and those times in wants. As Co-Founders, let us keep it in our hearts such sublime message so wether we are now in time of prosperity or adversity we know how to be flexible or versatile in facing whatever comes into our lives. For the religious and for those familiar with the ways of God, we are in a better position in handling whatever situation we have than those irreligious or not equip with God's teachings. For God is the same yesterday, today and tomorrow and to acquire God's virtues we imitate also to stay the same wether we are in good times or in bad times. Much like Paul, we live in this ever changing world always stable and secure knowing we are always in God's loving and merciful Hands. Thus, when we are enjoying our lives here on earth do not be so attached to it for such sweet kisses came from the enemies of our salvation deceiving us that abundance will remain always with us which is far from the reality. Like that wealthy man who suffered adversity losing his son unable to assess that those wounds came from a loving and caring friend which is our God who is and will always be faithful to us even though we are so unfaithful to Him. Thus, whatever wounds we have now fear not for they are great grace where our great and good God is calling us to get closer or even closest to Him. Remember, what wounds we have know that they are much like the inflicted wounds our Lord willingly received knowing it will bring great healings to His Own Body which is us members of His Church. Without the wounded

God, there is no other way we can be healed and restored back to Him. Without the wounded Christ, who will heal us?

"But he was wounded for our transgressions, he was bruised for our iniquities: the chastisement of our peace was upon Him; and with His stripes we are healed." Isaiah 53:5.

Who are we? Who are you?

"Behold, I was shapen in iniquity; and in sin did my mother conceive me." Psalm 51:5.

This is truth. We are and always be a hopeless and helpless sinner. Ah, do not lose hope for sin is our greatest sanctifier and without sin we would have never saw the greatness of God's love for us. Sin is grace disguised depriving us of Light but His Wounds activated the Third Persona of God gracing every hopeless and helpless sinner to see a glimmer of Light slowly enlightening the soul of the greatness of its being. Thus, when the Holy Spirit came down during that Pentecostal season gracing mankind that Eternal Light inspiring them to seek, to teach, to share everything God taught in each one of us regardless of status. By His wounds, peace between enemies were accomplished and great satisfaction to the Father by the greatness of His only begotten Son's sacrifice and love for Him and for His love for us.

Who are you? Who we are? Indeed we are what we are and now we should have the fullest understanding that our own wounds is so essential and so necessary if we aspire and desire to be in unity with the Divine Healer, Jesus our Lord. Since the Head is the healer once you become one with Him healed from your wounds the whole Body of Christ will reap the benefits providing healings to the many many wounded members of the church. Thus, in this class formation we who are members of His Body but most importantly soon to be professed as Co Founders with our Lady must strive for our own healings from the many wounds we have received during our lifetime. We will discuss them after break.

Break for 10 minutes.

After the break sing "Immaculate Mary"

Reading of today's Gospel. Read it twice while listener takes notes about the message of the Gospel. After reading it twice, spent ten minutes recollecting the message and write your own understanding for sharing.

Twenty minutes sharing of today's Gospel. Could be extended thirty minutes if there is a need to.

After the discussion reader reads the passage below:

There is no one among us who did not suffer in their lifetime. Wether you are rich or poor strong or weak young or old man or woman each one of us one way or the other had been hurt or wounded. Being wounded meant our experiences that was not pleasant not desirable not agreeable to our senses and it also goes beyond our physical well being but into our innermost being. Physical well being involves all the pains and injuries we suffered in our lifetime. A broken leg or arm or an operation a painful recurring illnesses or our physical shortcomings perhaps the way we look or suffering from a severe handicap limiting our physical capabilities affecting the quality of our life. Then there is our interior handicaps such us our emotional, psychological and spiritual well being. Some of us suffered severe physical or verbal abuse during our lifetime damaging our inner self. For example those who were victimized by severe physical, verbal, emotional or sexual abuse will carry a wound that would be very difficult to heal. Other means that wounds us are the tragedies that came into our lives such us death of our loved ones. When a husband loses the wife he loves so dearly or vice versa such wound can not be quickly healed. Time may slowly healed its wound but the scar will never be healed. When someone loses a child such tragic event can never be erased in the memory that it even bring back the pains of such loss. But the worst kind of wounds are those inflicted by those whom we love so much whom we place our trust. They are so difficult to heal and when those ugly memories came to us it ignites the furnace of hatred and anger drawing the soul into the path of darkness and worst it opens the scar making the wounds worse. If not corrected or controlled it intensifies the pain of such wound that the soul cries out in agony.

"Why is my pain perpetual, and my wound incurable, which refuseth to be healed?" Jeremiah 15:18.

Therefore, as Co Founders we have the greatest responsibility that the wounds we received will not become a perpetual pain by the strength of our will. When bad memories invades our thoughts we can conquer it by simply controlling them by the power of our love of God and yes our neighbor. As we are taught, true and perfect love for God can only be proven by how much we love our neighbor. And when we forgive and forget those who inflicted the greatest wounds in our lives one has proven that its love for God is pure and perfect. When one truly loves God purely and perfectly it becomes easy and natural in extending mercy by one's act of forgiveness to the one who severely inflicted the greatest injury.

Father forgive them for they know not what they do.

This is the divine standard of mercy and that is why Sacred Scripture showed us the pure and perfect love of God for us and that we too if we aspire to become like Him must do likeness to extend mercy specially to those that inflicted the greatest wound to us. By doing so, you extended God's mercy to others and such act of love was provided by Him by making you an instrument of His love. As we are commonly taught love alone suffices because without love everything is nothing for to become like God we must love at all times at all cost even it cost us everything. Since every one of us are wounded souls let us spent 15 minutes recollecting our life specially in the past and write on the piece of paper those wounds and those people that hurts or inflicted so much pain in your lives those whom you can not forget nor forgive. Also, made a recollection also about those people that you yourself have hurt or have inflicted severe injury or pains. This too is very important because each one of us did hurt or inflicted injuries or pains to others. Remember, we are all filthy as rags in His eyes and to deny that we are clean and pure is a great lie.

Spent fifteen 15 minutes in silent and recollect the wounds you suffered and what you had also did to others. List them. Dig deeper into your soul and in your own heart you will find them. Be very honest and truthful and start listing them. Do not worry about them because you alone knew and most importantly God also.

After fifteen minutes together the community prays together the following:

Psalm 56
"Be merciful unto me, O God: for man would swallow me up; he fighting daily oppresseth me.
Mine enemies would daily swallow me up; for they be many that fight against me, O thou most High.
What time I am afraid, I will trust in thee.
In God I will praise His word, in God I have put my trust; I will not fear what flesh can do unto me.
Every day they wrest my words: all their thoughts are against me for evil.
They gather themselves together, they hide themselves, they mark my steps, when they wait for my soul.
Shall they escape by iniquity? in thine anger cast down the people, O God.
Thou tellest my wanderings: put thou my tears into thy bottle: are they not in thy book?
When I cry unto thee, then shall mine enemies turn back: this I know; for God is for me.
In God will I praise his word: in the Lord will I praise his word.
In God have I put my trust: I will not be afraid what man can do unto me.
Thy vows are upon me, O God: I will render praises unto thee.
For thou hast delivered my soul from death: will not thou deliver my feet from falling, that I may walk before God in the light of the living?"

SPRITUAL EXERCISE:

In silence, Recollect those terrible terrifying times in your life and how did you react to it? Certainly, we feel so down even depress specially when God was not present in our thoughts. We may even had lost our faith in Him even questioning why did it happened to you. Now go back to that moment and listen. Spent fifteen 15 minutes.

IN GOD HAVE I PUT MT TRUST: I WILL NOT BE AFRAID WHAT MAN CAN DO UNTO ME.

We all have the same problems why we are cast down for we are only good in saying that we trust Him but in reality we are so far in trusting Him. This is true because all of us is always afraid and fearful and anxious when confronted with difficult trials and obstacles. As the cliche says, we are only humans. But the truth is, we do not really trust Him fully. True we have some trust but in a certain degree that fear and anxiety still remains. But to those who have the fullest and complete trust in Him definitely will not be afraid nor be anxious in whatever kind of situation and trials it faces. Indeed, we are very good in reciting all kinds of prayers but what we say is far from the truth. This is why, when we pray let the words sunk into our heart and soul and IN GOD HAVE I PUT MY TRUST, then you put its meaning into action and when this is done you are free from all our doubts and fears. It will not disappear for God allows this to happen to us as a constant testing of our faith so it will get stronger and stronger and we will have a foundation standing on solid rock. This will happen only when we are in constant contact with God's Words and always applying it into our lives until our last breathe.

I WILL NOT BE AFRAID WHAT MAN CAN DO UNTO ME.

Once you master the application of His Words into your very own lives, then really there is not much to fear or much to worry knowing that He is with you protecting and preserving His treasure and inheritance.

Bring the notes where you have listed the wounds of your life and bring it to the Blessed Sacrament and review it and give to our Lord and humbly ask for His graces to heal all your wounds so you can start a new beginning where those wounds are now but a scar.

Closing Prayer
Sing Salve Regina

Eighteenth Class

Hymn: Hosea (Community sings together)
The Opening Prayer:

Period Of Reconciliation

"And the younger of them said to his father, Father, give me the portion of goods that falleth to me. And he divided unto them his living. And not many days after the younger son gathered all together, and took his journey into a far country, and there wasted his substance with riotous living. And when he had spent all, there arose a mighty famine in that land; and he began to be in want. And he went and joined himself to a citizen of that country; and he spent him into his fields to feed swine. And he would fain have filled his belly with the husks that the swine did eat: and no man gave unto him. And when he came to himself, he said, How many hired servants of my father's have bread enough and to spare, and I perish with hunger!" Luke 15: 12-17.

Ten 10 minutes of silent reflection on the above passage. Silently invoke the Holy Spirit for enlightenment and write whatever was revealed to you. Do you see any similarity of your own life with the prodigal son? Count your blessings and add them together and it is endless and just like the prodigal son there is no satisfaction in our lives. Like him we have to explore other pasture that we might find satisfaction. Share to the community your own thoughts.

Twenty 20 minutes of community sharing.

Reader proceeds by reading the passage below:

"I will rise and go to my father, and will say unto him, Father, I have sinned against heaven, and before thee, and no more worthy to be called thy son: make me as one of thy hired servants, and he arose, and came to his father. But when he was yet a great way off, his father saw him, and had compassion, and ran, and fell on his neck, and kissed him. And the son said unto him, Father I have sin against heaven, and in thy sight, and no more worthy to be called thy son." Luke 15: 18-21.

Ten 10 minutes of silent reflection. Again write whatever the Holy Spirit revealed. This scene in Scripture truly touches our hearts and soul specially to the most wretched and the vilest of sinners. For those who have not sin much cannot feel the greatness of God's grace and His merciful love. In your very own life, how this scene affected you? lightly or greatly? Like the prodigal son, we too have experience the lowest point in our lives when everything seems hopeless and we are so helpless and had no other choice but to call someone higher and greater than us. Once this happens begins the great period of our reconciliation with the Almighty God and Father. This begins true peace when God and man are on the way of uniting each other. The greatest moment of our lives where we are to be reconciled to the Almighty Creator where the joy of heaven slowly replaces what happiness we have on earth.

Twenty 20 minutes of community sharing about the second passage.
After the 20 minutes sharing reader reads the passage below.

Come back to me with all your heart don't let fear keep us apart. As Co Founders to our Lady let us always remind ourselves that His calling for holiness and perfection will always be the standard and when we have reconciled to Him through our conversion from the old and sinful life to a new life in His Spirit comes a new command to give all our heart to Him. Since our heart is the storage of our love we are now responsible in giving all our love to Him. Now, this is the most difficult and the most challenging for us the giving of all our love to Him. Sure it is so easy to say we love Him but in His Eyes it is farther from the truth. Our lying lips have the tendency to exaggerate our self worth when in reality we are so far from giving all our love to the One who gives us all His love. Yes, we do not have the capacity and the capability to give all our love to Him because in our hearts are all kinds of treasures that hinders us in doing so. It gives us true insight that indeed how truly difficult it is to get to heaven contrary to the preachings of some do feel good preachers hiding the truth. The truth of our salvation is very difficult thus we have been warned so many times in Scriptures. One example is that so very few enters the narrow way but so many enter the wide path of perdition. Recall also that where our heart is will be our treasure also. If we treasure the things of this world then we have condemn ourselves in choosing to do so. Curse to those who blame our good God in sending unrepentant sinners to hell when they were the one who made the choices in walking the wide path of perdition. For over two thousand years He gave us Sacred Scriptures to be our light, our guide and our life so we will avoid in walking and entering the wide path of perdition. Sacred Scriptures showed us the way how to enter the narrow way and we can be saved. How many of us are truly dedicated in knowing the way, the truth and the life? When you spent less time in reading Sacred Scriptures then your interest in the well being of your immortal soul is also less. We all have fallen to this deceptive trap and many have lost their soul because of our gross negligence in obtaining knowledge of Sacred Scriptures. Why is this? Because our heart belongs to lesser gods that captivated our love. He warned us that He alone is God and to seek other gods then we are truly in big trouble. We know that we are His treasure but do we treasure Him as much as He does? Unfortunately not. Are we hopeless and helpless? Yes, but we are not if we can come back to Him with a pure and sincere heart in trying to love Him above anything else. He will be so pleased anytime we come to Him and when do He assured us that we are so very welcome. God also knew our difficulties in giving Him all our love simply because we are so weak, so feeble and so unstable that for a mere single second we could lose Him by sin. He also knew the difficulties in getting rid of those little and worthless gods that are enthroned in our little hearts and that is why He gave us His Words Holy Scriptures so by knowing the way to Him we will be able to get rid of those worthless gods that possesses our impure hearts.

Don't let fear keep us apart.

When we are reconciled back to Him despite of our filthiness, vileness, impurities, imperfections and those little gods that enslaves us, God will never cast us away from Him because of His desire that we become one with Him. He will never separate Himself from us for we are bound to become His greatest masterpiece and when we are perfected we are just like Him where He will be greatly glorified and honored. He knew the great obstacles and the great difficulties we are facing in becoming one with Him but He told us so many times never fear nor be afraid for He will be with us in all our struggles and hardships. Sacred Scriptures if we religiously study them and with our strong resolution to live it then all the obstacles and difficulties we are facing in our journey to our heavenly home will now become much easier and much more attainable because once knowledge and love put together the soul will possess an ammunition that can annihilate all the enemies of our salvation.

Long have I waited for your coming home to me and living deeply a new life.

For forty years our Lord waited for His beloved children of Israel to come back to Him. Indeed He waited so long and will continue to do so for our sakes. But please do not take your chances because we know not the time that we are called to His judgement throne to account for ourselves. As Co Founder we are more privilege than the others who did not respond to Her calling for the formation Program provided for each prospective Co Founder. Many were invited to join our Lady of Unity but so many ignored it much like our Lord's calling for holiness and perfection. Most of us thinks that we have all the time to go to God but His calling is for us to repent now because there may not any tomorrow available to us. He had been waiting for so long for us to come back but like His beloved children of Israel they simply ignored Him as if He does not exist. We who responded to the calling of our Lady of Unity as Her Co founder will have the greatest advantages for She Herself will present us to the Triune God and as His special possession we are on the way walking with Her as our guide to the narrow way. We have responded and we received special gifts and that is the Three Persona of God living interiorly deep into our soul giving us a new life with Him.

Let us examine the lives of prominent servants of God and their reconciliation with Him. First, Mary Magdalene whose livelihood was a prostitute and she was possessed with so many demons and when she heard about Jesus having dinner in the house of the tax collector Mary Magdalene went directly to Him although she was not a welcome guest. She fall on her knees and wept on His feet and then dried it with her hair. She became His follower.

Peter, the chosen one to have His church built committed a very serious sin for his denial of his Lord. Full of shame and broken hearted Peter fell down on his knees and wept bitterly for his sin. He begged forgiveness and became fearless as leader of the new church.

Paul persecuted Christians but encountered Jesus on the road to Damascus and became blind and after he was healed he became the greatest apostle and greatest teacher of the Christian faith.

Thomas was with Jesus saw everything He did and heard about the prophesy of His resurrection but he did not believe that He did. He had to touch and feel His wounds then feel on his knees proclaiming "My Lord and my God."

This very small example of reconciliation gives each one of us the greatest hope and a great inspiration that there is no sin how grave or great it was, God's grace always triumphs over sin. Each one us in formation after looking back at the past all those terrible sins and crimes we have committed can now look forward with the greatest hope that everyone of us have the chance to become not only a saint but even a great one. This becomes possible because of the precious period of reconciliation between us hopeless and helpless sinner and God's infinite mercy.

From the example, we knew that the tears of a repentant sinner brings joy in heaven such as the sincere tears of Magdalene and Peter. And David who committed serious sin of adultery, lust, sloth and murder was inspired by the Holy Spirit to write Psalm 51 knowing the seriousness and gravity of his sin that he accepted God's punishment knowing he was deserving of it. He was beloved by God because David's heart was just like Him and by David's confession, the Holy Spirit taught him the perfect prayer for penitents that the Church used it as a universal prayer every Friday morning of the Liturgy of the hours.

"Wash me throughly from mine iniquity, and cleanse me from my sin" 51:2

Such truthful confession touched Him knowing how sincere David was since God knew David loves Him. He understood that despite our love for Him, we all are subject to fall down quickly and as quickly as we separated ourselves from God quickly also does He calls us so we can come back to Him. God loves us so much that He does not want anyone of us to die in sin and to be forever separated from Him. That is why it is so grave injustice done to our God when we blamed Him if we go to hell. Again, God does not want us to be separated from Him and if we only knew how He works unceasingly so hard to save us, we would respond with the greatest love we can give Him. Unfortunately, our vision for God and heaven is so limited for we set our heart and sight on the things seen and the things of this world.

"For I acknowledge my transgression: and my sin is ever before me." Psalm 51:3.

Holy Mother Church by the guidance of the Holy Spirit perfectly chose this prayer every Friday in commemoration of Good Friday where He offered His Life for the sins of humanity. By His willingness to accept the horrible death on the cross all of humanity's sins in the past, present and in the future had been justified. They are fully paid by God Himself for we could never pay ourselves. Even though our sins continued His death is an eternal seal acknowledging that we have been set free from our eternal debt.

"My sin is before me"

We members of His Body the church kept on sinning and she confesses before the Throne of God that Her sins is always before Him and through the Sacrament of reconciliation we can never be separated from Him because of the absolving power of this sacrament restoring immediately the sinner back into His friendship or in the state of grace.

"Against thee, thee only, have I sinned, and done this evil in thy sight: that thou mightest be justified when thou speakest, and be clear when thou judgest" Psalm 51:4.

"Be clear when thou judgest"

A certification of how the Sacrament of reconciliation free us from the possibility of the severest form of judgment and that is being cast into hell. Again, it was repeated on the Psalm how this powerful sacrament of reconciliation easily freed us from being cast into eternal separation from our God.

"Hide thy face from my sins, and blot out all mine iniquities." Psalm 51:9.

Our Protestant brothers and sisters falsely accused that the Catholic Church invented the Sacrament of Confession was man made but they simply cannot see that only God can think of such way to make it more easier for us to obtain salvation. Simply because of their rebellion and disobedient they are deprived what is the fullness of God's truth. We who remain faithful to Holy Mother Church clearly knew how this beautiful and powerful Sacrament can quickly reconcile us to God. We who frequented the Sacrament of Reconciliation knew how it brings so much peace and joy after the priest gave his absolution.

"Restore unto me the joy of my salvation; and uphold me with thy free spirit." Psalm 51:12.

Indeed once absolution was given we no longer fear death because of the greatness of God's grace instituted in this saving sacrament.

"And uphold me with thy free spirit"

The cleansing and the purifying effect of the sacrament of reconciliation clearly restores us quickly to God's friendship but most importantly the Holy Spirit immediately and freely enters into our soul.

Ten 10 minutes break.
After the break, sing the hymn, Immaculate Mary.

Reading of today's Gospel.

Listen very carefully what is the message of the Gospel Write them down. Spend ten 10 minutes in silence and write whatever the Holy Spirit reveals to you. Share to the community your holy thoughts and inspiration. Twenty 20 minutes time sharing today's Gospel.

After finishing the Gospel sharing leader reads the passage below:

We continue discussing this period of our reconciliation. We learned from Scriptures that we can never be reconciled to God unless we must initiate the move. God is always waiting for us to come back as we all know. Free will is a powerful force that can change the destiny of our being. As we are all enemies of God, He does not force Himself in us for He had already made His great move by giving us the Messiah opening wide the gate to heaven. God will not come to the separated sinner specially those who refused to receive His Peace. Peace had already made available through Christ our Lord and for the unrepentant ones who remains in their state has now the greatest responsibility in humbling itself before the throne of mercy. God's perfect humility has its own limit. He had humbled Himself beyond the limits of humility by what He had to undergo for our sake. Now, like that prodigal son, let us follow what he did.

Father I have greatly sinned against you and heaven.

Once the unrepentant sinner call and cry out to God, grace follows and the heart is broken and the spirit is crushed and tears are shed and begins the reconciling period where the soul will be guided and lead by the Holy Spirit as to what kind of action to be taken. Light starts to shine in the heart, mind and the soul where the purgative stages had been slowly replace in the illuminative stage where the Spirit of God will be very active in bringing the soul into the different stage of life, embracing the Life of the Spirit. As Jesus was lead by the Holy Spirit to the mountain to be tried and tested as He begins His ministry, the penitent soul is now lead to a new life and in this first step the soul will be introduce to the light slowly and surely that makes the path of righteousness and justice desirable. Taste and see. The soul is now experiencing a much beautiful and a much desirable Life of God untasted before for the sinner was blinded by sin unable to see how beautiful it is to have the life of God in the soul. We have witnessed how a new convert is on fire to become a powerful witness of its conversion. They started their own ministry by witnessing how God made them see and taste His goodness. Compared to those devout religious who spent thirty years or even more of their lives praying and praying but their spiritual growth remain static because they were deprived of conversion. They are like the brother of that prodigal son.

"And he answering said to his father, Lo, these many years do I serve thee, neither transgressed I at any time thy commandment: and yet thou never gavest me a kid, that I might make merry with my friends." Luke 15:29.

I have known so many devoted and faithful souls who spent their lives praying, worshipping God but their spiritual growth remains stagnant meaning to say they have not seen nor tasted the fullness of God. This is what a Carmelite theologian defined as the unitive stage of one's spirituality where union of soul to God had been achieve and nothing can separate such union but sin. The unitive stage is the highest spiritual plateau one will have in this life and the soul in itself became the bride of Christ. So many tried to enter in this stage but so few achieve it simply because of the impurities of our heart denying the stained soul in entering the chamber of the bridegroom. Even those who answered the calling of the priesthood or even those who have been elevated to the most prestigious office of Church be it a bishop, a cardinal and even possibly the Pope. Simply stated our position here in this world are nothing else but an empty shell and our religious status can only bring us vain glory and applause in the world we live in. Much like the Pharisees and Scribes being honored and looked up but in the sight of God were very repulsive. Being religious merely is an entrance to the spiritual world where one seeks the invisible and unreachable God and most if not all of us desires but we could also easily get lost. By establishing the true church where He is always present we are more safe than before.

Thus, in Scriptures we all should never ignore the greatest spiritual direction and the simplest one and that was, unless we are born again we can not enter into His kingdom. Simply, unless we are converted we cannot advance spiritually. We need to be born anew in His Spirit. Our spiritual stagnancy can be traced by our own pride believing that having spent most of our lives practicing religion instead of seeking sincere repentance by our confession of our sins there would be no reconciliation with God. Like the prodigal son sorry for his sin and David broken in spirit and heart reconciliation with God was accomplished. Now serious theological thought comes to our mind about those devout and religious person who spent most of their lives praying and worshipping God but had no real conversion or was born anew in spirit wether salvation will be theirs. So long as they live always obeying God's commandments treating their neighbors justly and embracing a righteous and blameless life salvation can be theirs.

"And he said unto him, Son, thou art ever with me, and all that I have is thine." Luke 15:31.

Reassurance to the eldest son who never did wrong to the father unlike the prodigal son who was completely lost. He does not need a period of reconciliation because he had never separated himself remaining faithful and obedient to his father. In other words, he was always in the conformity with his father's will. Although he never did experience the joy of conversion having a new life in the spirit, the spirit was always with him since his very own life was live in the spirit of God. However, the element of self righteousness can stunt spiritual growth on the eldest son by complaining that he was unjustly treated.

"And he was angry, and would not go in: therefore came his father out, and entreated him. And he answering said to his father, Lo, these many years do I serve thee, neither transgressed I at any time thy commandment: and yet thou never gavest me a kid, that I might make merry with my friends: But as soon as this thy son was come, which had devoured thy living with harlots, thou hast killed for him the fatted calf." Luke 15:28-30.

A just complaint from the righteous son but it is evident that although he was living in the spirit he committed a sin of anger and jealousy whereby the Holy Spirit left which also exposed that God's love was not exercised in accord to His holy will. To become holy and perfect, this older brother although he is a good man failed to love like the love our Lord Jesus taught us.

"It was meet that we should make merry, and be glad: for this thy brother was dead, and is alive again; and was lost, and is found." Luke 15:32.

To prove truly that we love God one must love his neighbor and the older brother failed to love his very own brother. Like the father, he should also be rejoicing that his lost brother was found and he should have welcome him with the greatest love and joy. By doing so, this brother will receive the greatest reward for his pure and perfect love.

In closing, in order to grow and advance in the spiritual life, we need to be reconciled to Him by coming back through repentance as exemplified by the prodigal son, by Mary Magdalene, by Peter and by David. For God will never refuse nor reject a broken spirit and a contrite heart and for us members to our Lady's Order, our first step to holiness and perfection is to be reconciled to God by humbling ourselves that we are but always be a hopeless and helpless sinner and we need Him every moment of our lives.

Spiritual exercise:

At least ten 10 minutes by slowly and silently praying Psalm 51.
Closing prayer:
Sing, Salve Regina.

Nineteenth Class

Hymn: Morning Has Broken:

The Opening Prayer:

Birth Of A New Life

"Even so we, when we were children, were in bondage under the elements of the world: But when the fullness of the time was come, God sent forth his Son, made of a woman, made under the law, To redeem them that were under the law, that we might receive the adoption of sons. And because ye are sons, God hath sent forth the Spirit of his Son into your hearts, crying, Abba, Father. Wherefore thou art no more a servant, but a son; and if a son, then an heir of God though Christ." Galatians 4: 3-7.

Fifteen 15 minutes of silence meditating on such beautiful passage of which very applicable to us. Slowly and taste each words how we started our life. Recollecting our external life when we were slaves of sin. How our corruptible flesh kept overwhelming the life of God in our soul but praise our Savior who never stop interceding for His Body giving us that blessed hope that soon and very soon His grace will give us the strength and the courage to contain and restrain the sinful desires of our flesh. Without His coming to our land of exile there is no hope at all for us to triumph over our corruptible flesh. Indeed, we were given the law so we can restrain ourselves from committing sin until we will be truly be freed from its slavery. Now think of this truth that we are truly destined for greatness that we can never have in this world. Write your own thoughts about this wonderful passage of God's truth.

After 15 fifteen minutes community shared what their thoughts were. Thirty 30 minutes of community sharing.

After the community sharing, leader reads the following passage below:

Morning has broken like the first morning:

Once God commanded there would be light begins our creation. Everything that He said in His Words were good to His sight. He prepared the first morning of light and when Adam saw the light of that first morn he felt happy. And when Eve came into his life Adam was much happier sharing the abundance in the garden of Eden. Paradise on earth was a sight to behold. Both walked with God and conversed with Him and such closeness to the Most High was our greatest blessings and gift. But the question is, are they united with Him? This is a great question to theologians who studied God. Were they?

No. To be one with God, one has to undergo a process of perfection. Theologians and many of them thought Adam and Eve were perfect but they were not. In our limited mind, they were perfect since they did not suffer any physical or material wants and they have eternal life. If they were perfect, they would have never committed that sin against God. Much like Lucifer who was the prince of the heavenly having gifted with beauty, brilliance and honor was far from being perfect. Thus, both the prince of angels and both Adam and Eve were not perfect at all. Both have to be evicted from their lofty status and suffered the destructive consequences of sin. They were so far from being united to God because to be united with Him takes so much effort and God's greatest involvement to make us one with Him. God destroyed His first creation so their imperfection can be process so His greatest Works will become a perfected one. Sin brought death to Adam and Eve and although it brought so much pains and sorrow our death not only partially paid for our sins but it also started the process of our transformation into His Being.

Death brought us the birth of a new life where the first step begins in our transformation process. A Chinese saying reminded us that a journey of a thousand miles begins with a single step. In our journey to eternity begins with our choices as to what kind of a life we chose.

"For this my son was dead, and is alive again; he was lost, and is found. And they began to be merry." Luke 15:24.

Recalling Class 18, the period of reconciliation is the wisest option to chose where the greatest sinner repented and resolved to make drastic changes by abandoning its sinful and wicked way and living a life in conformity to the Holy Will of God.

For this my son was dead.

Sin brought death to Adam and Eve even though they were created immortal. Make no mistake nor doubt this absolute truth of our being that we are truly sons and daughters of God through adoption. Do not get down on yourself if you feel or think that you are not. We all were victimized by our sins that we all have great difficulties in believing that God is truly Our Father. Jesus Himself reassured us that His Father is also ours simply because through Him we became sons and daughters of the most High. Through His very Own Death brought His very Own Life to our dead bodies.

For this my son was dead, and is alive again.

Therefore do not waste the Life of God given to all of us through Jesus Christ His only Begotten Son for He took upon death in order to make us alive again for this God's will that we will live forever with Him. He does not wish sinners to die but to live. God made this possible for us but again the greatest problem God has is what choices we made. Recollecting the power of our soul how its third faculties which is our will determines what choices we do make in every aspects of our lives. Free will was God's greatest gift to us since it measures the length, the depth and the height of our love for Him. This is how God rewards those who chose to love Him by how it gives its own free will all to be God's Own. This is how one can become one with God how we can be united to Him by the complete giving of our own free will to Him. This is how to live God's Own Life into our own and this is the new life we are suppose to live. To live fully not in this world but to live fully for God alone.

He was lost and was found.

We all were once lost but by the love and mercy of God are found. We were dead from sin but now is alive by living the Spirit of God dwelling in us.

"Either what woman having ten pieces of silver, if she lose one piece, doth not light a candle, and swept the house, and seek diligently till she find it. And when she hath found it, she calleth her friends and her neighbours together, saying, Rejoice with me; for I have found the piece which I had lost. Likewise, I say unto you, there is joy in the presence of the angels of God over one sinner that repenteth." 15:8-10.

As Co-Founders with our Lady, we have found and we have a new life. By our confession and by our conversion the Life of God is in our soul begins to take into shape. As previously mentioned the three stages of our journey to God takes form in every moment of our life. We learned from previous class that our journey to our transformation begins in the purgative stage where the struggles between our sinful flesh and His Spirit takes too much of us. Since flesh and spirit is always against each other we experience a period of purgation and this can take any forms of sufferings or affliction where we are tested as to which side we chose to take. The life of the flesh or the life of the spirit. If one chose to continue to live in the flesh then the soul can not advance to the next stage since the will choses to remain stagnant in its physical life. But to those who persevere and endure in living in the spirit, it will enter into the second stage of one's transformation and such stage is the illuminative stage where the light of God starts showing the soul the path which leads to Him. Revelations comes slowly about the things of God and heaven and the soul can finally taste the sweetness and delights of His loving gaze and also His Presence. The illuminative stage is the final bridge that will connect the soul into God and this is a very crucial period because the testing becomes more stiffer and difficult. One important note we should keep in our hearts, mind and soul is that no matter what kind of hardships and difficulties we encounter one should never again never never to give up but to continue to climb the heights leading to union with God. It is also possible that during this period of illumination, the soul will also experience a step back to the purgative stage and we should never get discourage because this is for our greatest good. To make it clear, being on the purgative stage is not a bad thing because God saw in us that He wants to clean up so to speak so we can advance to the illuminative stage. For example, you love your spouse exceedingly that you will practically do anything to please her or him. If one is religious and trying to live in the life of God, He will lead the soul into purgation so He will become its All.

Of course, there is nothing wrong in giving our spouses love but there is a limit that it does not hinder or lessen our love for Him. There are thousands of purgative cases in our loves where the one we love so exceedingly will be taken away from us. Either tragically such us sudden death or incurable sickness are our period of purgation. True, it looks cruel and in-compassionate in our thought and conceptions but whatever tragedies and calamities we encountered in this life are nothing compared to what we will gain in the next life. If ever, something tragic happens to our very loved ones which they do not deserved, this is that purgative journey that each one of us must undertake even though it is very painful and difficult difficult to accept. To those of us who did experienced such tragic events in our lives be consoled that God is leading you to the purgative stage of our journey so we will reach the ultimate destiny for each creature - union with God.

"He that loveth father or mother more than me is not worthy of me: and he that loveth son or daughter more than me is not worthy of me" Matthew 10:37.

Our Lord's message and warning is very clear that He should and always be deserving of all our love. The truth is when one truly gives His all to God when one truly loves Him with all his heart, mind, body, soul and with all his strength we also did give our love to the spouse, children or the others. Even our enemies we did give our love. This is the secret of obtaining heaven and God while we are actually in this land of our exile and that is when one loves the Lord perfectly and purely peace and joy will accompany us to eternity where the fullness of eternal happiness, glory, honor and splendor will be finally be in our possession where no one can take it away from us. I have known quite a few devout person who experienced such tragedy even questioning the good God why He allowed it to happen but I also knew that the one taken away from this person had become an object of excessive love developing into idolatry. Or to put it properly, loving the creature more than loving the Creator.

Thus, in His great love and mercy, God is calling and correcting that person by this purgative action so it will enter into that first step towards the long journey to our sanctification and salvation. And even when there are so much trouble and serious division in our very own family is also God's calling so we can enter into that initial stage of purgation leading to the illuminative stage where God's revelation to the soul will draw it to Him. The knowledge of God and heaven are slowly implanted in the soul raising its divine life to a new level or heights where it can now taste the goodness of the Lord. If ever we did experienced so much problems with our families, friends or relations be at peace because it is God's way in bringing us closer to Him.

"For I am come to set a man at variance against his father, and the daughter against her mother, and the daughter in law against her mother in law. And a man's foes shall be they of his own household." Matthew 10:35-36.

Clearly be at peace with God and with yourself because all the troubles and divisiveness in our lives is merely a test as to how we can respond to such adversity and to measure how much knowledge we have acquired in the things of God and heaven and what actions we take. Truthfully, in this world there will be no peace because there are a zillion of us having each free will and certainly we are not on the same page thus troubles and division will always be in our midst despite the holy Presence of God and His prophesy will definitely stand until the the end of time. So be at peace if you have serious problems with any members of your family because if you are striving to love God above all things and your spouse or your children does not love Him then such division will remain until such time both sides will be on the same page.

Break ten 10 minutes.

After break community sing, Immaculate Mary.

Reading of today's Gospel. Read it twice slowly meditatively while listeners take notes about the passage. After reading it twice, spent ten 10 minutes recollecting what the passage is telling you. Write what the Holy Spirit reveals and share to the community.

Twenty 20 minutes sharing the messages in today's Gospel.

After the discussion, leader reads the passage below:

We continue to discuss the choices available to us for it will be the final and determining factor how we will end up our natural life. We heard many times that we need not to die to possess and experience heaven. What choice we made simply will be our eternal lot. Repeating what we learn is that if we live in the flesh we will reap the corruptibility of the flesh and if we never make changes to the way we live then it is so easy to judge that we will reap eternal death meaning to say, we will forever lost the loving and good God. Why is this? Simply stated flesh and spirit is always be in others throat. The Spirit's way of life is so different and so opposite to the life of the flesh. We know how we live and most of us are under the influence of our flesh and naturally we do give in naturally to what its cravings and desires. We need to rest our bodies after working hard the whole weak and yes there is no sin in resting our bodies but most of the time the flesh demands exceeded what is just and right. For adults 6 to 8 hours of sleep is normally enough to replenish and heal the body. However, the desire of the flesh kept us tied to the bed since for the flesh it is pleasurable and comfortable to stay longer and to those who are not spiritually minded will surely give in. Before we know it, we have spent 12 hours or longer and we know what is wrong with it.

"I do not have enough time to pray nor read Sacred Scriptures. Even for twenty minutes I do not have."

Sounds familiar? We should love the Lord with all our heart, mind, body, soul and with all our strength. We can show our love for God when we spent time praying, thanking, praising, adoring and worshipping Him. He wants us to spent more time with Him not because He needed your time. He owns time and eternity but why He wants us to spent time with Him because this is our greatest gift to spent time and get closer to Him. He wants us to spent time with Him for our greatest and highest good. Time with God is an eternal treasure that we can draw when we are facing Him in His judgement Seat. How much time did you spent for your own highest and greatest good. When one spent time with God, He will show you why we must. Time for God is your love for Him. Remember those time when you want to see and speak to your first love? How we want to be with our spouse? But who is our spouse but only a creature who in time we probably fall out of love and affection. Observe those married couples say twenty years or more and their desire to have their own space. I remembered a friend looking forward for retirement and he had been married forty years and when he retired I found out how depressed he is because he and his wife whom he had loved for a long time can not seem to enjoy their lives together when they were both looking forward to his retirement. Clearly it showed that loving a creature does not bring that inexpressible joy and peace when one gives all its love for God. I also know someone that when his wife died friends and relatives took pity and compassion on him because they thought he was full of pain and sorrow knowing how much he love his wife. They tried to invite him and they tried to find someone to replace his wife thinking of how lonely and miserable he was. But they could not see the spiritual side of this man and after talking to him I found out that he was very happy alone and when I also found out how dedicated and devoted he was to God was the reason why he found peace and joy not because he was alone but the fact was he was always with God through prayers and meditation and contemplation. I found out that we were the ones who are really lonely and miserable because we do not spent much time with God. I learned something very special with my encounter with him that the more time we spent with God it increases the fervency of our love for God and we will received that signal grace that nothing can disturb the peace and joy of being always in His blessed company. Thus, I found out that truly we can have heaven and God now and there is no need to die to be in heaven and to be with God. He did shared to me such lofty thoughts that I did tried my best to imitate what he taught. By following his example I did find something that I am sharing to you. In this world, if we work so many hours we get paid much more increasing our financial capacity. The same simple principle is also applicable if we spend too much with God we gain more of Him and the reward is that I found everything in this world and in this life were all rubbish. And my thoughts and my attitudes were confirmed when I read what St. Paul had said that he too found that everything in this world are rubbish. When you have Christ in you, really fully in you you know what I mean. Thus, when we received the grace of conversion much like the examples previously mentioned we will have a different kind of life, a new life of Christ living in us.

This is what we are discussing in this lesson, the Life of God wanting to transform us wanting to become one with us. Conversion then is conceiving God in us. We all heard, born again.

"Jesus answered and said unto him, Verily, verily, I say unto thee, Except a man be born again, he cannot see the kingdom of God." St John 3:3.

How could a man be born again and how could it possibly enter into his mother's womb? Such question came from the deeply religious Nicodemus of the Jewish faith who had no understanding of the Word. He simply could not get what Jesus meant because Nicodemus in spite of his religiosity was deprived of the Holy Spirit. Even today, the Jewish and Islamic faith had no clue about the arrival of the long awaited Messiah and because of their spiritual stagnancy in no way they can embrace nor accept our Lord as the Savior of mankind. Worst, they are deprived of becoming a part of His Body the Church and they will encounter severe difficulties entering the kingdom of God of which our Lady of Unity must enter into the salvation equation so they too will be save.

"Jesus answered, Verily, verily, I say unto thee, except a man be born of water and of the Spirit, he cannot enter into the kingdom of God. That which is of the flesh is flesh; and that which is born of the Spirit is spirit." St John 3:5-6.

Thus, the birth of a new life. Most if not all of us are familiar of life in the spirit. Quite a few servants of God did seminars and retreats about life in the Spirit because of how important this concept of truth that salvation is not possible at all if we live in the flesh. How many years or even if one spent a lifetime of being deeply religious but there was no conversion salvation would be very difficult. As a devout Catholic and I considered myself as very deeply religious I found myself in circle as far as my spiritual advancement. I known so many devout and very religious friends and even in my family but had not experience conversion or the birth of a new life in the Spirit. Thus, on the first class was about religiosity and how we can get stuck up and somebody ask me wether those soul who are so devout but did not experience conversion will they be saved? I responded that God's mercy is unfathomable and I always keep in my heart and soul that His judgement belongs to Him and not my business. However, like the prodigal son's story, the older brother who was very faithful and obedient to his father was given reassurance that while his younger brother was lost, he the older was always with Him. Meaning to say, he was never lost and from such assurance even though he did not experience conversion, it is logical to say that religious and devout Catholics who persevere in their religious practices through prayers and living a blameless life God then in His perfect justice will certainly be very merciful to them. However, having been baptized (be born of water) satisfies the first requirement and one's religiosity and perseverance in a life of goodness and righteousness then certainly the Spirit of God is already presence in the soul even though one did not experience conversion. This is the saving mystery if one is baptize in the true church be born of water integrated to His Body member of His kingdom here on earth. This is a very consoling fact for those who have never experience conversion specially we Catholics having all the sacraments and having our Lady of Unity, Mother of God and also ours.

As Co-Founders with our Lady, let us remember these two kinds of our spiritual lives. First is that prodigal son who squander its time seeking the world's pleasure neglecting his spiritual life. He was dead but now he is alive. The converted son had a new life now. Second was the good son who never left his father's house always obedient and faithful. He was righteous and never offended his father. From this information, it is obvious that the Spirit of God was in him for he live a life blameless and acceptable to his father. Thus, the life of the Spirit was with him and because he remain steadfast and faithful there is no need for him to be converted because there was no need for he had been living a just and righteous life which is pleasing to God. The story between this two brothers is an example of how God's graces is always available and accessible if we are aware of such gift that is freely given. What is important for us to remember that once we have the life of God (Spirit) in us we should take great care much like a baby sitter always watching and caring for the little child making sure he or she is safe and secure. Worth repeating is that this little child we are baby sitting in our soul is the Life of God wanting and desiring to dwell in us because we are the house of God.

Spiritual Exercise:

At least fifteen minutes:

In silence, slowly read the following words below and keep it in your mind, heart and soul.

I AM THE RESURRECTION AND THE LIFE. BY MY DEATH YOU ARE RESTORED TO MY OWN LIFE. WITHOUT MY RESURRECTION YOU DO NOT HAVE LIFE. THE NEW LIFE WHICH IS VERY PRECIOUS TO THE FATHER BECAUSE IT IS THE LIFE OF HIS ONLY BEGOTTEN SON SACRIFICED FOR YOUR OWN HIGHEST AND GREATEST GOOD. YOU ARE CREATED SOLELY BY OUR FATHER TO BE HIS VERY OWN SPECIAL CHILD. THIS IS THE ABSOLUTE TRUTH OF YOUR EXISTENCE.

Read the passage again and imagine that you are not what you think you are but you are what God wants to you to be. You are His belonging, His treasure and His inheritance for your greatness cannot be seen until He had completed you into His Very Own Likeness.

Pause two 2 minutes and recollect what you have known about yourself. Read again very slowly.

UNLESS A SEED FALLS TO EARTH AND DIES, IT SHALL REMAIN BUT A SEED. BUT IF IT DIES IT SHALL BRING NEW LIFE.

Read it slowly and see why Jesus the only Son of God came down to earth joining us suffering severely and finally giving up His Life so we can have a new life. If you do not believe this then there is no hope for you since the life, death and resurrection of Jesus our Lord was done for your own sake so you can come home to our Father who is in heaven.

Closing Prayer:
Community together sing, Salve Regina.

Twenty Class

Hymn: Christ Be Our Light

The Opening Prayer:

A Devout Life

"By night on my bed I sought him whom my soul loveth: I sought him, but I found him not. I will rise now, and go about the city in the streets, and in the broad ways I will seek him whom my soul loveth: I sought him, but I found him not. The watchmen that go about the city found me: to whom I said, Saw ye him whom my soul loveth." Songs 3:1-3.

Spent 15 fifteen minutes in silence meditating on this Scripture passage listening to the silent Voice of the Holy Spirit. Before you do, pray in silence invoking the Holy Spirit to come into your soul so He can reveal to you about the passage. Write whatever what you received from Him so you can share it to the community.

Thirty minutes 30 of community sharing on the passage, Songs 3:1-3.

After the community sharing, leader reads the passage below:

Being born again the life of the Spirit and the life of the flesh will persists in battling and tormenting each other and this unending conflict will not go away while we are still alive. This will be our daily battle with the sinful desires of the flesh and we will be struggling in every moment of our lives and this is how we are tested and this is how we can prove our love to our God. We will fail sometimes but do not let it get you down or do not be discourage because our struggle is part of His process in transforming us into His likeness. Faithfulness is God's never failing assurances that He will always be with us and in whatever situation we are in He is in us. This is the beauty of God that He will always remain with us so long as we remain in Him. Many times in Scriptures we read His faithfulness and that all He promises to us will be fulfilled. The problem is, us. Because of the darkness that envelop us and because of the burden of our sinfulness have cheated us of that joy, peace and unity with our Triune God.

Our sins are too heavy for us, cried the afflicted sinner. Indeed the burden crushes our spirit diminishing and weakening our wills into the point of desperation. But to those who are faithful to Him God never fails in coming to our assistance by means of His consolation and inspiration accompanied by the strength of His Holy Spirit so it will triumphed over the weariness of our body, mind and soul. It is in our darkness that will test our faithfulness. Remember when we were little children most if not all of us is so scared of the dark. There is something in darkness that brought fear and truly when there is darkness there is uncertainly as to what is in it. We do not know what awaits and it is in uncertainty that makes us anxious and fearful of what lies and what awaits in us.

It is the fear of not knowing wether our Lord is with us or that great fear that He might have abandon us and will never be with us.

By night on my bed I sought him whom my soul loveth:

Fear not for I am with you always. We remembered His promises never to fear anything because He is with us and to alleviate our fears and anxiety we induced into our sinful hearts the love He installed in us making our soul to seek the one during such darkness that covered us. Knowing He alone is our hope, our light and our salvation we exercise the power of our will to seek Him in the most darkest moment of our lives when we are at still in bed waiting for His Help.

I sought Him, but I found Him not.

When we can not find the One whom our soul loves how does one responds. We asked ourselves why I can not find my beloved when I seek and search for Him? If He is with us as promised why then I can not find my beloved.

Perseverance is an assurance for our salvation because of what is being promised that those who persevere will be saved. As Co Founders with our Lady let us never compromised our faithfulness by not giving up our search seeking the beloved of our soul. In this class, we must always practice and acquire that great virtue of faithfulness, fidelity to our Lord and Lady by living a devout life centering everything on Him. Despite our failure to find Him it does not mean God is not with us. He allowed us to feel that way so to continue to test and to draw us even much closer than we want to be. He alone knew what are lacking in us and God alone knew how to fix our shortcomings and defects. As Scripture taught us:

I will rise now, and go about the city in the streets, and in broad ways I will seek Him whom my soul loveth: I sought Him, but I found Him not.

We all experienced those moments when God is too far remote and all our prayers with our constant calling and crying out to Him had fallen into deaf ears. Again, for those unfamiliar of His Ways they gave up their faith in God and even dangerously falling away from Him. Reminiscent of God's chosen people who completely abandon their God when Moses their spiritual leader and guide did not show up after forty days in the mountain thinking he was dead and in their darkness without their leader they started looking and searching for another god made of silver and gold. They were tested and miserably failed simply because they have lost their leader. Much the same way now that Jesus is with us He constantly tests His devout if they will not seek for another foreign god to replace the one true God. Thus, for the devout if they could not find Him the first time one must never give up by rising and look for Him in another place or in the community one belongs which of course for the devout soul one will certainly search Him in the church. Still, the devout soul could not find the beloved. Of course God intentionally made us think that He is so far and remote and unreachable which make us much more stronger spiritually because one is no longer seeking God in the flesh but in the spirit reminding us that to pray and worship God in spirit and in truth. Thus, when we pray and seek Him in baseness we could not find Him although He was with us. Simply we cannot discern that everything we ask and prayed God heard it all but because of the condition of our wretchedness and of our sinfulness we think our prayers were not heard or answered. The truth is God never stops in shaping and forming us in accordance to His Own Design but because He is Spirit His Actions in us is not seen because God is an invisible powerful force that can destroy or transform anything He wish. How long then we keep looking and searching for Him?

In the city where the soul keep searching and seeking the Beloved, a city watchman found him and the soul asked the watchman if he had seen the Beloved. God can never be found in the flesh but in the Spirit. If we seek God in the flesh there is no way to find Him and that is the greatest reason that it took a lot of effort a lot of searching and seeking until the baseness of our existence have been extinguished where the Holy Spirit begins to take over our very own lives leading and guiding it to the Holy One to the Beloved.

"It was but a little that I passed from them, but I found him whom my soul loveth; I held him, and would not let him go," Song 3:4.

Once we live fully in the Spirit although we can not see Him the union between our spirit and His can be an experience beyond our existence. Saints wrote about such union where a mystical marriage between the chosen soul and God become One. Once this is experience the chosen soul experienced supreme delight and brought to an ecstatic state that the soul seems to lose everything and have tasted that divine delectation a tiny preview of what will be like when we get to heaven and become one with One. What earthly divine ecstasy one experiences here on earth is merely a tiny fraction to the infinite perfect happiness and joy prepared to those who loves Him. Our happiness, joy and reward corresponds the greatness or the littleness of our love for Him. Simply said, the great is our love for Him so does our reward and little is our love for Him little is our reward but to the recipient of God's reward will be forever happy for they know His reward is perfectly just and right.

"The Lord recompense thy work, and a full reward be given thee of the Lord God of Israel, under whose wings thou art come to trust." Ruth 2:12.

To encourage us and to be inspired by God's reward the Apostle preached of the greatness of His reward.

"But love ye your enemies, and do good, and lend, hoping for nothing again; and your reward shall be great, and ye shall be the children of the Highest; for he is kind unto the unthankful and to the evil." Luke 6:35.

Clearly as we answer Her call to be Her Co Founder and Co worker in bringing and uniting all God's children under One Shepherd as promised we will be rewarded. As previously taught each member does not have to do the most difficult and challenging work in Her Order for we shared all its treasury of merits and what is most important is our obedience to the community rules.

Thus, in Class Twenty, we will embrace a devout life centering solely on doing God's will and perfect obedience to our rule. Do not expect about experiencing ecstasy or visions for God's ways in drawing us to Him will always be contradictory to our will or senses since the physical or the life of the flesh will never agree to what the life of the Spirit and such conflicts between these diverse beings can only be made possible when the Fullness of God's Spirit dwells in the soul. When this happens although the life of the flesh keeps rebelling it's power has no effect because in the Spirit is the power of the Most High and with such fact everything will be under its subjection. Even the powerful demons are powerless when confronted with the power and authority of God.

"And there was in their synagogue a man with an unclean spirit; and he cried out, Sayings, Let us alone; what have we to do with thee, thou Jesus of Nazareth? art thou come to destroy us? I know thee thou art, the Holy One of God. And Jesus rebuked him, saying, Hold thy peace, and come out of him. And when the unclean spirit had torn him, and cried out with a loud voice, he came out of him." Mark 1:23-26.

And if the powerful evil spirit is easily subjected to His power the flesh will also be easily under its control because of God the Holy Spirit presence in the soul. There will be that instant in our spiritual life that we are constantly harass through temptation and obstacles from the enemies of our salvation to prevent us from advancing but when we experience such moment there is no greater weapon than the Words of God where the enemies of our salvation will have no chance in defeating us. Observe and learn from this important scenery in the Bible.

As Co Founders to our Lady, these are the three enemies to our devout life. Remember, once we are converted the new life of the Spirit starts to take over our life and this will be the most crucial point as to how truly we are in our commitment to our Lady and to the Triune God. These enemies of our salvation had practically enslaved most of us here in the land of our exile. Let us carefully learn from the following situation.

"For what shall it profit for a man, if he shall gain the whole world and lose his own soul?" Mark 8:36.

Think, are we not all been through this? How the world deceives us like a strong magnetic force that it is very difficult for us to detach. This is the cause why so many souls are lost to eternal perdition because we are enslave to it. If you have been to Wall Street, the financial district where stock brokers and traders converged how they acted like animals screaming and trading their hearts for money that such obsession had practically chained them to serve money instead of God. These people had already accumulated great wealth and this millionaires and billionaires are not satisfied with their wealth that they keep on and on even in their old age. Money indeed draws us all simply because with it we gain power. The more money the more power and those of us who are having difficulties to pay our bills could not comprehend why they are so engross with making more. Most of us with financial problems would be greatly relieved if only we have a few thousand dollars but these wealthy people that control the financial markets simply epitomized what this Scripture passage.

As Co Founders each one of us knows how we are in the financial spectrum but in our journey to holiness and perfection wether one is rich or poor it does not matter as long our aspiration was to imitate our Lord's ways and the example of our Lady. We want to accumulate heavenly treasures not worldly treasures because if one chose the later, one's soul is risking eternal perdition as warned by our Lord.

Many souls continue to be lost because of their excessive love for the things of the world; such as money, pleasures, honor and fame. By choosing earthly treasures, the soul rejects heaven and God. We cannot have both.

"No servant serve two masters; for either he will hate the one, and love the other; or else he will hold to the one, and despise the other. Ye cannot serve God and mammon." Luke 16:13.

God's first commandment demands we should give Him all of our love and if our love is in the world then our soul is in big trouble. When our love is not God obviously, our hearts belongs to the enemies of our soul. If so, God is no longer our treasure but an enemy.

"And now, Israel, what doth the Lord thy God require of thee, but to fear the Lord thy God, to walk in all his ways, and to love him, and to serve the Lord thy God with all thy heart and with all thy soul." Deuteronomy 10:12.

How can we love and serve God with all of our heart when we are seduced and enslaved by the power of money. In our world, money is god not God. And everyone of us is drawn to it. Even how religious we are that even the priests, nuns, bishops and even the Pope Himself are drawn to it. There exist that extreme deception tied to money deluding us that it will solve our problems. We are tricked that money can obtain happiness. True but in material things only where its happiness is as brief as a second. Once we acquired the most lovable and expansive things in this worlds we felt happy but once we possessed it how quickly our interest wane. Once I bought an expensive gold coins and it made me happy but now it does not. My sister bought me a brand new SUV and I was so happy but now no more. As Co Founders where our goal is holiness and perfection let us be careful how the world traps us into their maze of misery. Money is needed while we are in this our temporary time but do not let it enslave you. For if one is devoted to God and living a devout life then one is indeed very secure and stable and one with God's grace can easily conquer the world's trappings.

Break Ten 10 minutes:

After the break community sing, Immaculate Mary

Reading of today's Gospel. Read it slowly two times and everybody listen taking notes about the message of the Gospel. After reading twice, spent ten 10 minutes silently meditating and write whatever the Holy Spirit reveals.

Twenty 20 minutes of sharing about today's Gospel. How does the message draws you. Does it tells me something in my own spiritual journey?

After the sharing and discussion, leader resume Class Twenty about the devout life.

Returning to the enemies of our new life we did discuss how the world deceives us all into thinking that we belong to it. Even the deeply religious and the pious can become victims of such severe deception and we have constantly bombarded by the news media how many so called religious and servants of God were victimized by worldly allurements and pleasures that led them to commit despicable and horrible sins. Since we are living a new life in the Spirit in essence we are truly an extension of God and as such we are His participating Body in accomplishing His greatest Works - us. The problem is, each one of us will encounter what our Lord Jesus encountered when He participated in doing our Father's will. Before He started His ministry or mission, He was tried and tested and what He experienced will be ours also. He was tempted three times.

First, after fasting for forty days and nights, He was very hungry and the devil challenged Him that if He is God to turn the stone into bread. Matthew 4:3. On the second one, the devil challenged Him to cast Himself down the cliff where His angels will catch Him. Luke 4:9-11. And the third temptation was the devil promised Him that everything on earth will be His if Jesus will worship him. Matthew 4:9.

The devil fled after Jesus rebuked the devil by His Words which we now have in Sacred Scriptures or the Holy Bible.

Thus, in our devout life, the world is indeed like the third temptation of Jesus where the world is inviting us as an oyster where we will have everything if we do give ourselves completely to possess everything on it. But, the word of God said:

What does it profit for a man if we gain the whole world and lose our immortal treasure. Because so very few of us dig Sacred Scriptures and God's Word, we have no defense against our enemies. Jesus knew how to triumph over everything simply because He was and is the Word made Flesh. As Co Founder with our Lady who will participate in Her last and greatest mission, we will certainly encounter what our Lord did when He started His greatest mission and ministry which was and is the salvation of all souls of which our Lady together with the Triune God completes His Masterpiece.

After the world, our second greatest enemy is the devil. He hated us so much because we will become like God once we are perfected and completed. What an irony indeed that Lucifer lost God because he wanted to become God and we lost God because we do not want to be like Him. God's perfect Will was that Lucifer be the prince of the heavenly host but not like Him and for us to become like Him. So to become a saint, is God's will not ours. So if it is God's will that we will become like Him then we should be rejoicing for such lofty calling not to make excuses for doing so we imitated Lucifer by ignoring His Holy Will. Although the devil is one powerful enemy of our soul we should never be afraid because if we are with Him who can be against us? Thus, we must equipped ourselves with all the holy armaments of the Church and His Words. The devil fled by using the Word of God and likewise he will flee from us if he tried to tempt us to do something evil and sinful.

The reason why tens of thousand lose their soul because we do not use the sacraments available to us and worst we are not literate in God's Words. The devils keeps winning the war because of our nonchalant attitude in taking great care of our one and only immortal soul. We seldom goes to church where the Holy Mass is our greatest weapon against the devil. We do not pray often nor pray fervently. Yes, we pray vocally but our mind and hearts are not in it. Like the warning said, we must work diligently our own salvation with fear and trembling. Such warning is not a joke. It is the truth and we must seriously keep that warning otherwise it will be too late for our own salvation. How we can defeat the devil is by studying how Jesus defeated him during their encounter. As Co Founders be not afraid if ever you will be tempted by the evil one because we not only have our Lady and Mother but also the full protection of the Holy Trinity to whom the professed member is consecrated. If one is always faithful to the community's rules then it is a guarantee one will have the greatest chance to become a saint.

Even a great saint. This is not a delusion nor a pipe dream but the absolute truth.

Be holy and be perfect for our Father is.

He commanded us because it is God's will that each one of us should become a saint.

Now, the last and the most powerful enemy of our salvation is none other is us. Our very own flesh. As previously taught our sinful flesh never stops in pulling down our spirit. For example, knowing that it is Sunday morning and the spirit calls us to get up early and attend Holy Mass but decided to sleep another hour and when the hour passed decided to attend Holy Mass in the afternoon but when it is time to go some other distraction which made us miss the Mass. Many souls are lost not because of the world's or the devil's fault but the blame is solely on us. Familiar saying, We are our own enemies. The flesh is so powerful an enemy because they never stop they keep on fighting and rebelling God's Spirit in us making the flesh our greatest enemy. The flesh is on fire with lustful desires that overwhelms not only the weak but also even the powerful and strong.

"For the flesh lusteth against the Spirit, and the Spirit against the flesh: and these are contrary the one to the other: so that ye cannot do the things that ye would." Galatians 5:17.

Having reached to this point in our formation this is our turning point wether we are all for God or against Him. A very strong warning but because of my love for God and for your soul I must repeat the truth which comes from God and not my own. You have made your journey to this point and you have learned enough what is at stake and the community's prayer is for all of us that we persevere and stick together until we accomplish God's will, our sanctification and our salvation. And to help our Mother, our Lady of Unity in Her final mission, calling and uniting all God's children into His Flock.

Spiritual Exercise:

At least fifteen 15 minutes:

In total silence slowly read and meditate His Words: I AM YOUR GOD. Pause and present yourself in His real Presence and in your heart and soul tell Him. "Yes Lord, in my mother's womb you formed me and called me by my name. I (state your name to Him) am drawn because you called me to join this community so I can dedicate my nothingness to the service of the Blessed Virgin Mary and to be consecrated to your Three Persona with the greatest hope that through Our Lady's intercession I will become a faithful and obedient servant always willing to do your Will not mine. Listen to Him, I FORMED AND CREATED YOU NOT TO BE A WASTE BUT TO GLORIFY AND GIVE ME THE GREATEST HONOR. We do think that we do God a favor in giving Him honor and glory but......... MY SON WAS GLORIFIED AND RECEIVED THE GREATEST HONOR BY DOING MY WILL. YOU WILL HONORED AND GLORIFIED WITH HIM BECAUSE YOU ARE HIS BODY AND YOU CAN ACCOMPLISH IT BY FOLLOWING HIM IN DOING MY WILL. Now, think about this greatest and one time opportunity you have. This is your moment of great grace that by giving your self to the One that created you is not a waste but the greatest thing that will ever happen to your life. You have reached to this moment gaining precious knowledge of who you are knowing that your sole purpose in this life is to give God the greatest glory and honor and to do so you too will share what is His. He give us this choice and we can never blamed our good God if we wasted the greatest opportunity we will ever have. See how the world and its people operate? See how hard they tried to gain something of no value. Now listen to Him, MY GRACE IS ALWAYS FREE. YOU ARE IN THIS COMMUNITY BECAUSE OF THE GRACE OBTAIN FROM THE MERITS OF YOUR MOTHER'S INTERCESSION. Think why you are here. It is our Lady and your mother drawing you so you will receive the triple crown of God. Now listen to His Direction. IN THE LAND OF YOUR EXILE

NOTHING WILL COME EASY. THIS IS THE LOT OF ALL MY CHILDREN SEPARATED BY SIN AND EITHER YOU CHOSE ME OR NOT EVERYONE IS NOT EXEMPTED BY THE CONSEQUENCES OF YOUR FALLEN NATURE BUT I PROMISE TO THOSE WHO CHOSE ME DOING MY WILL RECEIVES ALL THE GRACES NECESSARY FOR YOUR SALVATION. LIVING A DEVOUT LIFE WHAT IS LACKING TO GAIN HEAVEN AND ETERNAL HAPPINESS IS THE VIRTUES OF FORTITUDE AND PERSEVERANCE. IT WAS AND IS MY PROMISE THAT THOSE WHO PERSEVERE IN DOING MY WILL SALVATION WILL BE THEIRS.

Closing Prayer:
Hymn: Community sing Salve Regina.

Twenty First Class

Hymn: Come Holy Ghost
The Opening Prayer:

A Prayerful Life

"And when he had sent the multitudes away, he went up into a mountain apart to pray: and when the evening was come, he was there alone." Matthew 14:23.

Spent fifteen 15 minutes in silence meditating what was the message tells us. What was the reason why the scene was included? What does it mean he went up to the mountain? When we go to the mountain isn't it we are ascending? Jesus was all alone to pray all evening. How do you compare your very own prayer life with our Model? In your own words do share what is your own thoughts about prayers? Why is it so very important in our spiritual life? A prayerful person had the greatest chance of salvation than the one who does not pray. A saint said this. Do you agree. Share your thoughts why prayer is needed for our spiritual growth and most importantly for our salvation.

Thirty 30 minutes of community sharing about Matthew 14:23.
After the thirty 30 minutes of community sharing, leader reads the following message below:

Even though He was God noticed how our Lord Jesus seek the greatest solitude that he even spent much time and even effort to climb the mountain. It was not revealed wether it was a very steep climb or a natural ascent but the fact was that He does not want anybody with Him. Why is this so? Naturally, like us, distraction truly derails us from that exclusive connectivity to the unreachable God. Distraction brings us to our baseness. For example when we are inside the church praying fervently when suddenly a friend sits by your side and there start the distraction. Now, there is that disturbances that obstruct that connectivity between the two diverse spirit making it difficult to refocus. Once distraction sets in, the life of the spirit had been brought to baseness meaning to the life of the flesh and although we were distracted it does not meant that God is not please with us. Remember, we are taught and encourage to pray in spirit and truth. When we do pray in spirit and in truth we are truly united with the Triune God. Praying in the flesh does not unite us to God but to our baseness.

"And when thou prayest thou shalt not be as the hypocrites are: for the love to pray standing in the synagogues and in the corners of the streets that they may be seen of men. Verily I say unto you, they have their reward." Matthew 6:5.

Unfortunately, most of us suffered from this baseness. Do not be discourage that we are like this. As a creature we have that tendency to be praise to be notice. It is in our being to be connected with others or simply we are social animals and we do seek each others attention. Observe how our behavior changes when there is a crowd specially when a big crowd. Most of us wants attention and it takes a supernatural effort to get rid of them. But, it is God's grace that we can conquer those natural tendencies. Thus, even the religious people wether you are a priests, bishops, cardinals or even the pope is subject to such baseness. Of course there are those who are exempt whom God gifted a prayerful life where such soul and God are always united in prayer. But for most of us wether we like it or not we have such weakness that tendency to be notice to be praise. When we pray for the people's praises and applauses such piety brings nothing but our baseness. The people's admiration and praises will be the reward but if one truly prays in spirit and truth then the reward is God and heaven. Therefore, let us carefully listen to what our Lord taught His followers so they can profit from their prayers.

"But thou, when thou prayest, enter into thy closet, and when thou hast shut thy door pray to thy Father which seeth in secret shall reward thee openly." Matthew 6:6.

Our Lord shared the secret how to be truly connected to God the Father. In our life, realize that we are solitary soul meaning that there is nothing in this world that can truly and assists us in our eternal journey to God or away from Him. Keep it in your heart, mind and soul that the solitary soul have no one but itself and the One who created us. True that we have our family and friends with us here but in reality they are worthless as dust in regards to our spiritual journey simply for the fact that it is between us and God. We all heard this familiar cliche, between you and God. This is what it meant that we are solitary soul. We alone during our judgment will face Him and how many friends or family members one had they can not do anything because the solitary soul is solely accountable for its eternal destiny.

Thus, the time of our judgment is the most dreadful and what we receive is final and irrevocable that even God Himself can never change the outcome. So many of us failed to think about that dreadful moment because if we all think about the seriousness of the situation then most of us will truly seek a religious life focusing solely on loving, serving and worshipping God. Indeed the three powerful enemies of our salvation have temporarily imprison us and we can only be set free by the truth. And this truth is that Jesus Christ our Lord came down from heaven to rescue and ransom from the slavery of sin and death. Salvation is now ours. It is freely given and if we do not appreciate such greatest gift from God then such grave injustices and grave ingratitude deserves the greatest just punishment, the complete separation from our good God and this time there is no turning back. If all of us meditate and give time to think our eternity specially in judgement time, again, repeatedly most if not all of us will become serious religious.

Recalling a saint's teaching that those who pray will have the greatest chance of salvation than those who does not pray at all. What the saint shared is the truth (Matthew 6:6)

When one prays in solitude (secret or alone) the Father in heaven which saw the prayer in secret will be rewarded openly. Not only in corporal blessings but most importantly the salvation of one's soul. Prayer without stopping obtains whatever is best for us.

"Peter therefore was kept in prison: but prayer was made without ceasing of the church unto God for him." Acts 12:5.

He was freed from his chains and was able to get away from prison. And when we pray always for our salvation there is no doubt that God will greatly grant the graces freeing us from the slavery of sin and our salvation is sure. In our prayer life though we should never stop praying for this is the key to our salvation. Anytime one misses or neglect to pray one is subject to suffer some consequences because of the fact he or she had separated itself from God (losing connectivity) and when this happens one loses His friendship and even those graces essential for our protection from the enemies of our salvation. There was once a famous and well known priest and preacher who wowed the crowd by his charisma and eloquence but at the end abandon his priestly duties and ministry by committing sin of fornication. Many were shocked that such holy servant of God fell into disgrace. Many asked why did God allowed this thing to happen to him when he was so fervent preaching the truth. Only God knows. But some theories can be made that perhaps pride did him in. Perhaps, he had neglected his prayer life. Or he was in the wrong vocation. A holy saintly priest once made this lofty remark that the prayer life of priests and religious should be their highest priority that they should spend most of their time praying in truth and in spirit and without ceasing. In doing so, they are well protected by the One who will guard them like a precious jewel. In the modern times, many have left the church because of the horrible sexual abuses done not only by priests but also by bishops and such despicable crimes against the innocent truly destroyed confidence on the Church and in its clergy. Again, if all priests and the higher hierarchy dedicated themselves in fervent prayers then seldom those things happens. Some theory why so many of those in clergy committed such horrifying acts can be traced that they are in the wrong vocation. It is well documented that in third world countries some entered the priesthood for financial motives and security and some parents pushed their sons to enter the priesthood because of pride. When one is in the wrong vocation then there is that high probability that one will surely fail. But God alone knew why these so called chosen ones failed but those theories mentioned had its merits. And again, if prayer is our highest priority then whatever one's vocation is surely God will be with us and He will never allow us to stumble and to fall into the deepest ditch. As Co Founder to our Lady's Order this will be our highest and greatest priority and that is a prayerful life to ensure that we are on the same page with our Model. Do not be however get discourage of the message to pray without ceasing because we who are in the world serving our family and others could not possibly involved in such deep prayerful life but as member of the Order we have also the greatest privileges by our simple methodology in obtaining perfection and holiness by simply following our rules. Perfect obedience simply does it. We are not like priests or nuns who are fully called to devote and give all themselves wholly to God. Such calling demands extreme exercise of piety for they are supposed to be the light of the world and they should spend more time in prayer, meditation and contemplation. We however have the option in increasing our time for prayers and contemplation but in accordance to what the Holy Spirit inspires us to pray. Remember when we pray it is not us but the Holy Spirit inspiring and instructing us to pray.

"Likewise the Spirit also helpeth our infirmities: for we know not what we should pray for as we ought: but the Spirit itself maketh intercession for us with groanings which cannot be uttered." Romans 8:26.

Thus when David found himself in deep trouble with God for his serious sins of adultery, fornication, sloth and murder, it was the Holy Spirit that inspired and instructed him to pray

Psalm 51.
"Have mercy on me, God, in your kindness. In your compassion blot out my offense. O wash me more and more from my guilt and cleanse me from my sin"

God knew David's heart is much like His and because He loved David so much and saw his grief and sorrow the Spirit came to Him and uttered such beautiful prayer of confession. This is the greatest example of how kind and merciful God is that despite the horrible sins David committed mercy is always available and accessible at all times and all we have to do to make good with God was simply to fall down on our knees with the sincerity of our hearts crying and calling to the good God for forgiveness and His kindness. And God quickly will forget whatever evils we have done and not only that He freed us from our guilt and from all our sins. We all should believe this because this is the absolute truth for it is God Himself teaching us how we can make good with Him. God is making it so easy for us to obtain peace and reconciliation so we can again have the chance to be with Him and to obtain salvation and the eternal joys of heaven.

"Make me hear rejoicing and gladness, that the bones you have crushed may revive."

David knew that what he did also deserve just punishment and he expected that since his heart is much like his God and that justice must be served. And he willingly did endured all the evils that happened to him and to his household but he was rejoicing and even glad knowing that what he suffered was the result of his own folly and most of all what he received comes from God. Much like the righteous Job, David also understood the prayer of the Spirit, God gives us the good things in life should we not also accept the bad things? Therefore when we do pray it is the Holy Spirit that inspires us to do. Then finally, David prayed that he and God becomes one again through His Spirit.

"A pure heart create for me, O God, put a steadfast spirit within me. Do not cast me away from your presence, nor deprive me of your holy spirit."

Now, the Holy Spirit instructed David to pray that his impure hearts made pure and most importantly the possession of His Spirit so he will now have the power and strength to resist temptation and to avoid sin. Do not deprive me of your Spirit so I will always live the rest of my life in Your Presence. Indeed this perfect prayer became a universal prayer of the Church recited every Friday morning calling and crying out to God so we the Church member of His Body will continue to persevere and endure our difficult and most challenging journey to our heavenly home. It also a holy universal confession of all humanity's sin committed during the day which is Friday reminding the Heavenly Father the day of His Son's death on the cross when He pleaded for us.

"Then said Jesus, Father, forgive them for they know not what they do." Luke 23:34.

Thus by the inspiration and instruction of the Holy Spirit, the Catholic Church made sure that this beautiful prayer of mercy will be included in the Divine Office recited by the clergy and the consecrated religious. By doing this prayer, abundant graces are poured on the whole world preserving creation from the wrath of God due to our continuous sinful activities and obstinate rebellion and disregard of God's Presence in us. We indeed does not know what they are doing. It is the Catholic Church the real Body of Christ in unity to the Head who is now seated on the right hand of God the Father sharing His splendor and glory never stops in praying for us. Much like He did on the troubled Peter whom He chose to be His visible Vicar here on the land of our exile.

"But I have prayed for thee, that thy faith fail not: and when thou art converted, strengthen thy brethren." Luke 22: 32.

This great mystery of how powerfully and invincibly constructed is the Catholic Church that she alone is so instrumental in sustaining the life of creation as God continues His works in our transformation. In the Divine Office every member of the clergy including the heir-achy participated in calling and crying out for His mercy and with Christ the Eternal Priest now with the Heavenly Father never stops pleading for His separated Body still in exile and the union of prayers from the Head and the Body draws pardon and mercy to all. Thus, the religious life is the fruits of the Catholic Church incredible and powerful prayer machinery that enkindles the spiritual life of all religion. The Jewish, Islamic, Hindus, Buddhist and all other religions being practiced and exercised are sustained by the treasury of graces from the true church established by the Messiah not only to greatly benefit His Own Body (members) but overspill to other religions where the Spirit inspired the religious to live in the spirit not on the flesh. Thus, when you study the Jewish, Islamic, Buddhist and other religion it is obviously clear that moral decency, love, compassion, kindness and charity are the foundation of their faith.

If there are disagreements about such claim then just listen to what our Lord and God told Peter.

But I have prayed for thee.

As the appointed and anointed shepherd of His Flock, Peter and the succeeding popes are in the most need of the Messiah's powerful prayer so the church's faith will never failed so Its members will be converted. Since the journey from our conversion to our final transformation involves much obstacles, difficulties, hardships and unending struggles, our Lord's prayer to the Heavenly Father makes the greatest difference in obtaining pardon, mercy and grace to all creation.

But I have prayed for thee———— so we can have the strength to endure everything so we can finally reap the rewards promised to those who love Him to the end.

Thus, as Co Founders to our Lady participating the greatest mission entrusted to the community, we then look at the prayer life of our Lord Jesus and to our Blessed Virgin Mary and to imitate them if possible in accordance to what the Holy Spirit inspires us so by our fervent prayerful life we too can make huge deposit increasing our treasures in heaven effectually drawing graces for the conversion of those who does not belong to the Body of Christ.

Break for ten 10 minutes.
After the break community together sing, "Immaculate Mary"

Reading of today's Gospel. Read twice slowly while listening to the message. Write down what attracts you like sentences or phrases. Then, after reading, spend ten 10 minutes in silence recollecting the reading and write your understanding and your thoughts for community sharing.

Twenty minutes of sharing the Gospel message. In your own opinion how does it relate to you and to your life as member of the Order.

After the discussion and sharing, leader proceeds by reading the passage below:

Our prayer life definitely weighed heavily when we are to face the judgement seat of God. Just to remind ourselves the truth that each one of us is accountable with our life. And everything we did is recorded the good and the bad and because of our gross negligences and carelessness in our spiritual life most of us will have to suffer the consequences of all of our actions. O I thought God is so good, kind and merciful and that He loves me so much but why is it that I must be punished? In our human thinking we thought so but our ways is opposite to God causing us to fail to what He intended us to be. To be like Him. To live His Life in us to perfection. Previously discussed that once converted to God, our first step of transformation is underway and many of us thought that once we have accepted Jesus as Lord and Savior we are now save. Strong reason why so many souls went to hell because of such false conceived notion that all we need to do was to believe and accept Him as Lord and Savior. What was falsely taught had only a tiny amount of truth in it purely because once we do accept and embrace

Jesus as God and Savior it merely start that most demanding and difficulty journey of our transformation. Words alone does not make the cut nor faith alone does not. We have to face the truth that we all must work so hard and to keep on working very hard even if we keep failing because only in perseverance we can be save. When we received and accepted Jesus as our Lord and Savior then we become an extension of His Life where what He did we become His follower and recollect all He did for us while He was here. Did not He work so hard even under appreciated, rejected, maligned and even condemned as a criminal and a big fraud. Thus, maintain this teaching that we need to work hard for our salvation by cooperating to God's will and truly following our Lord Jesus in His way, His Life and in His truth. By doing so we will become like Him. There is no other methodology or way but only through Him, in Him, with Him that we can be perfectly transformed into God. Thus to be able to do so, our prayerful life will be our greatest weapon and constant support so we may be able to accomplish God's plan for us. We have discuss the prayer life of Jesus and our Lady and yes the prayer life of the saints. As we also aspires to become a saint, then we can make it through our prayer life. Our prayer life is that constant communication and connectivity with God and when we keep it up for the rest of our lives salvation is truly be ours. To those who does not pray salvation and their transformation would be impossible. Only in the extreme mercy extended by God that one can be save. But why take the risk by not praying. Why be smart and wise by imitating the prayer life of our Lord and to our Lady.

In our religiosity, these are the kinds of prayer we do. Vocal prayers and silent prayers where we can be alone or with others in the church community. When one starts to pray it was the Holy Spirit that initiates the action. This is the goodness of God by the action of His Third Persona. Most of us think that when we pray we initiated it and not God. When we think that way we marginalized the goodness and mercy of God for without the Holy Spirit we do not know what to pray or how to pray. Thus, the Catholic Church to whom the Holy Spirit is its perpetual guide as members of His Body we place the highest value or merits in the following prayer below:

The Holy Mass: This is the highest and greatest form of prayer that reaches quickly to God. In the Holy Mass we participated with our Lord Jesus offering to the Heavenly Father thanksgiving, praise, worship and glory. God the Father was greatly glorified by His only begotten Son when He gave up His Life for the sake of all His children. This is the most difficult part in our transformation when God Himself has to give up His very Own Life for our sake so we can be justified, ransom and restored back to Him. Again, reminding us that only Lord Jesus can do this task and no one else and for such love and obedience to the Father, He was greatly honored and glorified by Him. When we do attend Holy Mass we too give glory and honor to God the Father for our participation with the Head. The Holy Mass alone is and will be the greatest and the highest form of prayer and the most powerful ever kind of prayer we can offer to God. Remember when somebody dies, we immediately offer Holy Mass for the soul of the deceased knowing such powerful prayer of the Church can make the greatest difference in obtaining God's mercy. But of course, not a guarantee since we all are judge by the way how we live our life. Therefore, as Co Founder to our Lady of Unity aspiring to become more holy and perfect and to obtain our salvation then I guarantee you that going to daily Mass and receiving Jesus in Holy Communion every day in the state of grace will do. Highly recommended to all professed and consecrated member of the Order but this is optional. The Order's rule is never to miss Sunday Masses and other holiday obligation prescribed by the Church.

The Liturgy of the Hours: (The Divine Office)

This is the second most powerful prayer of the Church. Religious and members of the clergy are familiar with this prayer for they all prayed the Divine Office as the great part of their prayer life. This is the official prayer of the universal church where participant's prayer is united to all who prayed. Again, this is not required in the Order but recommended. An option because most of us are busy either working or serving our families that maybe become a burden or a restriction in fulfilling servitude to those truly in need.

The Holy Rosary:

As Co Founder to our Lady, every professed and consecrated member should pray it everyday. Every Catholic knew how this prayer obtain abundant blessings and graces because the Mother of God and our own mother will help us getting what we need both corporally and spiritually. Millions can testify how the Holy Rosary produced all kinds of miracles by the intercession of the Blessed Virgin Mary. Again, as part of the Order's rule, members should never miss praying it everyday. It was St. Dominic founder of the Dominican Order that the Blessed Virgin Mary inspired and instructed to promote the prayer of the Holy Rosary of the Blessed Virgin Mary and such prayer had become a universal prayer of the Church and all devout and faithful Catholics recited daily. Repeating its benefits, millions will testify how Her intercession through the Holy Rosary did obtained corporal and spiritual benefits. In Her apparitions, the Blessed Virgin Mary always instruct to pray this prayer for our benefits.

Again as reminder, time spent in prayer is never wasted because time given to God will be our greatest benefits for He who will never be outdone in generosity will return more than a hundred fold. We may not receive what we ask for in our prayer but He will give you what will be our greatest and highest good for God alone knew what is the best for us.

Lectio Divina:

This prayer involves meditation and even contemplation and if one practice it every day spiritual growth becomes its fruits. Fifteen minutes or more reading Sacred Scriptures in the most quiet place where there are no distraction one gains more knowledge of God and His ways and because of the soul's inquisitiveness of the things of

God and heaven it will receive a reward from the Holy Spirit where He gifted knowledge, wisdom and those other gifts in accordance to His grace. This is how to do Lectio Divina.

Find a very quiet place, so that you will not be disturbed. Make yourself comfortable and clear the mind of mundane thoughts and cares.

Ask the Holy Spirit for the gift of understanding and knowledge so that you can grow in the love for God.

Sit in total silence and place yourself in God's Presence truly not imaginatively inviting Him to look at you with pity and mercy. Tell Him of your sincere desire to know Him more deeply so that you will know His Ways and humbly ask for the graces that you can love Him purely and perfectly. Then ask for His blessings invoking the Holy Trinity by making the sign of the cross.

Open the Bible and find a passage that attracts you and start reading it slowly. Pause. Meditate. The second time read it again slowly then pause and meditate. Then in total silence just empty your thoughts and just listen. Within three to minutes you should receive something. Get a piece of paper and pen. Write what was revealed. Does the Scripture passage say something about you? Or something for you to act on?

Example:

Be holy and be perfect for the heavenly Father is.

This Scripture passage never left me when I first read it. I asked why we should be holy and perfect when only God is. I thought such demand from Him is beyond our selves. How could we become holy and perfect when only God is. Quickly, it was revealed to this imperfect and unholy creature that because of my gross imperfection and unholiness I must strive to become holy and perfect otherwise if I do not act on it I will never reach the heights of divinity remaining in spiritual stagnancy and if stand uncorrected will definitely lead me to eternal death. In addition, it was revealed to this most vile sinner that by striving for holiness and perfection though impossible for us our sincere effort is meritorious in His Sight and in His love and kindness He will get Himself involve by leading and guiding us to become holy and perfect. Our efforts even though we could never become holy and perfect, It is God who will complete the transforming process so we can become holy and perfect. By our holy perseverance even how many times we kept failing we gain graces that eventually we will become like Him. Also revealed that we should always set our spiritual goal to the highest level because even though we will not reach it we did something that brings pleasure to God and when one pleases Him it is guaranteed and He will be intimately involved in your divine transformation. Would not a loving father do everything for his children specially those who gives him the greatest pleasure?This is the secret to be shared to all so salvation will be ours by doing what He taught by striving to become like Him. By not trying one becomes a disappointment separating itself from God instead of trying in getting most closest to Him. By not trying to be holy and perfect the soul is risking itself to eternal death.

Lectio Divina is so sacred because God and the soul is in constant conversation back and forth with God revealing something that an ordinary person could never understand. Contemplative prayers create great intimacy between God and soul. Great saints and mystics received their rewards because of their intense intimacy with God making their union impossible to break. Therefore, when you do Lectio Divina every day guaranteed that one will be truly intimately united with God and salvation is ours. It is highly recommended to the Co Founders if they truly desire to be one with the Holy Trinity to practice Lectio Divina and if you do it makes the greatest difference in our spiritual growth and advancement. By incorporating all the prayers mentioned the soul is on the sure path of salvation.

SPIRITUAL EXERCISE:

When you get home after the lesson or after at your most convenient time, do read a passage from Sacred Scripture and do the Lection Divina. Or if you are drawn to it then do it.

Closing Prayer:
Community Sing Salve Regina.

Twenty Second Class

Hymn: Take Up Your Cross
The Opening Prayer:

A Mortified Life

"And he that taketh not his cross, and followeth after me, is not worthy of me. He that findeth his life shall lose it: and he that loseth his life for my sake shall find it." Matthew 10: 38-39.

Spend fifteen 15 minutes meditating the Scripture passage. Slowly repeat in the silence the severity of God's demand in our spiritual journey to our salvation. Pray in silence invoking the Holy Spirit for His enlightenment and write His revelation so you can share to the community.

Thirty 30 minutes of community sharing so each one can learn from each other. Discuss your own opinion and thoughts and write for whatever important points so we can apply it in our journey to holiness and perfection.

After thirty minutes of community sharing, leader reads the passage below.

The Catholic church teachings is so different from our protestant brothers and sisters specially those who preach the prosperity gospel where those ministers who had their own ministry and even their own mega churches and followers. They did attracted a large number of followers because they rarely mention the above Scripture passage. They love to preached that those who give God will be rewarded a hundred fold. I saw on television how they wisely manipulated the holy Words of God into their advantage where money freely were sent by old retirees and hungered souls longing to listen and hear the Holy Name of God preached to give them comfort and assurances that salvation is freely available to anyone who repent and to accept and receive Jesus Christ as their personal savior. This model had been copied by ambitious ministers and preachers so they will have large followers and of course financial security and stability and obviously fame. We all are subject to this trapping, fame and fortune. But only God can judge these ministers and preachers who preached the truth of Jesus as Savior but hid the fullness or the truth. They are also good psychologist by feeding their flock or followers by preaching the bountiful blessings of God. Prosperity in this life and also the promise of eternal happiness in heaven makes that perfect formula in drawing and attracting many for it is our human nature to seek the good and pleasurable things in life. Rarely, they mentioned what it truly takes to be our Lord's disciple and follower. Sure, during the time of Lent they followed the lead of the Catholic Church by preaching the passion of Christ but to a lesser degree. They recognized and acknowledges the suffering and death of Christ as a ransom for our sins and that only through Him salvation is possible. Good and attracting theology but again it is surface surfing where they do not dig into the deepest part of the truth.

He that loseth his life for my sake shall find it.

Teachings by the saints and in their writings are the foundation of salvation and when you examined the lives of Saint Francis of Assisi, Saint Theresa of Avila, Saint Therese the little flower, Saint Rose of Lima and thousands more like them exhibited a life beyond and over their own. They mortified themselves by the death of their own life and acquiring another life much higher and greater than their own. The Life of the living God. They were able to write and share their experiences what it takes and what it is like to live Jesus life in them. No one I repeat no one can enter heaven unless one has the life of Christ living in them. Losing one's life in exchange for the highest life in God is indeed a no brainer but seldom practiced by most of us. It is our sinfulness and imperfections that blocked our vision to see our lofty mission in acquiring and living a new life in God. Remember, once we repented and decided to make a change in our sinful life that begins our transition towards our highest transformation. We did discuss that period of reconciliation and also the birth of a new life. Therefore, once we are converted the life of God begins to operate and function and the Holy Spirit starts involving Himself by His guidance and leading us to a different path of life reserved to those who answered the call of holiness and perfection. This new life of God now living in us will be our ticket to heaven because we did made the trade by losing our very own life for the sake of gaining the life of God. Thus, in this class, we are emphasizing the great importance of knowing that a mortified life is the key to heaven. This class teaches us the methodology of why the cross will be our salvation. On the cross our Lord Jesus did the holy will of God by giving His life so the Father will gain many lives where He will be greatly glorified and honored by the many many sons and daughters gained by His Son. And the truth is, we can not be His followers if we do not embrace the crosses sent to us as our greatest gift.

"Then said Jesus unto his disciples, if any man will come after me, let him deny himself, and take up his cross, and follow me." Matthew 16:24.

Please take a little time and do figure this out. Was our Lord serious about this? Or He was merely talking in parables? What kind of denial was He talking about? We therefore cannot be called His true follower and disciple unless we also take on whatever unpleasant and bad things that enters into our life with peaceful resignation. Clearly, we can never ignore what He said to His followers. As Co Founders to our Lady, clearly we should also embrace the crosses that our Blessed Virgin Mary accepted specially at the foot of the Cross. Thus, the Catholic faith never failed in preaching and teaching the fullness of truth by never deceiving its flock that the salvation of our soul involves our greatest commitment in working for it in cooperation with the graces of God. It is the complete dying of self in order to do so. The death of self is that denial our Lord was looking and demanding in us to prove how we really love Him. There are some who argue that there is no need for us to bear the cross for Christ had already died for us and all sins had been wipe out. Many do believe such tricky theology trapping so many soul having such excuse in living a sinful life without guilt because of that belief. They were easily sold the false grace of not doing anything depriving many souls in giving their very best for the sake of Christ and for the expansion of His kingdom. Thus the Cross is the greatest symbol of love between God and us. Let us examine why the cross is the real tree of life where the fruits will transform us into God. Remember how humanity lose God by eating the fruit of that tree in the garden because the devil tricked them that by doing so will transform them into like God. The liar was deceived that by his lies he was telling the truth. Our fall was designed by God so to advance His ultimate plan in transforming us into God. Without the fall, it is impossible to be transform into God. For only the coming of Jesus and by incorporating us into His body that our transformation be accomplished. Thus, God used the devil in fulfilling His will.

"And whosoever doth not bear his cross, and come after me, cannot be my disciple." Luke 14:27.

The addition of St. Luke's message again confirms that only through the cross one can become one with God.

The word cross in this context represents the many trials, tribulations and frustrations Christians must bear in their lives. It is a symbol of service, sacrifice and sufferings. To do the will of God, that is to know, love and serve Him, is to carry one's cross with peaceful resignation. To do so, involves the death of self. Selfish that we are, we tried to find an easy and comfortable life free from troubles and worries but in doing so we gain a life that is not of God and if we find ourselves in such position then we should be worried because we could be living a life destined to be lost forever. But if we accept everything that is so unpleasant and disagreeable to us then we have succeeded in mortifying ourselves. When we accept everything that is contrary to our will that is a mortified life. Yes, to carry one's cross is to perfectly obey His commandments, to turn away from evil and to forgive injustices done to us as Jesus forgave those who nailed Him to the cross. There is no doctrinal teaching that is so sublime and superior to what was shown on the cross where our God died for the sake of love. All that was written in Sacred Scriptures can be easily absorbed and understood by looking lovingly at the cross where the death of Christ brought us back that greatest opportunity to gain Him and to become inheritor of the greatest kingdom ever imagined. If you are lost and hopeless and you really want to find God then look at Him and reach for the cross of eternal life and He will give you rest from all your burden. We have to climb the cross so we can be united with our God. In the blessed cross awaits the One who will save us and who will take us home with Him. Back to the Father where paradise lost became the greatest paradise one could ever invented and forever and never again will there be any sorrows, pains, sufferings but only eternal happiness and joy that cannot be explain in words but can only be enjoyed by experience.

A mortified life therefore teaches us the fullness of the truth in regards to our salvation and in regards in how we can become like Him. If you lose your own will and only do the will of God what do you think becomes of you? You need not to be a great theologian to logically say that when we live a mortified life it is logical and safe to say that it is no longer you living but God in Three Person living in you. Paul testified that it is Christ living in Him but correcting the greatest apostle that it is the Triune God actually living for where Christ is so does the other two Persona.

Recalling our new life in the Triune God involves our full attention and dedication in living our life in the Spirit. Paul truly understood why so many failed in mortifying the flesh because of their lacked of serious commitment in living fully and perfectly the life of God. If we meditate and looked deeply at the cross clearly it showed that the death of His Flesh brought a new life of His Spirit. The Flesh of Christ died and was buried and without the Spirit it is not possible that He would rise again. The same principle applies to our spiritual life that we cannot get into heaven and be united with God unless the Spirit is in us that we live in the Spirit not by the flesh. This is supposed to be the life of all who professed that they are Christians.

"And they that are Christ's have crucified the flesh with the affections and lusts." Galatians 5:24.

And as Co Founders with our Lady then we should always be aware and be prepare to live a mortified life by imitating and following our Lord and God to the blessed cross where our salvation can be found and nowhere else.

Since the salvation of our soul involves the cross let us together study its mystical theology where hidden is the secret of sure salvation and our perfection transformation us as true and real children of God. Sin is un-erasable staining us and the only remedial way was to have someone somebody whose power is absolute and unrestricted and here enters the Almighty God who alone can fix anything and everything. But His way was so terrifying and horrible that even His very Own chosen people could not accept or believe why He let Himself reduced debased beyond description of His Divinity, Power and Might. Yes, they could not recognized that it was Jesus Christ their Messiah had finally come to redeem and save them but being crucified worse than a criminal they simply could not accept this man on the cross. What they were waiting and expecting was God in His mighty army saving them from their oppressive enemy reminiscent of how God liberated and freed them from the mighty power of Egypt. God only knows why they are deprived why He had to die in the cross for our freedom and salvation.

"With his own self bare our sins in his own body on the tree, that we, being dead to sins, should live unto righteousness: by whose stripes ye were healed." 1 Peter 2:24.

On this Scripture Passage, testified the man chosen to head the true Church founded by the Messiah. This summarizes why salvation is only possible by the love and sacrifice of God in His Second Persona so that un-erasable sin of all humanity can be fix through His Body (His humanity). The death of Christ erases all humanity's sin in the past, present and future. The Trinitarian theology brilliantly revealed to the true church can not be seen to those whose religiosity embracing the monotheistic theology as the only way to our full transformation into the Oneness of God. The death of the humanity of Christ will also be our triumphant transition from our sinful humanity to our new life of His Spirit. A mortified life defines such sacred transition from lowly dust to divinity. Since death is the penalty for sin a mortified life resurrects the life of the Spirit making us sons and daughters of God. The death of our body (flesh) removes the stain of sin that corrupted it much like our Lord's death on the cross universally removes all the stains of sin that humanity accumulated from the beginning of time until the end. Thus, when we are alive in the Spirit, it will be the Triune God living in us leading and guiding us into a life of righteousness and justice making us holy and perfect in Him because of the indwelling of the Blessed Trinity.

With His Own Self Bare Our Sins In His Own Body.

Obviously, when the stain of sin is not remove from our soul it is perfectly right to say that our debt was not paid or satisfied. This theology of justification could never be accepted nor embraced by other religion simply because of their lacked of knowledge about the concept of the Trinity that it takes His Three Persona not One for our transformation into God becomes reality. They are deprived of the most beautiful and most wonderful teachings of the Church why such concept of the Triune God as the only way to make possible the impossible. And the God man is the key to our transformation or in other words He alone is the bridge that enables humanity to enter divinity. With His Body and ours on the cross complete that perfect partnership between God and us to do the mission of saving us and bringing us back to God never again be separated but to be forever one with Him.

As Co Founder with our Lady, it is then our greatest and highest goal to live a mortified life because this is our goal to become a saint. In our spiritual journey to heaven and God there is no half bake nor un spirited passion in this goal in serving Her Order solely for the greater glory and honor of God simply the reward promised can not be measured nor quantified for it is humanly unfathomable. For those who do so will have something they never had nor will they ever had because the glory, splendor, majesty and honor of God will be ours also. You can not imagine such rewards awaits to those who chose to give its all to the One who gives His All. And to those who chose otherwise, the consequences is an eternity of regrets of missing such grandiose offering that we could ever receive from anyone.

Community together discuss the topic of our subject, A mortified Life. Spent twenty 20 minutes by discussing the following. 1. Express your own thoughts and opinions on the concept of our justification. Do you believe or agree with this doctrine that only the death of our Lord Jesus can pay the penalty of our sins? Why is it so difficult for other religion to accept such theology of justification. Why is it that it takes the Three

Persona of God to transform us into like Him? 2. Why it is so essential and so necessary to live a mortified life after our conversion to the life of His Spirit? 3. Explain why the seven sacraments of the Church heals and sustain us member of God's Body. Discuss briefly Baptism, Confirmation, Sacrament of Reconciliation, Holy Communion, Holy Matrimony, Holy Orders and Anointing of the Sick. How each heals and sustains us.

After discussion community takes ten 10 minutes break.
After the community break, community sing "Immaculate Mary"

Reading of today's Gospel. Read slowly twice and listen attentively and carefully write what the Holy Spirit inspiration. Spent ten 10 minutes in silent recollection and continue writing whatever additional messages you received.

Twenty 20 minutes sharing of today's Gospel.

After the community sharing, leader reads the following passage below about the class, A Mortified Life.

We all have experience life in poverty or in abundance a life of comfort and hardship a life of pain and pleasure. No one in his right mind chose to live a life full of pains, afflictions, sufferings, poverty and all kinds of miseries that weighed us down. We all want to have a life of comfort, abundance, ease, good health and pleasant things. We have been blest by God all kinds of material blessings and abundance that inspire us to give thanks and praise to Him that took care of all our needs. When we are so happy and when we are free from all unpleasant and tragic things in life where troubles are so far away we looked at the skies and think of how good is God for all the benefits we received from Him. We praise Him because we are so blest that we do not have any kinds of sufferings or afflictions unlike the others who are so unlucky and so unfortunate to have all kinds of hardship and difficulties in life that nobody would be in their places. No one of us would like to be in Africa to see malnourished children so paled and thin with bloated stomach with eyes so sullen filled with sorrow and sadness. We who are so blest with good job living in a nice comfortable homes with all the modern conveniences and food in steady supply of abundance that we never seem to go hungry or in want. To see widows with their children roaming through garbage bins looking for their meal and others cooking mud pies to fill their empty stomach and drinking polluted water as their daily routine is what we see everyday in this world we live in. The rich and the poor. In this life, there is great inequality or it would be great injustices to see such contrasting life of the haves and the have nots. Those who have a shallow knowledge of God will be so easy to say, If God is good why this poor hungry and starving people are suffering like this and even such little ones that looked so helpless and hopeless why does God allow this to happen? Such unjust accusation to God deserve severe punishment for such stupid judgement about our great and good God. He is not responsible for all the injustices and inequalities that is in our world. We and not God are to blame. When there are a zillion free wills executing and operating every second surely will result in all kinds of injustices and inequalities because of our very own selfish and evil will. Again, if each one of us does the will of God to perfection then we need not die to go to heaven. Heaven will be brought down to earth if we all do God's will. But such was not the plan of God. He gave us free will so we all can make all kind of mess for our greatest and highest good. Sounds like a silly stupid statement but true. By having all kinds of sufferings, miseries, afflictions, trials and tribulations conceives the tree of life which was and is will be the Holy Cross and each one of us had already been fitted in accordance to God's divine design so to accomplish a mortified life. A mortified life therefore the soul had passed in flying colors all the trials and tribulations gifted by God.

"If ye endure chastening, God dealeth with you as with sons; for what son is he whom the father chastened not? But if ye without chastisement, whereof all are partakers, then ye are bastards, and not sons. Furthermore we have had fathers of our flesh which corrected us, and we gave them reverence: shall we not much rather be in subjection unto the father of spirits, and live? For they verily for a few days chastened us after their own pleasure; but he be our profit, that we might be partakers of his holiness. Now no chastening for the present seemeth be joyous, but grievous: nevertheless afterward it yieldeth the peaceful fruit of righteousness unto them which exercised thereby." Hebrews 12: 7-11.

This Scripture passage summarizes the mortified life. We now know the answer to that question that if God is so good why did He allowed all kinds of sufferings and pains? Read the passage slowly and meditate each words and sentences and we have the perfect answer why God allows evil to happens all the time. It is the chastisement of humanity's uncontrolled and ongoing sins that if no correction surely will be our ruins. We are bastards not sons of God. Sons of the flesh offsprings of corruption deserving to be thrown to the eternal fire. For the worldly and enemies of God, mortification is not their cup of tea for they lived fully in the flesh intensely involving themselves in a lustful life seeking all kinds of pleasure to satisfy their never ending lust. But to those who loves God, they welcome whatever kinds of sufferings and afflictions that comes in their lives knowing that a mortified life will be most profitable for it purifies leading to our sanctification making us holy and perfect now truly acceptable to God. True, a mortified life is not pleasant nor desirable but such sacrifices is too little for the greatest reward waiting to those who partakes in the life of the Spirit. But, remember whatever we suffer in this life it will always end while those who avoid to live a mortified life they will have to account for their avoidance and the consequences would be an eternity of unending torments that their regrets of choosing a corruptible life made it even more painful and unbearable. But to those who chose to live a mortified life for the sake of God's love then the passage below will be our greatest consoler knowing that His assurance will be ours.

"But the souls of the righteous are in the hand of God, and no torment will ever touch them. In the eyes of the foolish they seemed to have died, and their departure was thought to be an affliction, and their going from us to be their destruction: but they are at peace. For though in the sight of men they were punished, their hope is full of immortality. Having been disciplined a little, they will receive great good, because God tested them and found them worthy of Himself; like gold in the furnace He tried them, and like a sacrificial burnt offering He accepted them. In the time of their visitation they will shine forth, and will run like sparks through the stubble. They will govern nations and rule over peoples, and the Lord will reign over them forever. Those who trust in Him will understand truth, and the faithful will abide with Him in love, because grace and mercy are upon His elect, and He watches over His holy ones." Wisdom 3:1-9.

If anyone of us experience the severest form of suffering and affliction the passage above should give us the greatest consolation and confidence that to accept and embrace it makes us holy and He will be One with us. The God of truth always fulfill what He promised. Therefore, as Co Founder with our Lady whatever we will encounter in our journey to God and heaven if we remain faithful and true to Him the assurance of His presence and involvement is guaranteed and if God is with us we will overcome and triumphant in any obstacles and trials.

The love of God for us is everlasting and He never give up on us even though we give up on Him. Thus even if those soul chose not to live a mortified life God can still accomplish His plan on them. How? Through the means of applying forced mortification. In our journey to heaven and God in the greatness of His love and mercy He will do everything He can to make sure the soul will be save. A mortified life is not definitely agreeable to anyone of us simply it is natural for we are alive in the flesh and the spirit could not live to its fullest potential unless through mortification. Paul preaches and teaches to all this truth.

"For if ye live after the flesh, ye shall die: but if ye through the Spirit do mortify the deeds of the body, ye shall live." Romans 8:13.

Thus a mortified life is truly the answer if we want salvation and eternal life with God. A mortified life can be classified two ways.

The first one is called forced mortification. This kind of a mortified life was forced by an event that is not acceptable nor we desired. Let us see the severe sufferings of Job of which most of us Christian knew. He loses practically everything he owns because God allowed the devil to do everything evil not desirable to Job. A great example of a forced mortification where he lose all his children whom he loves and all his possession. He even suffered boils and his mental and emotional health was a burden to him. Isn't this so familiar with our very own lives. I knew someone who had everything wealth, position and beautiful wife and adorable children and his family seems to be free from all troubles of which most of us desired until one tragic day the van they were riding crashed into the desert ditch killing his beautiful wife and all four of his children. He alone survive but he was hospitalized for a few months in a coma and partially paralyzed. Why does God allowed it to happen to such a beautiful and good family when they does not deserved it? Simply God applied forced mortification so He can take away the life of the flesh and breathe a new life that would lead to sanctification and of course salvation. Unlike Job, who did accept everything (he was a just and righteous man) this one took awhile before he realizes that God did the right thing. He confesses that he was so preoccupied with the things of the world and its pleasure that seldom he even think of the goodness and the bountiful blessings He received from God. The more wealth he accumulated the more he desired to have more that eventually lead to a life contrary to God's will. They never put the highest priority with their spiritual life and religion was never on their agenda. He have so much wealth and all he cared was to enjoy his riches and to make his family happy. Then, God intervenes through what we called forced mortification that also leads him to think about God and it did lead to his conversion to a new life of the Spirit. He accepted his infirmities with faith, hope and love knowing now the what happened to Him was coming from the loving Hands of God.

The Lord gives and He takes. Should we also not accept the bad things in life? Blessed be the name of the Lord.

The converted man echoed the prayer of the holy man Job. Job, though accepted immediately his misfortunes and tragedy because he had a faith stronger than death and he knew that God is always with him. The other incident was different because the man was not religious and he was so far away from God. But in His great love and mercy He will always intervene by means of forced mortification and if one sees the light of grace then salvation is now possible.

The other kind of mortification is called voluntary mortification where one simply chose to do so for the sake of God's kingdom. Thus, you can see these beautiful souls seeking a religious life where they want to give their all to God. They entered a religious Order where they follows a strict rule of poverty, chastity and obedience. Such voluntary mortification is not required for Our Lady's Order for we are lay religious in the world but our rules are simply to do the holy will of God by striving to give our all to Him in accordance to His plan for each Co Founder. However, below is an example how a simple voluntary mortification can become so pleasing to God and to our Lady.

By rejecting and striving to conquer the following deadly sin is an admirable and acceptable form of a mortified life where we give glory and honor to God.

To have a mortified life, we must strive to conquer our pride and this sin is very difficult to conquer and such sin causes many to lose their soul. Do not expect we can get rid of this but our efforts to avoid or even minimize it is a great mortifier leading us to Him. Pride is an exaggerated opinion of one's own worth. We are surrounded in an environment where pride reigns but as Co Founder let us always pray to our Mother for the precious virtue of humility. When someone hurts or insults you rejoice for your acceptance you gain that virtue of humility. Always think of you as lower than the others and by doing so abundant graces you will receive.

We live a mortified life when we control our desires to possess more either in wealth or material things in this world. Avarice if uncontrolled will derail anyone's desire for God risking the soul to eternal death. As Co Founder, we imitate our Lord and our Lady by living a simple and unpretentious life focus primarily on seeking our salvation for the sake of God's love. Instead of desiring worldly wealth and pleasure cultivate the virtue of generosity by always practicing charity.

When we practice the virtue of chastity and purity and avoiding the lustful inclination of our sinful flesh we have lived a mortified life.

We live a mortified life when we chose to be calm when somebody provoke us. Anger makes us displeasing to God unless it is just anger. Our Lord Jesus shown us what is just anger when He was driven to rage when the merchants turn the sacred temple a marketplace. Every time we exercise patience and fortitude in this life we lived a mortified life.

When we spent our time in serving others without expecting any rewards and by always busy in doing our work well is also a mortified life.

When we are always in control with our passion such us over eating or drinking exceedingly or seeking excessive pleasure contrary to moderation then we have lived a mortified life. When we refrain from excessive talking or involved in gossiping or when we exercise meekness and gentleness then we lived a mortified life. To summarize a mortified life is simply to control the ordinate desire of the flesh and to bring it to submission. Repetitively, Saint Paul simply summarizes the mortified life as:

"For he that soweth to his flesh shall of the flesh reap corruption; but he that soweth to the Spirit shall of the Spirit reap life everlasting. And let us not be weary in well doing: for in due season we shall reap, if we faint not." Galatians 6:8-9.

As Co Founder we will strive to live a blameless life pleasing and acceptable to God by simply following and obeying the Order's rules to perfection but never giving up if we fail for what is needed in us is perseverance and when we do we live a mortified life.

For fifteen 15 minutes community discuss our mortified life.

SPIRITUAL EXERCISE:

In your spare or in your most convenient time search and read in Sacred Scriptures our Lord Jesus words when He was dying on the cross. Seven of them for you to meditate and pretend you are present at the foot of His cross. Does any words of Jesus affected you?

Closing Prayer:
Community together sing, Salve Regina.

Twenty Third Class

Hymn: Whatsoever You Do

The Opening Prayer:

Labor Of Love

"For God so loved the world, that he gave his only begotten Son, that whosoever believeth in him should not perish, but have everlasting life." John 3:16.

This Scripture Passage is a constant reminder of how God loves us beyond our understanding. All Christian knew this verse and as Co Founder we should also. Now, spend fifteen 15 minutes meditating this passage and lovingly invoke the Holy Spirit how God's love drew you to Him. Listen to the silent Voice He whispers in your heart, mind and soul and wrote whatever He reveals to you so you can share to the community.

Thirty 30 minutes of community sharing. Knowing how much God loves us now it is our turn to give Him love. This is our greatest challenge as to how deep how sincere how pure and how perfect is our love for the One who gives all His love for you and me. Remember on the previous class that we are to be rewarded in how we love Him. Little love gets little reward and obviously great love reaps great reward. Again if we sow little, little we get and sowing more abundance is the harvest. Thus, as member of our Lady's religious Order as Co Founder participating in Her last and greatest mission in uniting and bringing all God's children into the true Church deserves great reward a privilege for answering Her call. Again, just reminding that a Co Founder need not do great works but to simply be obedience to the Rules. As St. Theresa of Avila, the great Carmelite Doctor of the Church reminded members of her religious Order that by obedience to the rules makes one a saint. Just like St. Therese, the Little Flower who was doing nothing much inside the Carmelite convent but surprised many when she was declared a great saint and even the title Doctor of the Church by simply doing the little things but with the greatest of love. A sister who once said that Therese never did anything spectacular or anything showing greatness but only God saw the greatness of her love for Him. She was not a show but a hidden star of God teaching the whole world that it is not necessary to preach brilliantly or to convert millions of soul or to become the greatest missionary but what God wants on us is simple pure and perfect love of which she did. Therese became Patroness of the Missionaries and became the Doctor of the Church for teaching little and ordinary soul the perfect way to God was nothing else but love. Like John's message about God's love Therese brilliantly executed to perfection how to love Him. Thus, in this class as we are about to end our formation classes ready for profession, this class is very important so we too like Therese can give that pure and perfect love to our God.

After thirty 30 minutes of community sharing, leader reads the passage below.

Love is not a show. It is an action motivated by the heart to do what is necessary to make others happy or better. Love can be best shown not by words but the actions. How easy and casual for us to say that we love God but our actions reveals the contrary. This is the greatest problem we all have and as Co Founder each member must strive to love purely and perfectly and yes it is truly difficult and challenging. We all have this problem in loving our neighbor. Why is this? As we are imperfect so does everyone else. When we see someone (neighbor) whose behavior or actions is repulsive there is the tendency to dislike them or even hate them. When someone did us something wrong or did hurt us through their words or actions we are subject to our emotions leading us not to like them. Simply to love the unlovable is very challenging and very difficult for us stalling our spiritual growth and advancement. Simply to see the imperfections and repulsiveness of others also reveals that we too are also repulsive and imperfect to others. We failed to love purely and perfectly simply because of our inherited impurities and imperfections and it will take great efforts and the grace of God to attain holiness and perfection. Again, to remind ourselves that our impurities and our imperfections was perfectly designed by the Divine Architect so He Himself can make us pure and perfect. It sure is so discouraging when it is impossible to be holy and perfect but this is the journey God encourages to take for this is the only way we can be one with God. Since God is Love He demanded us to love like Him. Once we can love like Him then we are transform into God. There is no other way we can become like Him unless we love. Thus He gave us that two greatest commandment to love Him with all our hearts, mind, soul and with all our strength so by doing it we have become like Him. God is all love and truthfully He does not need our love for He is full and complete love. He was demanding such love because it is for our greatest and highest good if we are to inherit and become heirs being His children by adoption. He really and truly wants us to become like Him so we can experience what is like to become God. When one loves purely and perfectly the experience can not be described for how can anyone describe what God is. Going back that most of us so easily and casually say we love Him but it is a lie.

"If a man say, I love God, and hateth his brother, he is a liar: for he loveth not his brother whom he hath seen, how can he love God whom he hath not seen." 1 John 4:20.

Therefore it is wise to refrain in words that we love God but instead let us show love by how we treated everyone. By our actions and behavior is enough to reveal how we love God and neighbor. Remember, the second greatest commandment is to love our neighbor as we love ourselves. Or putting it simply, we must do the very best that we do not inflict injury to anyone regardless of their race, culture, religion or status. Thus, it was written in stone to never steal, cheat, bear false witness, lie, murder or commit any sin towards them. Once we do injury or harm them it is God whom we must answer for an accounting of our deeds. Thus, our entrance song is indeed appropriate in teaching us how to love our neighbor and they are also our church teachings so we can be laborer of God's love.

As Co Founder to our Lady we adhere to labor of love by doing the following:

Whatsoever you do to the least of my people, that you do unto me. How we treated everyone is a testimony a great witness of how we love God.

When I was hungry you gave me to eat. Did you ever refuse anyone who beg bread? You will never be save if you persistently refuse anyone who beg for food specially the beggars or orphans. By your lacked of mercy it will also be your lot once you face judgement.

When I was thirsty, you gave me to drink. We should always gave drink to anyone who ask for water otherwise we will never receive mercy when we too are in need during our accountancy with God.

When I was homeless, you opened your door. If someone who needed a shelter we should do our best to help them so they will not left out in the cold specially in the severe storm or freezing cold.

When I was naked, you gave me your coat. If God clothe the meadows with flowers should not we also do the least of our brothers who had no clothes. What an injustice done to God if we failed to do so.

When I was weary, you helped me find rest. We should always help those who needed our company when they are alone. We should give comfort and consolation to those who are inconsolable.

When I was anxious, you calmed my fears. We should never abandon those who are suffering emotionally or psychologically by assuring them that God will always be with us and He will be our helper and deliver from all our afflictions.

When in a prison, you came into my cell. Remember during His Passion our Lord spent in a tiny cell so dark and damp alone in His severe suffering where no one can console Him nor no one can give Him consolation and company. There are so many in prison who experienced what our Lord had and because of what that, He commanded us to become Him by our love and compassion towards them. True, they deserve their punishment but again if we want to become like Him then we must come and visit them sharing them faith, hope and love and from our labor of love they will experience the real presence of God's love represented by us.

When on a sick bed, you cared for my needs. Although our Lord was not on His sick bed, His dying on the cross where He is so helpless and hopeless and although a few were on the foot of the cross unable to help Him, their presence was enough to give Him the consolation He need. And when sickness sap the strongest they too became helpless and hopeless and when we take great care of their needs we become His instrument in providing love and compassion and such action glorifies Him. Such is the labor of love that each of us should never failed to do.

Now enter into the home of my Father. Such assurance from God should inspires us to do His works being His Body. Now, enter the home of our Father. Who would not be inspired by such sublime statement. The Apostle Matthew taught that what works we do here in this land of our exile weighed heavily on what kind of rewards we get or not get.

"For the Son of man shall come in the glory of His Father with His angels and then He shall reward every man according to his works." Matthew 16:27.

This is not a parable but factual truth. According to what we do here now measure the length, the width and the depth of our love for God and yes our neighbor. We have free will that what we chose will be justly weighed by our perfect Judge.

As Co Founder to our Lady's Order, we focus on our labor of love because this is it!!! This class is so important in our formation and nearing our profession and enrollment in Her Order we must truly learn and absorb what is being taught.

And so, whatsoever we do the least of our brother that we do unto Him. When you love your brother purely and perfectly then you did love God also purely and perfectly and indeed you deserve to received the Triple Crown reserved to those who are consecrated to the Most Holy Trinity. Let us pay much attention to the Sacred Scripture passage below.

"For I was an hungered, and ye gave me meat: I was thirsty and ye gave me drink: I was a stranger, and ye took me in: Naked, and ye clothed me: I was sick, and ye visited me: I was in prison, and ye came unto me." Matthew 25: 35-38.

We must keep it in our hearts, mind and soul the above passage for such is the labor of love the key that opens the door for us where awaits the Father ready to give everything that belongs to Him. By serving our neighbors in great need you took His place in dispensing His Divine Providence and then He will.........

"And the king shall answer and say unto them. Verily I say unto you, Inasmuch as ye have done it unto one of the least of these my brethren, ye have done unto me." Matthew 25:40.

This is the greatest reason why the Ten Commandments should be meditated day and night so we can perfectly obeyed not 9 but all ten. By perfect obedience, we have perfectly love our neighbor and we have also love God perfectly. What we did to the least of our brother surely we do have that reward promised by the Lord. This labor of love is what Holy Mother Church taught its flock and they are called the Corporal work of mercy. Worth repeating they are seven listed below:

1. To feed the hungry.
2. To give drink to the thirsty.
3. To clothe the naked.
4. To visit the sick.
5. To visit those in prison.
6. To shelter the homeless.
7. To bury the dead.

If we do all these things then we have indeed deposited a chunk of charitable works noted in heaven amassing treasure that towers over earthly treasure and because of your corporal works of mercy in God's perfect justice you will also receive His mercy and whatever debit or credit balance one have determines the reward. But the Catholic Church additionally taught the spiritual works of mercy where its rewards are much much more greater than the corporal work of mercy simply because this kind of labor is truly geared as the highest labor of love. Why is this more and greater? The corporal works although admirable is simply earthly where we participated in providing what is essential in our worldly life. The spiritual work of mercy is much more meritorious because it involves the salvation of one's soul. Did not God gave His very Life to save soul? What did our Lord received from the Father? He received all the Father's glory, splendor, majesty and honor. What was the Father's All the Son received All of the Father. Can you see the greatness of your reward if you imitate our Lord's passion in saving soul? See why our Lady is greatly honored and revered by His Son and why did she received the Triple Crown because she labored unceasingly for the salvation of souls. Thus, we members of Her Order will have the greatest chance and opportunity in receiving great rewards by our participation in Her last mission of drawing and saving souls specially those who belongs to the Jewish, Islamic faith and those other religion where our Lord and Savior is not honored nor received and embraced as the Messiah. And by teaching others the concept of the Trinitarian God its reward is immeasurable. Therefore pay very close attention the following spiritual works of mercy below:

To admonish the sinner. When you know someone who had an illicit relationship with a married man and warn her of such sin is deadly, you have exercise spiritual works of mercy. Even though she will not listen to your warning and continues to live in accordance to her evil will you will still gain merits in the eyes of God. Thus Scripture reinforces such principle that when we warn someone of their deadly sin and yet persisted in doing so the obstinate sinner goes to hell but the one who made the warning certainly saves its soul. And additional merits is gain if that sinner listened and turn away from its sinful life.

To instruct the ignorant. The lacked of knowledge of God and in His Ways are the major causes why we do not have that love our God deserves from us. There is such a saying you can not simply love if you do not know the object. Nobody would love money if they do not know its value. The same thought is applicable in loving God. How could anyone love Him if they do not know about God. In our world we are filled with innocent and ignorant people and as its result so many are lead astray specially in the area of religion and of God. Familiar saying, ignorance of the law excuses no one. Will such saying also applicable to our relation with God? If we are ignorant of God and His ways, are we too inexcusable for such defect. Unless you are in the deepest jungle or in the remotest place in the world unless you are deprived of missionaries preaching and teaching about God then there is merit that one will be excused from his ignorance otherwise everyone of us is accountable. Simply this is God's way of justice and no one of us can escape or make excuses if are negligent in knowing Him and His ways. If we are in a place or in an environment where churches are in our midst where the mass media made available to us then certainly we are accountable for our negligences. Seek and you shall find. If the Holy Name of God is spread and one heard about Him then one is responsible to seek this Holy God that loves us and who only wanted the very best for us. Or ask someone so one will have the opportunity in knowing God. Thus, by asking someone then one receive some information and knowledge about Him. Once knowledge slowly fills the mind and heart then one will start praying and by knocking on His Door God will definitely open His grace and assistance providing the innocent or the ignorant that amazing Light leading the soul into a relationship with God. As Co Founder, we have the greatest responsibility to our families and friends making sure we can give some instruction about God. Such action delivered definitely reaped rewards beyond our expectation.

To counsel the doubtful. We were given the greatest opportunity by our loving God so we have gain even more treasures in heaven by being a counselor to those whose faith is weak. Everyone of us have the same problem being doubtful about God and the things of Heaven and believe me nobody is immune from such weakness. Even those who were supposed to be very close with our Lord were victimized by doubt. What made Judas betrayed his Master could be traced that there is doubt that this is not the Messiah. Worst, even Thomas would not believe that his Lord resurrected from the dead even though he heard that He will rise again on the third day after His death. However, to be doubtful can become an instrument in increasing our faith. Truthfully, it is so difficult and challenging for us poor and helpless humans to possessed the strongest of faith since we are in an environment that constantly challenges and test what little faith we have. In Scripture in order to strengthen our faith, we were instructed to encourage each other so when we falter someone will come to our assistance sustaining us to never give up the race. When our Lord Jesus commanded His apostles to go out and preach and teach about the Gospel He dispelled them two by two. You know why. And you know why religious Orders produced many saints? They encouraged each other when one's faith is weakening or faltering. Thus, being member of the community of our Lady one has the privilege of receiving support by inspiring and encouraging each other to go on with our mission. In our world, a vast ocean are filled with doubters and each one of us has the greatest opportunity in reaping great rewards by counseling and inspiring those who are doubting about God.

To comfort the sorrowful. We have so many kinds of sorrows in this life and it affect the emotional and psychological well being of a person. Divorce, death of the spouse, financial calamities, loss of loved ones and other tragedies definitely dragged us to sadness and depression. Such sorrow state are not of us is immune to it. Simply, this is life and they are naturally a part of the equation. There are times we are happy and sad. Times of sorrow and joy. Isn't it this particular work of spiritual mercy be classified as corporal work of mercy? In the surface of our humanity it is but in the spiritual sense this is most applicable to those on the way to the new life of the Spirit where the converted soul will be filled with sorrow from its previous life of sin. We called this a grieving heart and a broken spirit prayed by the Psalmist in reference to his new affliction. Thus, as Co Founder to the Order, we give the greatest comfort to those who newly convert knowing they are introduced to a new different kind of life of the Spirit. The new convert will experience sorrow for leaving the old life into this new life of God. Therefore, give comfort, encouragement, inspiration and consolation so they will proceed and keep on living this new life of the Spirit. Your concern and support surely great rewards awaits. For you have become an instrument of their salvation.

To bear wrongs patiently. Every second in our life all kinds of injustices are being practice in this land of our exile. Again, this is simply the part of the process in our transformation into the likeness of God. Just a few example: Your best friend borrowed 5000 dollars from you despite of your financial hardship you took a cash advance from your credit card with a 24 percent interest so to help him out. You told the situation and he promised that he will make the monthly payment for you. When you received the bill you gave it to him. A few months later, you received a phone call in the place of your work and the credit company was cancelling your card because for two months they did not received any single payments. You called your friend and he reasoned that he is still having financial difficulties and promised to make the payments once he is able to do so. Most if not all of us will be angry even enraged for the wrong done to us. Justifiably will be our anger. This kind of wrongs done to us gain so much merits by simply accepting it and patiently prays to the one who committed the wrong. Such action is what we called a heroic virtue present in the very few for our humanity reacts so differently from those who are spiritually advance. But believe me, if one have this beautiful virtue then one had deposited greatly in the treasury of heaven.

To forgive all injuries. Looking at example number 5, if we do not harbor hate or resentment to our friend who failed in honoring its pledge then great merits are again deposited in your vault in heaven where no moth or thieves can take it away. Your friend inflicted injury to your relationship but because of your act of mercy through your forgiveness what you did was simply imitating our Lord Jesus when on the cross He said Father forgive them for they know not what they do. In essence, each one of us did all kinds of injuries not only to our family, friends, loved ones and even to strangers without even knowing it or being aware of what we did. There was a saint that complain that why he was so treated badly and maliciously by the one whom he did so many good things and he heard the Lord told him that the saint himself did the same thing many times over. Confused and shocked, the saint finally saw the past where he was enlightened of the many injuries he caused to those who loved and cared for him. In sorrow and full of tears he dropped on his knees and prayed for pardon and mercy realizing he was a terrible sinner who did so many injuries to others. If ever you experienced that injustices or injuries be assured that this was allowed by the good God so as payment of your own injustices and injuries you did to others. And if you think you did no wrongs or injuries to other think of what injuries and injustices you had done to our good and loving God.

To pray for the living and the dead. This summarizes our great responsibilities to all our brothers and sisters and that is to pray for the living and the dead. We all know the power of prayers and once we pray wether we know it or not it will be applied to those who needed the most. If you prayed for the salvation of soul such prayer without your knowing did saved a soul bound for eternal damnation. Thus, a single hail Mary can be applied to either save a hopeless and helpless sinner or can be applied for the conversion of the most hardened sinner. It can also be applied in healings, prevention of accidents, wars, calamities and all evil that surrounds us. St. Paul taught and insisted that we all pray unceasingly for this will benefits all of God's children. Others who believe not purgatory will never pray for the dead but to those who does for sure once you are in purgatory it lessens and even shortened your stay because once you were alive you did prayed for the dead. Both spiritual works of mercy indeed should inspires us to pray more and unceasingly.

Break for ten 10 minutes.

After the break sing, "Immaculate Mary"

Reading of today's gospel. Read slowly twice and listen to what it says to you. Write whatever the Holy Spirit reveals so it will be shared to the community. Spent ten 10 minutes in silence and listen to His Voice.

Twenty 20 minutes sharing of today's Gospel. Could be extended to another ten 10 minutes if is an interesting discussion.

After the discussion, leader reads the passage below:

We do have the knowledge in applying what we have been taught in our formation as Co Founder of Her Order. We have the greatest responsibility in applying the seven corporal works and the seven spiritual works of mercy. Basically, our works parallel God's labor of Love. Beginning with the First Persona, our Father in Heaven driven by love begins His works by creating the world and all of its creatures and it took Him seven steps (days) before He rested. He needed the rest but in reality God does not rest but what it meant He had completed His work the first stage of which was recorded in Sacred Scripture. He was so pleased from His works because it was done with perfect love. As He created everything in the world for us, we too if we want to be like Him must also labor for love although ours is only a dot compared to His we will receive the greatest and biggest reward we could hope or expected since we will have all of Him as ours. Thus, by doing all the seven corporal works of mercy inspired and taught by the Church we have imitated our Father's works making us pleasing and acceptable to Him as real children and heirs of His kingdom. And so when God created all the fowls, fishes, livestocks, trees and vegetation for us we too should have no problem in feeding the hungry or giving drink to the thirsty. Indeed, what our God demanded from us is so easy and so simple but there are so many of us who could not share what they have for the least of our brothers. We can see the many billionaires and millionaires in our world who shared the smallest portion of their wealth. They filled themselves with their own insatiable wants and desires forgetting their obligation and duty to dispense what God had entrusted or gifted to them. Thus, the prophesy of our Lord is fulfilled when He said that it is much easier for a camel to enter the thread of the needle than the rich to enter His kingdom. This was also revealed when a very rich young man who desired to follow our Lord simply could not do so when He asked him to give all his possession and give to the poor. True, there are so many generous billionaires and millionaires who set up foundation and charitable organization but what they contributed to the welfare of the poor is only a dollar to the million they have. And if you take into account of the benefits of tax deductions and honor they received truly what they gave was so little in comparison to what they received from God. Thus, we can see the continuing wretchedness of the poor in the third countries struggling every day for a meager meal. Although in the eyes of the world they looked so pitiable and miserable they are the Lazarus exemplified in the Bible. Yes, the billionaires and the millionaires who had it all does reap what they sowed here on earth but in the final analysis of our finite existence they are the most repulsive the most despicable and heinous creature for they will end up swimming in the eternal fire that will blanket their bodies and soul and its torments will never end. To avoid such eternal miseries, the Church teaches the great important of doing the corporal works of mercy because this is the labor of love demanded and required by God in each one of us.

As the Father in heaven never stops in providing all our corporal needs, Jesus too did showed us the importance in doing it. When He saw the multitude gathering to see Him, Jesus knew how hungry they were and immediately He performed the corporal work of mercy by multiplying the loaf of bread and fish and everybody was filled. When the tribe of Israel where complaining that they do not have any meat or bread God the Father rain manna and quail for their satisfaction. And when there was no water in the desert, He instructed Moses to strike the rock and there water flowed like a river. Thus, for fulfilling everything in the seven corporal works of mercy we will receive His rewards for what we did to the least of our brother we did it to Him.

As to the spiritual works of mercy, again let us examine how the Father in heaven performed His task by giving Moses the Ten Commandments so to admonish the sinner, instruct the ignorant and most importantly He gave His only begotten Son our Lord Jesus as the greatest spiritual work of mercy because without Him no salvation to the whole human race. And to make sure we all get it, Jesus showed us the way, the truth and the life so we can reap the benefits of great spiritual value and treasure not taught by anyone except by the Perfect One.

Our Lord and Savior as part of His mission showed us how to bear wrongs patiently when He endured all His suffering and finally in His crucifixion and death on the cross. And most of all He showed us how to forgive each other by forgiving those who murdered and butchered Him. And when He ascended to heaven, as His greatest spiritual work of mercy He established His church with all the powerful sacraments of our salvation so again to benefit our spiritual life. Finally, His works of mercy continues by giving us His Third Persona the Holy Spirit and He teaches us all how to pray not only the living but also the dead so she can reap the great benefits of our spiritual work. The spiritual works of mercy will be our primary focus being Co Founders with our Lady and for such participation of Her last mission we do shared what great harvest of soul be accomplished. But let us never ignore the corporal works of mercy. For us who strive to the live the life of God in our soul to do the corporal works of mercy should be considered easy and even normal. Our greatest challenge however will be the most difficult and most demanding spiritual work of mercy because like the old cliche that the most difficult challenge also reap the greatest reward. Or no pain no gain. But be assured that as a community, our greatest responsibility was to do the rules and to do what one is capable of doing but doing everything for the love of God.

Twenty 20 minutes discussion about the corporal and spiritual work of mercy.

Discuss why both works of mercy is so necessary in our journey to God. In what way that by doing both works we are on our way to become like God. Knowing that each one of us must do the labor of love as the way to enter into God's kingdom, does it convince you that faith alone does not cut in with God and it must be accompanied by a lot of works? Share your thoughts and opinions.

SPIRITUAL EXERCISE:

For fifteen 15 minutes in silence slowly and meditatively read this Scripture passage:

"BUT ALL THEIR WORKS THEY DO FOR TO BE SEEN OF MEN: THEY MAKE BROAD THEIR PHYLACTERIES, AND ENLARGE THE BORDERS OF THEIR GARMENTS."

You are almost done with your formation as Co Founder. God's grace made it possible that you are so close to your profession. You will be involved in our Lady's last mission. Think and meditate about our Lord's warning about spiritual pride. Humbly pray always for the virtue of humility that you are only an instrument of God and nothing else. Be careful about the sin of pride and never think that you are better than the others. Many priests, bishops, cardinals, religious and servants of God were and are victimized of their position as leader or models deluding themselves that they are better than those who are lower than them.

I AM THE HANDMAID OF THE LORD LET YOUR WILL BE DONE UNTO ME.

This is the humility of our Founder. This will be our motto. WE ARE ONLY USELESS AND WORTHLESS WORKERS OF OUR LORD'S VINEYARD AND WE CAN ONLY DO IN ACCORDANCE TO HIS WILL.

AND WHOSOEVER SHALL EXALT HIMSELF SHALL BE ABASED; AND HE THAT SHALL HUMBLE HIMSELF SHALL BE EXALTED.

In closing let us always remind ourselves of our motto and always keep in mind that in everything we accomplished in our labor of love that they are worthless if we do for our own glory and honor.

Closing Prayer:
Community Sing Salve Regina.

Twenty Fourth Class

Hymn: Lead Me, Lord
The Opening Prayer:

Preparation For Profession

"Lift up your eyes to the heavens, and look upon the earth beneath: for the heavens shall vanish away like smoke, and the earth shall wax old like a garment, and they that dwell therein shall die in like manner: but my salvation shall be for ever, and my righteousness shall not be abolish. Hearken unto me, ye that know righteousness, the people in whose heart is my law; fear ye not the reproach of men, neither be afraid of their revilings. For the moth shall eat them like wool: but my righteousness shall be for ever, and my salvation from generation to generation." Isaiah 51: 6-8.

Spend fifteen 15 minutes in silence invoking the Holy Spirit for His gift of understanding, wisdom and knowledge listening to the words of the prophet since the message carries weight as we prepare to be professed as member of Our Lady's religious Order. Prepare to write whatever the Holy Spirit whispers to our mind, heart and soul.

Thirty minutes community sharing on the Scripture passage Isaiah 51:6-8.

After thirty 30 minutes of sharing leader read the passage below:

Truly the Lord had chosen you and it was His grace that you are now ready to enter the Order of our Lady of Unity. And it was the prayers of the community and through the powerful intercession of our Lady of Carmel its Founder that obtain those graces. Now, it is time to prepare with the greatest expectation that we will be soon professed as Co Founder to our Lady in Her final mission. We all should be humbled from such gift and graces and before we proceed let us together pray the following: Pray slowly saying every words with emotion and passion.

"Lead me Lord, lead me Lord to the light of your Truth." Pause.

In silence, see His Light in your soul. In your memory, remember all the formation classes you have attended where His Words taught you how to dispel the darkness of your soul. Our Lady showed you that His only Son is the only light that can conquer any darkness that covered us. He is that eternal Shepherd that lit your path so you will find and know the truth.

"Lead me Lord, lead me to seek the narrow way where so very few can find it."

In silence, your memory stored the truth of His teachings that so very few entered the narrow way. In your understanding, you know why so very few walk His ways and most if not all of us chose to walk the wide path. Our Lady showed you why so many lost their souls to eternal death because they chose to live fully their lives here on earth neglecting the highest life of their being and that was and is to live fully in the life of the Spirit. You knew that the only way we can walk into the narrow way was to walk with God and He will be the only One who can lead us the way.

"Lead me Lord, Be my way, be my truth, be my life, O my Lord lead me today O lead me Lord now."

In silence, your will alone can make possible the impossible and that is our final transformation to be like God. You have been formed to lose your own life so you can have His Life. By losing your life your will too becomes the will of God. You have united your will to God and perfection is now your standard. God's way is your way now. God's truth is yours now. And God's life is yours now.

"Bless us Lord we who are poor in spirit longing for You alone."

Pause and in silence contemplate that you are one of the blessed if you find no happiness and contentment except for your strong desire for God and in His infinite mercy. You are so blest if you find yourself in the greatest need of His mercy and love. In constantly seeking His mercy you are among the blessed for in your humility you have found the truth that no one can save you except the Lord. By your poverty in spirit you have gain His Eternal Kingdom. Persevere in your calling and you will be there.

"Bless us O Lord and grant us the graces to be merciful always loving and forgiving."

Pause and in silence contemplate that you are among the blessed if you always extend mercy to those who asked. All sins how great and grievous will be forgiven because you never refused to grant mercy to those who seek your forgiveness. You have been formed into the likeness of God's Son by your formation to be merciful always because this is the key to our salvation. This is the key to our transformation to become like God and when you are always merciful you have become like God. The greatest virtue that most pleasing to God is when you pardon those who committed the greatest crime against you. When we forgive the unforgivable we have lived His Life to perfection. Remember, when we are always merciful God will be very merciful to us.

"Bless us O Lord by giving us the graces to have the purest of heart solely giving all our love for You."

Pause and in silence humbly begged Him for the graces of detachment to all things that is not pleasing nor agreeable to His Holy Will. Think of how impure is our hearts with so many things we desired that is not for out greatest and highest good. Scripture reminded us that only those who are pure in heart can see God. Sounds contradictory when there is a passage in Scripture that no one can see God and live. But there is no contradiction to such truths. Simply said, when one had completely detached itself from other things ungodly or worldly, one's heart becomes pure and clearly one can see God in the Spirit. One can see that God is living and operating in itself by all the good things one did to others that truly such truth can be substantiated by what Paul said, that it is no longer him living but Christ in him. Because of Paul's pure love for God and for the salvation of souls he did saw God though invisible truly alive and operating in him. This will be our utmost goal to acquire the purest heart by giving all our love to Him.

"Bless us O Lord who hungered for righteousness by giving us the graces to become holy and perfect for such command is Thy Will"

Pause and in silence, humbly begged our Lord for such graces since we can never be filled and be satisfied in this life unless we have become holy and perfect. Such struggle will be ours until our last breathe to become holy and perfect but when we do strive for it and even though we come up short God will fill us with the greatest satisfaction and we will have that peace and contentment that the world tried to take it away from us. Whatever will be our lot meaning to say that whatever we will encounter in this life either bad or good desirable or undesirable what matters the most is that we are One with Him to that transforming journey to our eternal happiness.

"Lead me, Lord, lead me Lord, by the light of truth to seek and find the narrow way. Be my way, be my truth, be my Life, my Lord, and lead me, Lord, today. I want nothing else but to be all Yours and I want You to be all mine now and forever Amen."

Pause and in silence meditate and contemplate your very personal covenant to the Holy One who will do everything to lead and guide you to our greatest and highest good. Since our greatest desire and ultimate goal was to become one with God we will never stop seeking Him even though we can never see Him. We can never see Him because He is Spirit but He is alive and again repeating that once we have completely purified our hearts then we will be able to see Him in the Light. Once the darkness of our hearts had been dispersed by the light of His truths then we will be able to see Him living in us. We will always be aware of His Presence in every moment of our existence because the Life we live is His not our own. We become the living God and others will see His Light shining on us by the way we act, behave and how we exercise God's love to all we met. Once our hearts are purified we all can see His Works through us and once this union materializes His way will be our way His truth will be our truth and yes indeed His Life will be our life.

In preparation for our profession let us keep in our hearts, mind and soul the following holy instruction so we will never quit the race in obtaining the greatest crown awaiting for those who answered the call to become Co Founder to our Lady's last mission and to never leave this Holy Order founded by Our Lady of Mount Carmel.

To know wisdom and instruction; to perceive the words of understanding. Proverbs 1:2.

All the classes we have gone through is nothing else but to seek holiness and perfection and such wisdom should keep us in the straight path leading to the narrow way where so very few can pass through. Do not be influenced by the teachings of others of the easy way to our salvation for in Scriptures the demand clearly indicates the contrary. By the great intercession of our Lady and in Her community the light of understanding will lead you to the summit of knowing the fullness of truth about our transforming journey to eternity.

To receive the instruction of wisdom, justice, and judgement, and equity. Proverbs 1:3.

Our Lady of Unity's community rules is the absolute instruction about wisdom which was gifted by the Holy Spirit to ensure we will never go astray to the wide path of destruction. We must live our lives justly contrary to the way of the worldly and the unjust where selfishness supremely reign denying justice to others. Example is to live our lives by not taking any advantages on the goodness or in the weaknesses of others for such selfishness profited nothing else but displeasure from God. Let us remind ourselves constantly the karma-tic effect of all we do in this life that sooner or later we have to be accountable of all our deeds, words and thoughts. Those who thinks that judgement will not come to them are truly fools as warned in Sacred Scriptures. Let us not forget the concept of charity and as Co Founders we should shared everything we received specially the gift of our ministry by inviting and inspiring them to participate to our Lady's closing mission in uniting all God's children under one shepherd.

A wise man will hear, and will increase learning; and a man of understanding shall attain unto wise counsel. Proverbs 1:5.

Once professed, we should never abandon reading Sacred Scriptures and reviewing the formation classes for in doing so should strengthen our resolution in applying what we learned to our daily lives where we will encounter so much opposition from the world, the devil and from self. St. Teresa Avila advises her members never abandon reading Sacred Scriptures and other holy books not only to maintain and stabilizes our spiritual life but increase our knowledge of God and the things of heaven. She always carried with her holy books to occupy herself when she is waiting or have free time. The saying that knowledge is indeed power is certainly true. If we have tremendous knowledge about God and the things of heaven then such understanding should give us tremendous wisdom that we will become wise counselors to those who needed the most. For example, Saint Teresa of Avila became a great saint and doctor of the Church for her wise counsel about our spiritual lives. She became a master of the spiritual life because she was avid reader of Sacred Scriptures and other holy books. What she learned and what knowledge she had about God and the things of heaven she eventually shared to all by the books she had written. Books like "The Way to Perfection" "The Interior Castle" became spiritual classics benefiting us in how we can be holy and perfect. Thus, as member of

Her Order, we too should strive to be an avid reader on Sacred Scriptures and other good spiritual books so we can never be deceived from the darkened deeds of the enemies of our salvation.

The wise shall inherit glory: but shame shall be the promotion of fools. Proverbs 3:35.

When one is learned one is considered wise and such wisdom will be more than enough to bring itself to the right path of holiness and perfection. As Sacred Scripture taught the fear of the Lord is the beginning of wisdom. The foolish professed that there is no God and such lacking of knowledge and comprehension about God is what made them fools. And when one have no fear of God they simply do everything their evil will desired leading them to offend and sin grievously against Him. But to the one who fears the Lord knew the severe consequences of His judgement to the fools and the ungodly. The wise will never compromise the light of wisdom knowing that it will lead to true salvation. And the wise truly seeks its own greatest and highest good and that is to share the glory of God. Who then shall inherit God's glory? None but only the wise and the fools can only inherit the fullness of shame.

For I give you good doctrine, forsake ye not my law. For I was my father's son, tender and only beloved in the sight of my mother. Proverbs 4: 2-3.

As we are ready to be professed as Co Founders to our Lady's last mission, let us religiously focus on the rules of the community so we can promptly obey them making us pleasant to our Lady of Unity where the Holy Trinity will make us shine like stars for having this grand virtue of obedience. Again, reminding all professed members that obedience to the rules of the community suffices sure salvation of our soul. For we were taught good doctrine where the law of God will be perfectly obeyed through our love for God through our Lady. Reminding members that our Lady will never forsake nor never cease in pleading for our salvation. She promised that she can guarantee salvation to those who obeyed the rules of Her community although she can not promise prosperity or happiness in this life but she will always assist us in our temporal needs but not our wants. Obviously, when we perfectly obeyed the rules of the community including perfect obedience to our Father's Ten Commandments we all became His children and being sons and daughters of God we are beloved by our mother who never abandon us through Her presence in our community. In all the formation classes we received was more than enough to make us holy and acceptable to the Holy Trinity. For good doctrine was implanted in our mind heart and soul and with the help of God's grace we should bear much fruit glorifying and honoring God of which we in turn will be honored and glorified for the labor of our love.

Take fast hold of instruction; let her not go: keep her; for she is thy life. Proverbs 4:13.

Finally, the last passage should always be in your heart, mind, soul and spirit for this will be your greatest treasure leading you sanctification and glorification as true and faithful children of God. You have been formed through those classes leading you in your transformation to become like God. In addition to your twenty four formation classes, the Order will be providing professed members On going formation classes to ensure continuity of one's spiritual well being and advancement to the highest level of union with the Triune God.

Important things to do prior to profession and consecration.

Make sure ceremonial rings are ready for the solemn ceremony.

Make sure the three consecutive day visit to the Blessed Sacrament was made giving thanks to our Lord for the graces received- soon a professed and consecrated member of Our Lady of Unity's Order.

Make sure name, address, phone number and e mail address had been submitted to the Order's Apostolic Administrator so certification and verification be completed.

Make sure to go to confession a day before profession to ensure one is in the state of grace.

Spent a few minutes in the Blessed Sacrament a day before profession not saying anything but to listen to whatever He reveals. When you enter, kneel and like a good and faithful servant simply say gently, "Lord, here am I presenting my poor self so you will lead me to do Your will." Sit silently and empty your thoughts and be still.

Make sure you received copy of the profession ceremony.

Try to come early at least twenty minutes before the start of Holy Mass so we will be on the same page.

Break ten 10 minutes.

After the break sing, Immaculate Mary.

Reading of today's Gospel. Read it twice while listener takes notes about the message of the Gospel. After reading twice spend ten 10 minutes recollecting the message and write whatever the Holy Spirit revealed, then share to the community.

Twenty 20 minutes of community sharing and could be extended thirty minutes if needed to.

With the book, Our Lady of Unity's Co Founder's Formation and Mission Handbook, leader turns to the Table of Contents, Part Four and read all The Holy Rules of the Order. This will be the standard of our spiritual lives and repeatedly, obedience to our rules guarantees salvation. Please do not get discouraged if we failed some times but to stand tall and keep on persevering always confessing our failures and imploring our Lady for Her intercession that we may be able to obeyed all the rules to perfection. Do not let the enemies of our soul drag us down to the pits of defeat because only those who give up the race are the real loser. How often we failed does not matter but how we keep up the fight is the key knowing that God never wants us to quit. Remember this, Did God Ever Quit On Us Despite All Our Failures? NO!!! NEVER!!! SO MUST WE.

TO GIVE UP ON HIM MAKE US FOOLS AND QUITTERS NEVER WINS. BUT TO PERSEVERE WE ARE WINNERS WITH GOD AS OUR GREATEST REWARD.

There are twenty four 24 Rules with leader reading slowly each rule. Spend at least two 2 minutes or less discussing each rule.

Closing Prayer
Community Sing Salve Regina.

PART THREE

Our Lady's Last Mission

The Religious Order of our Lady of Unity's mission will also be the Catholic Church final mission in drawing and bringing all God's children into the true Church established by God's Son, Jesus Christ. When He gave up His last breathe, Jesus willed to His mother His redeemed to be Her very own children. Every creature is always drawn to its mother, as its life came from the womb that form and shape its existence. Our Lord was formed on that holy and blessed womb of our Lady where God's DNA was knitted into humanity's DNA as the only way that we all can be integrated into the Body of His only begotten Son. Such unique and unusual blending of completely opposite being pave the path to the way, the truth and the life which was accomplished by the coming of the Messiah that through His Life, Death and Resurrection will also be our legacy where we can freely enter to the house of our Father making us truly sons and daughters of the Most High. Thus, truly, the womb of our Lady became the land of our birth. As the Son of God and Son of Mary, Jesus the Lord became our real Brother through the marriage perpetuated by the Spirit of God and the flesh of humanity (Mary) making our adoption real and divinely documented when Jesus during His ascension to the new heaven brought with Him, us, His Body so we can dwell with Them for all eternity. But, only to those who truly love God with all their hearts, mind, body and soul.

Indeed, our Lady's first important mission was to say yes when she was chosen to be the mother of God and after bringing in the God man she also received another mission when her Divine Son entrusted us in her care as our powerful help and intercessor knowing the degree of difficulty we all are facing in our journey to our salvation. Thus, once the true church was commissioned by Christ to Peter establishing the hierarchy to govern the spiritual formation of God's children so they can also participate the saving mission of His church so all will be save. And part of that Body is none other than its mother which our Lady was given the title, Mother of the Church where her children continuously prayed the Holy Rosary in response to our Lord's ordaining will that His mother will also be ours.

In the history of our salvation, none can compare to what our Lady had accomplished and also what she will be accomplishing. Catholics are so familiar with the powerful influence our Lady has on the Triune God that it is impossible to deny her when she ask the Blessed Trinity whatever she wants. Millions of Catholics and even non Catholics testified how this Great Lady of our race did helped them in their corporal and spiritual needs and for the skeptics just go and visit those famous shrine of our Lady where she was honored for the miracles she obtained from the Triune God. Go to Fatima, Portugal and see what she did for God's people. Go to Lourdes and see thousands of miraculous healings made possible through her intercession. Go to Guadalupe in Mexico and learned how millions of innocent people with no religion was converted into Catholicism making this country the cradle of Catholicism. Such powerful massive conversion started when our Lady appeared to a lowly man Juan Diego requesting his help in building a chapel and from that point on millions join the Church. And in Simala, Cebu, Philippines our Lady's shrine became a large church where millions of visitors came to pray and do homage to the Mother of God where thousands testified how she interceded for them. The above places mentioned was only a tiny fraction of the thousands of places she appeared bringing the same message her Son did while He was with us here. Pray, do penance, repent and be converted and live a holy and blameless life for the salvation of our souls and others. We can not marginalized our Lady's participation in saving souls that even the Church unofficially gave her the title Co Redeemer and even though un biblical and theologically unsound such title is fitting to the holy one groomed by our Father in heaven so with her all God's plan will be accomplished by the lowest and humblest creature. Therefore, let no skeptics disrespect nor dishonor this great Lady who is God's only ordained daughter, who was ordained spouse of the Holy Spirit, who was ordained to be the Mother of God. She deserves whatever title one can think of simply because she was crowned queen of heaven and earth and such sublime enthronement overshadows whatever title we can give her.

Since our Lady was the land of our birth and as the greatest participant in our redemption and salvation it is also fitting that she will be the one who closes the curtain of of our salvation. Thus, the Lady of Unity was entrusted to be the finisher of God's Masterpiece by the grace entrusted to her by the Father, the Son and the Holy Spirit that through this perfect union with the Triune God she will be the one who will bring all God' people back to the One who created us. Since this will be Her last mission and as Mother of the Church she is calling all members baptized Catholics to be an active participant by becoming a Co Founder of Her religious Order, Our Lady of Unity which will be the greatest source in drawing and converting those religions where Her Divine Son was not received nor accepted as the Messiah. As a devout practitioner of the Jewish faith, our Lady's affection to the children of Israel still remains very close to her heart knowing that they were the chosen race to made known that God truly exists in our midst giving creation the chance and opportunity to rise above their human baseness into the sublime heights of divinity. The Jewish religion shared to the whole world what God revealed to them and we all should be very grateful and thankful to the children of Israel for their love and devotion to God and to us. For His very unfathomable reason, the chosen race of Israel were deprived of something greater and nobler when they missed their Messiah was in their midst stunting their spiritual development and advancement unable to understand the Trinitarian concept of their God. And as member of the real and true Body of Her Son, we have the great responsibility in returning that favor extended to us by the children of Israel by making known to them that the long awaited Messiah had already come and had already established the greatest kingdom not only in heaven but also her on earth through the existence of the one and only true church certified and validated by the Most Holy Trinity. Not only for the Jewish faith that concerns our Lady but also to the Islamic religion and those other religions deprived of knowing the truth that Jesus Christ is both Son of God and man and only through Him that salvation is possible that no one can come the Father except through Him. Although God can easily grant graces to all for our salvation in His perfect justice He will not interfere in our free will for we are constantly reminded that He is always present standing at the door of our heart always waiting for us to open it so He can enter and dwell in us but again, free will becomes a powerful stumbling block restraining His entrance to our life making our salvation very difficult.

Some theologians thought we could have been better of without free will which undoubtedly a silly statement for without such awesome gift of free will there is no way we can be transform or be save. We should treasure this amazing gift of free will because this is the most powerful part of our immortal soul making possible for us to become like God. We all should realized that our free will can accomplish whatever our hearts desired. Imagine if we do not have free will and we find ourselves like robots and vegetables unable to do or accomplish anything at all God gave us this precious gift so we will be judge in how we apply it during the length of life allotted to us. Know your free will is your most powerful possession and by exercising it one can accomplish great things that humanity will benefits. Free will is that powerful spirit if applied brought technological advances unimaginable to us an d it will be more amazing and magical in the future if we continue to use it for the greater good of humanity but the opposite negative action can also bring devastating destruction to our world. Case in point, if one's free will was possessed by the evil spirit then by the push of a button will launch powerful and destructive missiles which would certainly bring to the end of our world. But the most important and greatest use of free will when we chose God over anything else. When we chose to give our all to God then this is what transform into like Him. It was the free will of Jesus to do what His Father commanded Him that He was supremely glorified and honored not only by God but also His people. And it was our Lady's will to do everything she was ask by her Father, her Son and Her Spouse, the Holy Spirit that she was greatly exalted and honored not only by the Blessed Trinity but by the true church, the Catholic Church. And it was free will that produced thousands and thousands of Catholic Saints who chose to do God's will instead of their own.

And it was free will that made our Lady to call members of the Catholic church to participate in Her and the Church last mission for the unity of all God's people and for our salvation. And our very own free will can make the greatest difference in our sanctification and glorification with our participation in our Lady's greatest and final mission.

Co Founder's Mission Participation

After the two years formation program, the professed Co Founder can now participate in our Lady's mission and as mentioned previously there are three different level of defined missions where the professed will have the option which level to chose from. The first level will be the most easiest with the second level increasing in difficulty and the most difficult and most challenging will be the third level. What level one chose to participates receives the same merits since Her Religious Order shares all its treasury of merits and graces gained and obtained by our Lady and by every Co Founder. Such are the advantages of being a professed or consecrated member of a religious order. Hence, below are the three level of defined mission available to the newly professed and consecrated Co Founder.

Level One Mission Option

Number 1: In every last Saturday of the month, professed and consecrated Co Founder will carefully review the Holy Rules of the Order examining one's obedience and if there are infraction committed one must immediately go to confession for an absolution and to make the greatest effort in correcting the infraction.

Number 2: Co Founder's mission by going to daily Mass and daily reception Holy Communion and offering the Holy Mass and Holy Communion for the intention of Our Lady of Unity's mission.

Number 3: Praying the Holy Rosary daily all of the Joyful Mystery, Sorrowful Mystery, Glorious Mystery and the Luminous Mystery offering everything for the intention of our Lady of Unity's mission.

Number 4: One Hour adoration in the Blessed Sacrament three times a week offering one's prayer and adoration for the intention of the Order's mission.

Number 5: Daily Scripture reading and solemn meditation for fifteen minutes (15) offering one's meditation for the intention of the Order's mission.

Number 6: Weekly confession and after absolution, penitent prays for the intention of the Order's mission. Prayer must be silent coming from the heart.

Number 7: Fasting three times a week offering the sacrifice for the intention of the Order. Fasting can be made by two slice of bread and coffee in the morning, full meal during lunch limiting 1000 calories and dinner will be a bowl of soup and bread. Fasting days snack is not allowed.

Number 8: Praying the Chaplet of Divine Mercy three times a day offering it for the intention of the Order's mission.

Number 9: Praying the Station of the Cross daily and offering the prayer for the intention of the Order's mission.

Professed and Consecrated Co Founder can chose 3 (Number 2 to Number 9) in addition to Number 1 which is compulsory. Thus as example, one can do its mission by doing Number 1, Number 3, Number 5 and Number 8 or any combination totaling 4. Number 1 should always be included in whatever combination one choses.

Level Two Mission Option

Number 1: In every last Saturday of the month, professed and consecrated Co-Founder will carefully review the Holy Rules of the Order examining one's obedience and if there are infractions committed one must immediately go to confession for an absolution and to make the sincere effort and resolution in correcting the infractions. Number 1 is compulsory. Below are choices and chose 3 items.

Number 2: Going to daily Mass and receiving Holy Communion offering the Mass and Communion for the intention of the Order.

Number 3: Serve your parish as Eucharistic Minister offering the service for the Order.

Number 4: Serve the Order of our Lady of Unity by forming a community using own home or residence as the place of gathering and formation.

Number 5: Serve your parish as Lector offering its service for the intention of the Order.

Number 6: Go to your parish priest asking his blessings and permission to start a formation program and for the establishment of Our Lady of Unity's Religious Order in the parish.

Number 7: Pray the forty 40 decades of the Holy Rosary daily (Joyful, Sorrowful, Glorious and Luminous Mysteries) offering the whole 40 decades for the Intention of the Order.

Number 8: Serve your parish in the music ministry by becoming a member of the choir offering your service for the intention of the Order.

Number 9: Serve the community by organizing a food feeding program for the poor offering its service for the intention of the Order.

Level Three Mission Option

Number 1: In every last Saturday of the month professed and consecrated Co-Founder will carefully review the Holy Rules of the Order examining one's obedience and if there are infractions committed one must immediately go to confession for an absolution and to make a sincere effort in correcting the infractions.

Number 1 option is compulsory and necessary. Listed below are options where 3 more items are to be chosen.

Number 2: Going to daily Mass everyday and receiving daily Communion offering the Mass and Communion for the intention of the Order.

Number 3: To see the bishop of the Diocese informing him about the existence of the Order of our Lady of Unity asking his blessings and permission to establish a community in every parish with the participation of his priest as its leader in the formation of Co-Founders.

Number 4: To participate in teaching and preaching the charism of the Order by asking permission and approval from the bishop in doing retreats to parishes.

Number 5: To make an appointment to see the Cardinal informing him of Our Lady of Unity's Order to build a Cathedral in honor of Our Lady of Unity where Co Founder's congregate during the feast day of our Lady of Unity's feast day.

Number 6: Establishing a soup kitchen for the poor in the community offering its service to the poor and needy for the intention of the Order.

Number 7: Pray the 40 decades of the Holy Rosary (Joyful, sorrowful, glorious and luminous mysteries) daily offering all decades for the intention of the Order.

Number 8: To participate in teaching and preaching by doing retreats and spiritual seminars during Lent and Advent.

Number 9: To join the SOS Missionary in their mission by going to difficult areas preaching and teaching about the saving truth.

Number 10: To see the Holy Father and giving him the special messages and instructions from our Lady of Unity who is the Mother of the Church and Mother of Salvation in perfecting the Church to Its final formation and completion.

Again, Co Founders are reminded that whatever option one choses each shares the merits of the Order. What is the most important as Co Founder is perfect obedience to the Order's Rules and also its faithful participation in the mission one choses to do. Once one chose its mission after one year he can either renew or chose another level or option. May the Holy Spirit leads you which mission chosen that it may give greatest glory and honor the Holy Trinity through our Lady of Unity.

PART FOUR

Holy Rules of The Order

The holy rules are imposed not to restrict anyone's freedom but to give each member the greatest opportunity in exercising their free will to its highest degree through perfect obedience to the Order's rules. Perfect obedience to the rules simply frees the member from the chains that shackles and stagnates one's spiritual growth so it would soar to the highest level willed by God. Obedience was and is always that great virtue pleasing God as exemplified by our Lord Jesus and His mother, the Blessed Virgin Mary. Not far behind is St. Joseph who never disobeyed God and whose powerful intercession protects and defends the Church. Obedience made many great saints too long to be listed and one greatest doctor of the Church, St. Teresa of Avila taught to her community that in order to become a saint simply obey the community rules to perfection. Since every one's goal was to be with God in heaven then the surest and safest way to get there was our obedience to the holy rules. On the other hand disobedience brings the opposite result.

"And as many as walk according to this rule, peace be on them, and mercy, and upon Israel of God." Galatians 6:16.

Our Lady of Unity's Holy Rules:

Perfect obedience to the Ten Commandments of God. Co Founders should memorize them and kept them into the heart.

Pray the Holy Rosary every day.

Attendance of community meeting every month. Can be excused in difficult circumstances but member should prioritize such gathering by careful planning of one's schedule. Community meetings normally three 3 hours or even less. Two hours minimum is that not much to give to the community and to our Lady. We need each other for inspiration and encouragement and most importantly to share one's experiences as we journey together in our formation and mission.

Spent at least ten 10 minutes daily reading Sacred Scriptures for nourishment and inspiration helping one's growth and advancement. Remember listening to God makes us ponder what He wants of us.

Attendance of Holy Mass on Sundays and all holidays of obligation prescribed by the Church and for the feast day of Our Lady of Unity celebrated September 7. (Apostolic Administrator is still working for its approbation from proper authorities.)

To always pray the Order's Consecration Prayer after reception of Holy Communion.

Co Founders should go to confession every month or every time serious sin was committed.

Co Founders who had chosen their mission option should strive diligently to fulfill them.

Co Founders should enthrone in their residence portrait of our Lady of Unity and venerate by praying the Memorare.

Co Founders should visit the Blessed Sacrament at least once a week at its most convenient time staying at least fifteen 15 minutes praying for the Order's mission. If possible frequent visit is encourage but once a week suffices.

Co Founders should obey the teachings and precepts of the church which includes obedience to the Pope and the clergy.

If possible, volunteer your service to the church if there is a need.

Co Founders should imitate and emulate the life of our Lord and our Lady by always saying yes to His holy will.

Co Founders should always practice and embrace the virtue of humility remembering how God resists the proud and the arrogance giving God all the credits in everything we have done or everything we have received.

Co Founders should always embrace and practice the virtue of poverty preparing one's soul to detach itself from the trapping of the world and materialism so it will advance and grow spiritually into the image of our Lord and Lady. There is no sin if one is blest with wealth or riches but by practicing such virtue one will not be attached to it since it will impede one's growth. Such example was about the young rich man whose wealth he could not detach brought sorrow for not able to follow our Lord. To desire only what we need and avoid to desire what we want.

To embrace and practice the virtue of chastity and purity. We all are tempted at all times with impurities in thoughts, words and deeds and we must always strive with the strength of our will to resists them to never give in to sin. Temptation in itself is not a sin but to give in is.

To practice and embrace the virtue of meekness preferring to always practice the virtue of patience and fortitude when confronted with negative company and all kinds of adversity. Obviously, we all have this problem by always complaining and to become pleasing and favorite of God that we should strive to never complain for by doing so one truly becomes like Jesus for he is so meek and humble at heart.

To practice and embrace the virtue of generosity exemplified by our Lord and Lady. They were extremely generous in giving themselves completely to God without any hesitation. Co Founders should never refuse to extend helping hands specially to the truly needy and helpless. As professed and consecrated members, your giving of yourselves by obeying its rules and performing your chosen mission makes one generous.

To live life in the spirit of love and unity by never getting jealous or envious on other's successes or possessions. Every talent or riches were God's allocation to whom He pleases as Scripture taught that God alone makes the rich and the poor. If we are jealous and envious makes us very displeasing to God for opposing His will. Brotherly love should always be in our lives appreciating every one even those we do not practically like knowing the truth that we are all brothers and sisters in Christ wether we like it or not. By practicing brotherly love fulfills the second greatest commandment by loving our neighbor as self.

Be always active and industrious in your undertakings specially in your chosen mission. Refrain from taking so much rest and relaxation for in doing so is an open invitation for the devil and for our own sinful flesh leading us to sin. Prime example was David whose heart is like that of God where he was a passionate warrior fighting fiercely against the enemies of Israel but when he took rest and relaxation David was victimized with lust and sloth leading him to commit adultery and murder. As Scripture warns us that sloth is the devil's workshop. Therefore, as Co Founders keep busy with whatever mission you have and most importantly keeping busy in taking out the mote in your eyes instead of telling others their motes. In short, work out your very own salvation before you tell others how they can be save.

As Co Founder to our Lady, be a servant to all as she was and is. Serve those who needed you specially those who are spiritual bankrupt by teaching and showing them to the way, the truth and the life. As Scripture said, those who aspire to become great in the kingdom of God must become a servant to all. When you inspire or enlightened those in spiritual darkness leading to their conversion you are certain of your very own salvation as Scripture taught.

As professed and consecrated member of this holy Order, like our Lord and Lady love should always be our way of life for nothing else can transform us into their likeness until we ourselves have become love. Like Paul said in his holy preaching that love alone suffices and nothing else.

Be holy and perfect for our Father in heaven is. This will be our greatest challenge by always trying to be one and never giving up such lofty command for this will be for our greatest and highest good. For trying and striving fulfill this rule.

In times of prayer and meditation think always of our Father, His Son and the Holy Spirit giving thanks, praise and honor to each Persona for their works in making us like Them. May the Most Holy Trinity be with us in our participation with our Lady of Unity's last mission that we may give Them the greatest honor, glory and splendor. Amen.

Prayers to Our Lady of Unity

This novena prayer to our Lady of Unity will be heard and she will promptly intercede for her Co Founders petition to the Most Holy Trinity since we are consecrated to our Triune God. It is advisable that petitioner should go to Holy Mass for nine consecutive days receiving Holy Communion in the state of grace. After the Holy Mass, pray the novena prayers to our Lady and you will receive signal graces and blessings which will be very beneficial to our greatest and highest good. And if we do the nine novena prayer starting August 30 ending September 7 greatly honors and glorifies the Holy Trinity for she will fervently intercede for us Co Founders who are faithful and true to her. In petitioning her, do not be dismayed nor discouraged if your petition was not granted because like her our life as Co Founder is to do only God's Holy Will and never ours. By doing so, she promised that Our Lady will bring us to God's Throne and she will personally present us to the Blessed Trinity where we will be welcome by the Father, by the Son and by the Holy Spirit for we are His possession. And the triple crown will be ours.

First Day of the Novena:

O most holy daughter of God, beloved by the Father, called and chosen to be the dispenser of His graces, behold your afflicted children imprison in the land of our exile, be merciful to me as I call and cry out to you O mother of mercy that you will intercede to our heavenly Father the grace that my poor petition will be granted and in gratitude for His favor I promise to be faithful in my vocation. (Pause a few seconds and humbly present your petition)

Our Father
Hail Mary
Glory Be (3 times)
The Memorare
Our Lady of Unity pray for us.

Second Day of the Novena:

O Holy Virgin who bore the Son of God in your blessed womb, chosen to be the mother of God, look kindly on us specially on this helpless and hopeless child who is in need of your help knowing that you are the only one who is most powerful with God that in your kindness intercede for me that my petition will be granted and I promise to strive to live a blameless life pleasing and acceptable to Him. (Pause a few seconds and humbly present your petition)

Our Father
Hail Mary
Glory Be (3 times)
The Memorare
Our Lady of Unity pray for us.

Third Day of the Novena:

O most pure and most chase spouse of God, chosen by the Holy Spirit to be His only bride, I look up to you as my greatest helper knowing that your beloved Spouse would never refuse your request to affectionately intercede for me that my petition will be granted and I promise to Him that I will strive to avoid sin and to make my body pure and chaste for His dwelling place. (Pause a few seconds and humbly present your petition)

Our Father
Hail Mary
Glory Be (3 times)
The Memorare
Our Lady of Unity pray for us.

Fourth Day of the Novena:

Holy Mary ordained by the Father to be the chosen vessel of our salvation, have pity on us specially to this afflicted creature who is in the greatest need of your assistance, having known and witnessed how you obtained from God whatever you ask from Him that I come to present my poor petition with the greatest confidence that it will be granted. And for His kind favor, I promise with the help of His grace to be obedient to His Commandments.

(Pause a few seconds and humbly present your petition)
Our Father
Hail Mary
Glory Be (3 times)
The Memorare
Our Lady of Unity pray for us.

Fifth Day of the Novena

Lord Jesus Son of God and man, our Light and Salvation, you gave us Your mother as our very own to be our helper in times of our greatest need. In my pressing need, I humbly beg of You to grant my petition placing my hope and confidence of your love and mercy trusting that You will never fail us despite our constant failure in loving and serving you. O Holy Mother of God, my mother, mother of mercy obtain for me from your Divine Son to grant what ask from Him and I promise to strive to give all my love to Him. (Pause a few seconds and humbly present your petition.)

Our Father
Hail Mary
Glory Be (3 times)
The Memorare
Our Lady of Unity pray for us.

Sixth Day of the Novena

Come Holy Spirit and renew us with the fire of Your Love that through the assistance of Your beloved spouse we may live a blameless life worthy to be Your Dwelling place so we may give glory and honor to Your Holy Name. Lord, in the greatness of Your Love and mercy, do not reject the pleadings of Your beloved Spouse and grant to this poor sinner what I ask promising to live a pure and chaste life so You can be in me as I can be in You. May Your Most Holy Spouse, the Blessed Virgin Mary intercede for us. (Pause a few seconds and humbly present your petition)

Our Father
Hail Mary
Glory Be (3 times)
The Memorare
Our Lady of Unity pray for us.

Seventh day of the Novena:

Our Lady of Unity, chosen daughter of the Father, behold your devoted servant suffering from the thorns and thistles of our exile to plead for me to our heavenly Father for His graces to persevere and to endure and in union with your sorrowful heart for the conversion of the Jewish and Islamic religion to Your true church and in gratitude for His Favor I promise to serve Him through you. Beloved daughter of our Father intercede for us. (Pause a few seconds and humbly present your petition.)

Our Father
Hail Mary
Glory Be (3 times)
The Memorare
Our Lady of Unity pray for us.

Eight day of the Novena:

Our Lady of Unity, mother of God and our mother, like you did at Cana gently whisper and tell your Son, Jesus about all my needs specially my pressing problem knowing how obedient is our Lord to you that in His kindness and compassion He will grant my petition and I promise that I will visit Him at the Blessed Sacrament often to praise, adore and thank Him for such favor. Mother of God pray for us. (Pause a few seconds and humbly present your petition.)

Our Father
Hail Mary
Glory Be (3 times)
The Memorare
Our Lady of Unity pray for us.

Ninth day of the Novena:

Immaculate mother of God, honor and glory of our race, splendor of Carmel hear the cries of the children of Eve that with you and your Divine Spouse the Holy Spirit will renew and recreate us into a new being in the likeness of your Son so the most Holy Trinity will be greatly honored and glorified by the completion of God's work through the final mission of the Holy Spirit and the Lady of Carmel foundries of the Order of our Lady of Unity. In the greatness of your servitude to God, obtain for me the grace that my petition will be granted and I promise to love, serve and adore the Blessed Trinity all the days of my life. (Pause a few seconds and present your petition)

Our Father
Hail Mary
Glory Be (3 times)
The Memorare
Our Lady of Unity pray for us.

After the nine days novena go attend Holy Mass and offer it in thanksgiving for your petition and when receiving Holy Communion say to Jesus, "Thank you for hearing my petition and I receive you because I love you so much." Doing this special 9 days Novena to our Lady of Unity will be of your greatest benefit and know your petition is in the archive of the new heavens. In the event that your petition was not granted be assure that you will receive much much more greater things than what you ask.

Spiritual Exercises

If one does this spiritual exercises regularly (recommended once a month or any time faith is tested or severe temptation occurs and the soul weakens do not despair nor be desponded but rather run into an isolated room where you and God are alone. By doing this spiritual exercise stability, security and strength restores the soul into the divine zone where it is now safe and under the protection of God's grace. This spiritual exercise was inspired by our Lady of Unity specially for her Co Founders so they will have the courage, strength, energy and fortitude in living their vocation and fulfilling their chosen mission for the greatest good of Her Order. The Spiritual Exercise should only be done with no distraction and possibly in the most quietest place available. Remember just yourself and in the presence of the Most Holy Trinity. This spiritual exercise can be done at least an hour but for the serious contemplative will take more than that. The practitioner has the option as to the length of time spent in doing the exercise since the Holy Spirit will be involved knowing that He alone inspires us how much time we need in completing it. Our exercise was formatted to elevate us lifting our spirit.

Remember that this special exercise is for your soul. Again, to remind you that in our soul are three faculties. Co Founders should be more familiar with this concept of the three faculties of our soul. They are the memory, understanding or intellect and will. This is our soul and because of our fallen nature and our baseness our memory are filled with the good and bad experiences we had in our lives. Our understanding and intellect can be our greatest obstacle in knowing God's will and finally but the most powerful faculty is our will. Our free will, to remind us again determines our eternal destiny and most importantly measures the length, the height, the depth and the width of our love for God which also determines the greatness of one's reward. Therefore, below is our spiritual exercise:

Having found the most quietest and secluded place begin by invoking this prayer:

"Our Lady of Unity, mother of God and my mother humbly I ask of you to intercede for me to your Divine Spouse the Holy Spirit to help me see, understand and know what must be done in my life and in my vocation as your Co Founder that I may gain the wisdom and the courage that God's most holy will be done unto me."

Our Father, Hail Mary and Glory Be (3 times)

Then: Slowly pray to the Holy Spirt:

Come Holy Spirit, Lord and God of my life come to my assistance and enlighten my heart, mind and the three faculties of my soul so I may gain the company of Your Three Persona so God the Father who gave me my memory will always remind me that He created me in my mother's womb and called me by my name. Assist me Beloved Spirit to unite my intellect to the Word made flesh which my Lord Jesus empowered me in conquering the enemies of our salvation that I may have a body acceptable and pleasing to You so it will become Your Dwelling place. Come now come Beloved Holy Spirit possess me and unite me to Your Three Persona so I can clearly see the vision of who I am and that You alone is my God and Your Possession. Amen. (Make the sign of the cross in reverence to the Holy Trinity.

Now begin the exercise:

In the Apostles' Creed hidden the way to true salvation. This will make a perfect spiritual exercise incorporating prayer, meditation and contemplation of our true faith. Inspired by the Holy Spirit to His devoted and faithful servants its composition clearly and concisely how the Three Persona of God must enter into the equation of our salvation and finally our transformation into God.

I BELIEVE IN GOD.

Pause and re energized your faith in God. Then proceed by asking yourself why you believe in Him. Pause and offer your response why you believe in Him then pray and say, "I believe in You Lord because of the revelation that you enter into our world taking on our mortal flesh where You who is Immortal will taste the terror of death." Pause and enter into the realm of your imagination and think of you as Him. You govern and ruled everything with an awesome indescribable power then ask yourself why are you doing it when you are complete perfection in no need of anyone. What comes to your mind to leave your glorious eternal kingdom and to become a vile creature an inch higher than the beast. Pause and write your answer the reasons why you as God will step down so low.

I BELIEVE IN GOD, THE FATHER ALMIGHTY, THE FATHER ALMIGHTY.

Pause why our God is the Almighty Father. Ask yourself why we call God as Father? You have your own father and recollect your relation with him. Without him do you think you are here now exploring the realms of the spiritual life? Now, we believe that without God the Father we do not exist but because God exist we now have our being. Pause and meditate the similarity of our own natural father and to the One who is God and father of all. Now when you hear someone that there is no God logically you can now defend the thesis about the existence of God. In Scriptures, everybody knew that He created man first and took a part of him which became Eve. Why did God not form the woman from the dust? Pause and analyze why. God design that man and woman should come from the same being so this woman can inherit the originality and singularity of His greatest work. What was gifted to Adam Eve also received. Eve's immortal status came from Adam as a preview that man and woman are destined to be one through marriage which also a preview that God and man become one through the marriage of Mary and the Holy Spirit. With the birth of Jesus the marriage of God and man was consummated. The Father Almighty made the impossible possible because of His Mightiness. Without father nothing can exist. Therefore, without our Father in heaven there is no way created things will exist.

I BELIEVE IN GOD, THE FATHER ALMIGHTY, CREATOR OF HEAVEN AND EARTH. CREATOR OF HEAVEN AND EARTH.

Pause and retrace THE FATHER ALMIGHTY and now you saw His Mightiness when you saw the earth and heaven was created by Him. Foolish are the wise on this world by inventing their own tomfoolery that Mr Big Bang was responsible for the universe and such can be clearly and logically exposed as purely imaginative. If such theory can be proven true which is impossible, then it can also be logically explained that there exist a Supreme Being which by merely using His Word impossible things become possible. Mr. Big Bang was doing it for he heard the Word of the Creator. There can be no other true simple explanation in what it seems to be complex as the cosmos or the incredible existence of our being and all its amazing surroundings save God's own simplicity. It was and is the Mightiness of our God the Father that everything existed. It is our complexity that unable us to see God's simplicity. Pause and think why did He created heaven and earth? Dig deeply into your innermost being why? Isn't God is in heaven? Of course, we heard those preachers and evangelists preached that heaven was created for us. And we heard that our Father is preparing heaven for us. And the earth? Pause and think why the earth? Out from the dust God formed us. Therefore, He created the earth to provide that dirt or dust so God can shape it into His Likeness. He made heaven already and now God has its Own problem and think and pause what is His problem. Of course, as Christians we should all know His biggest problem was how He can bring us home. Even though He is the Mighty and Powerful God He simply can not just take us home for the simple reason that we are made of dirt or dust meaning to say we are nothing at all and God's greatest and hardest problem was to transform that nothingness into something great as He. Pause and think about yourself. You are nothing and now you just found out that God wants you to become like Him. Then say to our Lord. "O Lord my God, Beloved Father, I have sinned greatly against my loving and good God and in the greatness of Your Love and Mercy forgive my blindness for not clearly and concisely see the greatness of my destiny that the only reason I existed because of Your plan to make me as great as You. How marvelous are the works of

Your Hand Beloved Father and for knowing the greatness and potential of my being of which I was not able to understand nor fathom. Beloved Father, You are deserving of the greatest love and if ever I found favor with You make me Your greatest lover to compensate all my failures in giving you all my love." Try to pray this prayer with the greatest sincerity in your heart and soul.

I BELIEVE IN GOD, THE FATHER ALMIGHTY, CREATOR OF HEAVEN AND EARTH, AND IN JESUS CHRIST, HIS ONLY SON, OUR LORD. AND IN JESUS CHRIST, HIS ONLY SON, OUR LORD.

Pause and think how could God the Father can have a Son when He had no wife for in nature conception can only be made possible by male and female. In order to multiply ourselves or to conceive it is an absolute necessity that both male and female must come into the equation of conception as God exhibited when He commanded Noah to bring into the ark both male and female in every animal so the earth will be replenished. In the natural order of things everything was patterned in God for He is the Creator of all things visible and invisible thus in the natural order in conceiving so must it be in the supernatural thing therefore in Jesus Christ, His only Son can not be conceived without a mother which can be proven later. Indeed even though God is the most powerful and the most mighty He simply can not have a Son equal to Him creating Him mighty problem so to speak. How could God solve such impossible problem? If you are God think and pause how can you fix it with all your power and might. Know that you can not create a Son of God for being equal with the Father can not be created simply God is the Creator and can never or ever be created. If we can find a solution for such impossible problem then God have given you a mind like His Own. For us, such problem is impossible to solve but God is that Supreme Genius and easily He found quick solution. Now, before His holy Presence listen to what our Lord how He easily fix the greatest problem God ever faced.

"By Myself I can not fix such problem but even though I have all the power and might and even though by my Words I can create anything but to have a Son by Myself is not possible even though with me everything is possible. There are divine limits that even My Supremacy and Sovereignty can not intrude much like I can never intrude or interfere in your will." Again, in our lowliness pause and think how you can help Him or what kind of action will our God must take to solve the divine dilemma.

I BELIEVE IN GOD, THE FATHER ALMIGHTY, CREATOR OF HEAVEN AND EARTH, AND IN JESUS CHRIST, HIS ONLY SON, OUR LORD, WHO WAS CONCEIVED BY THE HOLY SPIRIT, BORN OF THE VIRGIN MARY. WHO WAS CONCEIVED BY THE HOLY SPIRIT, BORN OF THE VIRGIN MARY.

Indeed it was so quick and easy for the Supreme Genius to come up with something so incredible and impossible by the help of His Third Persona, the Holy Spirit. His Involvement by God's entrance into the flesh of man through the womb of a very simple woman can never be comprehended nor be easily accepted as truth or even fact for woman to conceived without man contradicts nature's way creating much conflict and even confusion in the world we lived in. Pause and reflect as your very own opinion if the virgin birth truly happened or not. Wether we believe or not the fact and the truth was it did happened for in the actual history of our salvation, the birth of Christ was real recorded and witnessed by many. It was not only recorded in Sacred Scripture but documented in our human history that the birth of Christ was factual and could not be denied. But how could anyone or any scientist or any biologist explained such phenomena and none could but to categorized such event as a miracle. Therefore when there is a miracle we have no choice but to accept that there is something greater than us that caused such event. Thus, in Sacred Scriptures or in the Bible it clearly defined that so many incredible miracles were recorded attributing such unexplainable event to God. We all knew how God parted the Red Sea and how many miracles Moses performed when he led God's people to freedom. Read the Old Testament the countless miracles recorded to convinced us that He exist. And in the new Testament also showed the countless miracles Jesus performed such us His rising from the dead. Even today many many more miracles are happening that God cannot be ignored and denied that He is alive and well in our midst. And if such incredible miracles kept happening then the virgin birth does not shock us specially when God is intensely involved in accomplishing His marvelous and incredible Work in our salvation and most importantly our very own transformation into God. Therefore, if God wanted a Son the only way He can be equal to Him was His Third Persona must inject Its divine Gene into the human gene through the virgin flesh unmolested or infected with sin otherwise God's Gene will not strive on the flesh contaminated with sin or impurities. Pause and meditate how hard and difficult indeed God's work in trying to save and transform us into His greatness. Such free gift to us should be meditated, contemplated and treasured like no other treasure because the greatness of our destiny should never be taken for granted nor ignored. When we do, we deserve to be in hell for our ingratitude and injustices to the holy and good God. Now, you knew why Jesus must become one of us and why He is called the Prince of Peace for with His integration to our humanity He accomplished in uniting God and man into one. Pause and meditate how much we owe our Savior for without Him we are as good as the lower creature just like the animals, fowls and fishes who will die with no hope or chance to live for eternity.

SUFFERED UNDER PONTIUS PILATE, WAS CRUCIFIED, DIED AND WAS BURIED;

Now, you should clearly understand the necessity of suffering even to die for our sake. Ask yourself why God must endured so much suffering for our sake? Pause and think and as a Christian the answer should be so easy why the Son of God must accept and do what God the Father set Him to do. Is there other ways for Him to save us instead of suffering and dying on the cross? If you are Him can you think if there are other ways. Then listen to His Voice. "What was done was the perfect way and the plan was revealed by prophets that my coming will be the redemption and salvation of all. And I must give up my Life for there is no one other than the Son of God and Son of man that justification, redemption and salvation is possible. I am that only One that can satisfy the penalty of all the sins committed in the past, present and future. Sin must be satisfied through death. I must enter into time and was conceived in the womb of a woman so I can unite humanity and divinity into one entity so Our Father in heaven can reclaim what was lost by our father on earth who was banned, exiled and separated until such time of My coming. My death is necessary not only as payment but also I represented all creation through my humanity so justly they can contribute in its redemption. By doing so, God and man once again become friends by satisfying what was owed and when I was buried I brought all of humanity so when the appointed time I can also bring them back to where they belong."

HE DESCENDED INTO HELL;

Although the flesh of man rested in the tomb the Son of God now in Spirit proceeded into the spiritual kingdom where the souls of the just are detained and immediately saw the splendor of His glory approaching and they knew that the long awaited One did come setting them free so they can finally enter the promised kingdom of God and to claim their expected reward of eternal happiness where no eye had seen nor words could describe- heaven. Why did the Apostle's Creed included hell where our Lord Jesus went during the three days period before He rose from the dead? Pause and meditate and explore His mysterious activities before rising from the dead. Then listen to His Voice. "I will reveal the mystery of my descend into hell. Hell is suppose to be the place where the reprobates and the fallen angels are sent for their eternal separation from Me. The misery and pain of hell can not be described and one will know what truly is its greatest pain - complete separation from Me where they can no longer be with Me. The fires of hell nor its torments can be endured for eternity but their separation from Me is the most difficult and most painful to endure. When I died, the Son of Man's body went to sleep for more than two days but the Son of God's mission continued for I will be the One who will set them free and bring them to heaven. They were the just and the righteous ones, the prophets and patriarchs and those who lived their lives blameless obedient to my Commandments can now enter the new heavens. They waited and waited for thousand and thousand of years for that blessed and glorious moment that the new heaven will open so they can be with Us and those times for them was indeed like hell because of of their deprivation and separation from Us whom they desired and gave their love. Once they saw Me there was that indescribable joy and happiness reserved to the faithful ones and they were all transformed into the splendor and glory of our Being. They were my inheritance and their voices sang their praises

BEHOLD, BEHOLD THE HOLY ONE, THE LAMB OF GOD WHO TAKES AWAY OUR SIN GLORY HONOR PRAISE AND ETERNAL THANKSGIVING TO THE LAMB OF GOD WHO WASHED US WITH HIS BLOOD MAKING US PURE AND HOLY WORTHY TO BE ONE WITH THEM."

Pause and recollect how indebted we are to our Lord Jesus for without Him there is no hope for us. Thus in gratitude, raise your eyes heavenward and pray slowly and silently. "Glory, honor, praise and eternal thanksgiving to my God who give me my freedom to love and to serve You. You are my light and my salvation and Your death on the cross opened the new heavens so we can be with You forever. Without You Beloved Jesus, I could never come to Our Father and I could never be His child. Eternal gratitude to my Redeemer for my integration to Your Holy and Pure Body so I will never be lost nor be separated from You. Now in splendor and glory seated at the Right Hand of the Father cease not praying and interceding for Your Body, the Church on earth suffering from our temporary separation that in His time we will join You and with all the saints in heaven echoing, Holy, Holy Holy Lord, Glory, Honor, Praise, Splendor, Power, Majesty and Unending Adoration and Eternal Worship to our Triune God forever and ever. Amen". Pause and contemplate that those holy people of the Old Testament waited for thousands of years before they can enter the new heavens but think of our blessed opportunity that we do not have to wait such long time for our Lord Jesus made it possible that we can now enter quickly but Are we serious to enter now or we are not too passionate to be there since we do love the world so much and creature that we prefer to remain in purgatory perhaps thousands and thousands of years or even more. Thus, indeed God justice is perfect that the faithful and just ones in the Old Testament and us will be waiting and waiting to enter His glorious kingdom. But, we have free will and we can chose to get to heaven much quicker if we will it. Think seriously about this.

ON THE THIRD DAY HE ROSE AGAIN FROM THE DEAD;

Had our Lord stayed in the grave, think and meditate about hell. Tens of thousands of years is not actually too bad when we compare it to eternity. But, our Lord is not a cruel and sadistic God for He is perfect love and goodness. His justice too is perfect where God equally dispense what is perfectly will be our lot. Most of us can only see the darkness that clouded our being that we even blamed God for all the bad things happening in our lives instead of going deeper in our soul to recollect and ponder how we are living our lives and how we treated the good and loving God whose only concern was for our highest and greatest good. Our ascension from the dead (darkness) would have never happened without our Lord's death and we should always praise and thank Him for raising us from the darkness of despair and hopelessness and giving us that blessed hope and that incredible opportunity to possess heaven. In our sinfulness we have destroyed the temple of God and Jesus our Lord did His mission by fulfilling His prophesy that in three days God's temple will be rebuild and with His descent to hell the work was completed by picking up the pieces and debris of the ruined temple. He gathered them children of the old covenant deprived of their Messiah into the sleeping Body (church in slumber) and brought them in so when He will rise from death.................

HE ASCENDED INTO HEAVEN

Thus the glorious celebration of Easter where the whole world are reminded of our Lord's Resurrection from the dead giving His Life to those who believe and follow Him. The Church's glorious moment when their Head showed mankind that Jesus our Lord did conquered not only sin but also death. Death is our greatest fear overwhelming us into such anxious moment not knowing what awaits us. Easter is a celebration of life a new life graciously given to us by the Son of God and Son of man where our corruptibility and His incorruptibility lifted us to a new level of life where member of His Body will also have the greatest privilege to enter the new heaven. The ascension of our Lord is the hope of all Christians that we too after our own demise will also be there joining our Head which is Christ Jesus who made everything possible. Think, meditate and pause about the ascension of Christ. How can we repay the Lord for this marvelous plan that we too after our death will also ascend to heaven where eternal happiness and unending joy will be ours. The children of the old covenant rejoices unceasingly when they saw the coming of our Lord finally seeing the glorious Face of the long awaited Messiah the Prince of Peace making them officially children of God. Remember His last command to His disciples and followers when He was about to leave earth for heaven. Recall His last message. Such message was the key how we can get to heaven. Baptize them in the Name of the Father, the Son and the Holy Spirit. No one can come to the Father except through me. These are very important messages why we should kept it in our mind, heart and soul. This is the mission of the church that all should be baptized otherwise they have separated themselves from the Body of Christ where it would be impossible for them to get to heaven. And before our Lord's ascension, Peter was chosen to become His representative so His redeemed will not go astray much like the children of Israel went astray when their leader Moses did not show for forty days. Our Lord made sure that His inheritance or His Body will not repeat what the children of Israel did by providing His ever present through the the establishment of the papacy so all baptized Christians will not go astray. Listen to His Voice. "I went to hell gathering the children of the old covenant and before I ascended to the Father during my forty days stay I showed them the essentiality and the necessity of establishing my Church. This is my greatest mission after your redemption the establishment of the Ark of the new covenant for my Church will be the source of salvation to all mankind. My Church will bring a multitude of souls honoring and glorifying the Father for without it my works of redemption will not bear fruit. The mystery of my Church can not be easily seen by the human eye but only to those who are enlightened by the light of the Holy Spirit. Even the children of the old covenant I carried with me during my resurrection making them witnesses in the building of My church. They themselves received the necessary sacraments making them members of My Body so they can be with Me ascending to the Father. My Church is my Bride and wherever I am there she will be and those who chose not to become My Bride they will sent their eternity according to My Father's will. Pause and meditate how absolutely necessary it is to become His Body (Members and baptized in His Church) so we too will be with Him as His resurrection we too are resurrected and then His ascension will we too be ascended to our Father in heaven.

AND IS SEATED AT THE RIGHT HAND OF GOD THE FATHER ALMIGHTY

Sacred Scripture showed us a mother's concern that her beloved sons deserved the best seat or position when they are in heaven that they be seated at God' right or left as long they are most closest to Him. All mothers desires and wishes are naturally inclined that they received the best in all things. But our Lord gently rebuked that it is not Him but the Father who decides which seat or place we are assigned. However, the mother's demand was prophetic because everyone who belongs to the Body of Christ will be seated on the Right Hand of the Father which in itself will be the best seat or the best place in heaven courtesy of our Lord Jesus Christ works in justifying, redeeming, shepherding, guiding and incorporating us into Himself. (Pause and meditate praising and thanking the Lord that you are baptized, confirmed as a member of the Catholic Church truly a part of Christ. Knowing this truth do not waste such dignity that you are a spiritual and divine treasure by invalidating the thing of this world and the things that are contraries to God's will. Be not afraid to live your baptismal vow by rejecting Satan and his deceiving works and that our Father is waiting for you with our Lord Jesus waiting for you so you can be united with Him and yes, you will be seated at the Right Hand of the Father where you will greatly enjoy the Beatific Vision of God since you will be the most closes to Him.)

FROM THERE HE WILL COME TO JUDGE THE LIVING AND THE DEAD

Believe it or not, as His saints, you will also become a judge when the time of His final coming executing judgement on the vile and the wicked specially the anti Christ who did deceived a multitude of souls. We ask how could this be? Know that it is and will be Christ the Lord who will be seated on God's Throne of justice and the One who will make the perfect sentence and just what the Revelation warns such time will be the most terrifying and dreaded moment because what we will receive will be irrevocable. (Pause and meditate about your own life and be honest and truthful how are you prepared to stand in His Presence and how would you respond when you are to be accounted for your life. Do not wait for the Lenten season where we practice and exercise fasting and repenting since as we all knew life can be taken from us any second or moment. Do not be deceived that you are very healthy and strong or you are still young for always we are warn that we do not know when is the time. This is the moment of grace that you are doing this spiritual exercise and now is your time to act to truly repent and be converted to the true life of a Christian not in brand but in deeds). As previously mentioned where the Head (Christ) is, we (Body) too will be there judging the living and the dead.

I BELIEVE IN THE HOLY SPIRIT

As Christian you believe in the virgin birth and it is Him who entered into the blessed womb of the Virgin Mary where implanted the seed of divinity forming the one and only Messiah though came from two diverse being defining that our Lord Jesus Christ is truly both God and man. As Catholic we then believe that the Holy Spirit is the Spouse of the Blessed Virgin Mary and He was the One who completed the mystery of the Incarnation. The Word made Flesh was proclaimed by His apostle. The Word of God is both spirit and life. The Father willed that His Word and His Will was to make visible what was impossible invisible so all of us will see God in the flesh. In the Old Covenant, we were warned that no one can see the face of God for surely we die but in His great love and concern for us He changed that condition with the coming of the new Covenant making Himself seen by the multitude. Once, an unbeliever said that if only God shows Himself everybody will believe but such statement was merely a cover up of a truly blinded soul where he exercised free will not to believe and not to accept the truth that God exist and He is present in our lives. (Pause and meditate in your own life how God is always present loving and sustaining you. Recall those moments when you were in deep trouble where it seems your problem can not be solved. Recall those times when you were so depressed and close to despair. Recall the worst moment in your life).

Now, you understood that God was truly there for you never abandoned you and you should now believe how God truly loves you and us. I believe in the Holy Spirit because He is God in our midst instructing and inspiring us to pray knowing what we need and it was Him who formulated those words so God the Father will hear and will respond to your prayers. We do believe that it is the Holy Spirit that will changed ordinary bread into the Body of Christ and ordinary wine into the Real Blood of Christ. This truth can not be accepted nor comprehended by any other non Catholics simply because they are not His Bride. So sad they chose not the real and true church but God must have the perfect reason why this is so.

I believe in the Holy Spirit who will complete to perfection the works of the Father and the Son. The Father started framing the foundation of His children by forming dust into flesh and permitted the great fall so His Son can participate by restoring us back to the Father. Both works were incomplete but with the Holy Spirit we will be brought into perfection and Their Works will be completed transforming us as sons and daughters of God where we will inherit and reign with Them forever. (Pause and contemplate this truth. Imagine yourself to be an heir of God inheriting the greatest kingdom ever. In our lives we are driven so success will be ours so we can have more of the things in this world. How we envied those wealthy and the famous and how we envy the powerful kings and presidents but their position and possession are worthless and they are just like dust when death claim them. However, for those who have faith, hope and love then we do not much envy them knowing their things are filth as Paul preached the truth). Finally, why is it that the sin against the Holy Spirit can not be forgiven? Theologians should clearly know why. Let us discuss why the sins against God the Father or God the Son can be easily forgiven. God the Father knew we are made of dust and the curses of sin is in our being and with this truth God the Father is very merciful and forgiving. God the Son easily forgive even those the greatest and vilest of sinners simply because He knew the great difficulties of our journey to our transformation into Their Likeness but They also knew that both of Their Works can only be done perfectly by the Holy Spirit. And His Works of perfecting and transforming us into like Them can not be accomplished if we persevere to be obstinate in living in sin for in doing so we rejected Him much like evicting the Holy Spirit from our being making us un savable therefore such sin against Him can not forgiven simply because we chose not to be forgiven. The Holy Spirit is all love, all good and all mercy much like the Father and the Son for our God is a holy and perfectly good.

THE HOLY CATHOLIC CHURCH

Those who believe that this is the one and only true church approved by the Father, the Son and the Holy Spirit will have the greatest chance of salvation and will have the greatest opportunity to be transformed into God. If we believe in those seven powerful sacraments as transforming gifts from God then our salvation is much nearer than those who does not believe.

The Catholic Church crowned and honored Mary as its Mother and even given the title as Co Redeemer and if we do agree and approve of Her dogma then we are so privilege of such grace and we are far more secure and safer in our salvation than those who are not. We believe that we are really and truly the Body of Christ where we are fully protected against all the enemies of our salvation for it was written that the gates of hell will not prevail against her. This is the only Church that the Triune God willed and to oppose His will certainly would face some unfavorable consequences detrimental to one's eternal destiny. Controversy did happened years ago when the Catholic Church proclaimed that only through Her salvation is possible which irked other religions making Her softened Its stand to ease and even erase the controversy. She did not made any mistake in proclaiming the truth. The Catholic Church was, is and will be the source of salvation and without Her presence the world would have destroyed many years ago. It was written that our Lord wanted to build and established His Church for nothing. God knew how feeble and naive we are that when we faced a situation where our faith is tested we have the tendency to abandon it such was the case when the children of Israel when they created their own god once Moses their spiritual leader did not come back after forty days in Mount Sinai. Knowing us, Jesus our Redeemer, made sure His redeemed and His Body will not abandon Him by the establishment of the Catholic Church where He is and always be present in the Blessed Sacrament where the faithful simply comes pouring all their problems and because of the reality of His Presence no one feel abandon because everyone who comes will be consoled and even inspired to come visit Him again. Millions who comes, converse and adore Jesus in the Blessed Sacrament will testify such truth that consolation comes immediately simply because our Lord Jesus is truly present because it was written that He will always be with us until the end of time. And what is so amazing in the Catholic Church was when ordinary bread and wine are truly transformed into the Body, Blood, Soul and Divinity of Christ and if one receives Holy Communion in the state of grace will be temporarily transformed into Him pleasing God the Father where He will continue to pour abundant blessings and graces to His creation sustaining the world giving everybody the opportunity so they too can participate in this great mystery of one's constant transformation of communicants reminding Him of the potentialities of our being. Thus, it was also clearly written during His last night in the Last Supper to do the sacred ritual of eating His Body and drinking His Blood as a reminder to us the essentiality and necessity to receive Him so we will live eternally with Him. There is not and there will never be another religion or church where we can consume the Real Body and Blood of God save in the real and true Church of God.

THE HOLY CATHOLIC CHURCH.

She is the real deal the complete package prepared by the Most Holy Trinity through our Lady of Unity.

THE COMMUNION OF SAINTS

We believe in the triumphant Church's unstoppable production of saints where they are now in heaven seated at the Right Hand of God through the courtesy of their Head, Jesus Christ. No other religion can come close in forming souls into the image of God. They could not simply because it is the Son of God and the Son of man's only responsibility to transform His members into like Him. In the Vatican, if ever you have a chance to stay there for at least a month and check in their library you will be amazed of the spiritual treasure in the Church's archive. Volumes of books and ancient documents reveals its amazing history and its amazing growth becoming the most powerful religious organization unmatched by any other. What truly thrilled me was how the Church kept and preserved documents about the lives of its saints. The thousands of thousands of recorded and certified miracles performed by the Catholic Church's saints reminded us when it was written in Scripture that our Lord's follower will do even greater things and more miracles than what was recorded in Sacred Scriptures. Before, I was so impressed with what the Old and New Testament taught but when I found out the history of the Church's Tradition I was even more impressed and dazzled how truly marvelous is this church built and established by none other, Jesus Christ the Son of God and man. I was so spell bound by this true and real church which compelled me to write "YBA Catholic". What I experienced and what vision I saw about this true and saving church made me rejoice but at the same time very sad simply because billions of souls are deprived of knowing that the Catholic Church alone stands above any churches or religion for She was chosen to be the One and only Bride of Christ, And to make this saving truth known to the world, thousands of canonized saints are raised by the Catholic Church to such sublime status to make the world see that everyone of us are entitled to become like them. Before they were canonized by the Church as saints, intense investigation are made by the "Devil's Advocate" to ensure that they truly lived the life of Jesus. This group was established by the Catholic Church as its microscopic lens trying to find the tiniest speck of dirt so to speak to the candidate of canonization. And if they could not find one, the Church with its power to bind and to loose approves the candidate but will not be finalized until such time that God ratifies it through a miracle in behalf of the candidates intercession. If one can see the tedious and meticulous process of the saint's canonization one will be amazed with the wonders of the Church's methodology in declaring a saint. (Pause and meditate about how this saints became what they are now. Think about your own life and reflect if you too can become like them. Do you think it is impossible? Do you think that only those who are chosen can become saints) Pray briefly this prayer. "Lord, I am not worthy that you should come to me but only say the Word and my soul will be healed" It is only in our blindness and extreme ignorance to say that it is impossible to become a saint. Remember all those holy and perfect saints were once just like you. What made them saints was their conversion to no longer live a life that contradicts the will of God. When you are healed, Jesus was the One who heals because it is God's will that all of us becomes saints and when such was and is God's will that we all should become saints then it is not impossible for anyone of us including you. Remind yourself that you are chosen to become a saint but our greatest hindrance and obstacle is us. We chose not to become a saint because of our ill will always preferring to live a life contrary to the Life of God entrusted to us. When we do oppose God's will then we are His enemies and such self prophesy that only the chosen one becomes saint are fulfilled. Or to put it simply, saints became saints because they chose to become a saint. And the reason why the Catholic Church constantly produces so many saints because they are the factory of God. As the Holy Trinity had Three Person the Catholic Church had its own three Body working as one in completing the perfection of our total transformation into God. We believe in the Communion of Saints because the Three powerful Bodies of the Church was one and its mission was to transform the imperfect and incomplete Church Militant so it can advance to the next processing stage where we members of the Catholic Church here on earth after shedding the corruptible flesh will enter into the spiritual kingdom so we can be process thus the Church Suffering became the final checkpoint to ensure that we are to be perfectly cleansed or purified to ensure that no speck or stain of sin remains. The Church Triumphant will be our final destination where our Father in heaven will say, "Welcome home and enter into My Kingdom for you have made yourself worthy of the Lamb who takes away all your sin so you will be with Us for all of eternity." This is what we believe that the communion saints are always working for each other making sure that members of His Body will finally make it.

THE FORGIVENESS OF SIN

We Catholics believe in the forgiveness of sin because this is the only way we can reach our heavenly home. Do not be afraid if your sins are so bad or you have committed the most gravest sin simply because God is greater than all the sins of the world put together. As Jesus taught us that He is the way to the Father, He showed that only in His mercy that salvation is possible and it is only by His forgiveness that we can enter into heaven. Thus, when the good thief cried and called to the Lord, Jesus remember me when you are in Your kingdom our Lord saw in his heart the desire to be forgiven and quickly mercy was given. Today you will be with me in paradise. When the prodigal son decided to return back to his father's home forgiveness was granted when he confess all his sins. Peter wept severely and with a contrite and sorrowful heart Jesus did forgive him. When David confessed his sins to God forgiveness was given. In our spiritual life and in order to receive salvation simply seek God's mercy and quickly He will forgive and even though your sins blackened your soul God will make your the whitest making you so beautiful and desirable to God. Although our journey to heaven is so difficult there is one easy way out of it and that is to sincerely seek God's mercy with a contrite heart and a broken spirit. Such claim can be certified in the crucifixion scene when Jesus assured the good thief that on that moment he sought God's mercy he receive it and his soul was saved. Theologians wrote many marvelous things about God and us but as I repeat the easiest way to be save was simply beg our Lord for it. Father, forgive them for they know not what they are doing. Every Christians remember the pleading of God the Son to the Father interceding for us His mercy knowing that through such plea will be receive and granted if one truly was sorry and to amend living the new Life gifted to the new convert. But to those who are proud and arrogant, their sins to the Holy Spirit will never be forgiven simply for the reason that they refused to seek His mercy and they have maliciously reject God's love and mercy and actually they were the one who choses not to have anything to do with God at all. Therefore such obstinacy simply the soul chose to delete God in their being.

As members of the Catholic Church one of the powerful sacraments that save soul is none than the Sacrament of reconciliation where the sinner goes to confession so the priest will give absolution making the sinner white as snow. All its sins are erase and the soul is so fresh and her fragrance reaches to heaven. During the Lenten season the Church emphasized the greatness of God's mercy and He will never refuse anyone who seeks it. (Pause and meditate with your own life and your sinfulness and wretchedness. Try to recollect the gravest sin you have committed and raise your heart, mind and soul and in the Presence of Jesus praise and give thanks to Him for taking away your sins and the sins of the whole world. Remember that the children of the Old Covenant waited thousands and thousands of years before they can enter the new heaven and now in the New Covenant of perfect love we do not have to wait thousands or even ten thousands of years to enter into God's kingdom because of our Lord Jesus who made it possible for all of us. Though very difficult and demanding, still we are in a much better and greater position because of this opportunity that our Lord Jesus had given to us, His Body, the true Church. Are you dismayed or discouraged about the graveness of your sin? Don't because all the saints that are now in heaven were just like you and there are saints which were worst than you.)

Pray, "Jesus, my Lord and Redeemer, I have sin greatly against you and I need your mercy forgive me my God and be my Light and my salvation and never permit me to sin against you." By your true and sincere prayer, you are already save much like the good thief on the cross. Like Mary Magdalene possessed by many demons was freed from her sins with her tears of sorrow and sincerity in living a new Life in Christ. And unlike the arrogant and proud religious bragging about himself while judging the publican as the worst of sinners, his religiosity gain negative merits in the eyes of God. The humble sinner who cry and call out for God's mercy was justified and like what was written in Scriptures that thieves, murderers and prostitutes will enter God's kingdom first before those religious who relied on their own righteousness but with a heart hardened by their sin of pride. Again, let us always remind ourselves that the forgiveness of our sin takes only a few second and by doing so, salvation is ours. However, in teaching and guiding us to the fullness of truth, let us remember and be aware that once forgiven that His Eternal Words remains in our heart, mind and soul when Jesus said to the adulterous woman whom He save from death. SIN NO MORE. By obeying HIs Words we are on the way to the new heavens always to sin no more and to live God's Life to perfection.

THE RESURRECTION OF THE BODY

We believe in the resurrection of the body when we sin no more. Although we are habitual sinners, never get down nor be discourage with our weaknesses and wretchedness for our sinfulness will be our greatest burden and there was a great saint that the heaviest cross he had to carry was not the sufferings or pains but the weigh of his sin and of the guilt that kept harassing him. Again, God desired mercy and not sacrifices. To Him sacrifices had no value in our spiritual life unless we did obtained His mercy and to live a resurrected life patterned after His Own. When we are in state of sin, our body and soul is dead. But by obtaining His mercy, grace comes into our being restoring us into His likeness in a resurrected body governed by the Head which is our light and salvation, Jesus our Risen Lord. We who are His Own will never die again if we keep His Body free from the corruption of sin. But even though we still sin glory and honor to our Lord for providing us those potent and powerful sacraments such as the sacrament of reconciliation where we are made clean again and again making us a prominent shining member of His Body. So when sin overcomes us quickly go to that sacrament of reconciliation and like the father of the prodigal son our God will quickly put on us His garment of immortality and adorn us with the ring of His eternal kingship. This is who we are that despite of our wretched and sinful nature God provided us with all kinds of remedy and the greatest of it all is our Lord Jesus Christ, His Church and His mother. Thus, Easter becomes the Church greatest hope that we who are so helpless and hopeless will indeed be made new in a resurrected Body where our Eternal Head will lead and bring us home to where He had prepared a place for us and that is in the Right Hand of God the Father. (Pause and meditate and whatever burden or obstacles that weigh you down do not let such shackling sadness crippled you for the power of our Lord's resurrection defies and defeats any obstacles and such hope will help us to a new life of the Spirit where once again will make us triumphant over sin and death).

A reminder that once we are pardon and restore to God's friendship and grace we have the greatest responsibility that this resurrection should be sustain and nourish so the Immortal and Glorious Life of God will be ours forever.

AND LIFE EVERLASTING. AMEN.

We, baptized and confirmed members of the Catholic Church do believe that after we are done in this life awaits another life that will never end. For those who are truly serious in getting to heaven without waiting a long time will obtain what they hope for His Words promised that those who eat His Body and drink His Blood will have eternal life with Him. There is no other religion where such devout practices are exercised every moment of the day because Catholic Churches are all over the world offering Holy Mass to the Eternal Father reminding Him of the the greatness of Jesus love and obedience and He will not be denied whatever He asked of Him. Thus, whatever you ask from Him in the Name of Jesus His Son will be granted that is if it is His Holy will or if such request will be for our greatest and highest good. Skeptics questioned eternal life and for thousands of years philosophers and brilliant thinkers wrote about their own theory if there is another life after this. Theologians did chose to believe that there is an eternal life based on their serious studies on Sacred Scriptures and also in philosophy. In studying theology and philosophy one dips and investigates our lives in this visible kingdom of the world trying to analyze the purpose of our existence with brilliant minds offering their conceived opinion while in theology one tries to fathom the mystery of the spiritual kingdom where its invisibility cannot be clearly define leading many minds to the pits of speculation. However, with the existence of Sacred Scriptures, the invisibility of God's spiritual kingdom have been clearly and concisely revealed by none other that the Creator Himself through our Lord Jesus who entered into our visible world so He can be seen. It was His coming as God and man that changes the world by offering us something incredible and unbelievable where we will be transform into the likeness of God possessing everything of God drawing billions fo accept and embrace His teachings so we will have an eternity of happiness where there are no more tears, pains, sufferings, afflictions, troubles, wars, pestilences, calamities, tragedies and death. (Pause and meditate. Think of God's promises to us. Do you remember how we could earn such undeserving reward? In our formation classes, we are taught and shown how we can gain God and heaven. Also, remind yourself that we are given this one and only opportunity to gain God and heaven but salvation can only be achieved by how much we love God by how much we give ourselves to Him. If you give your all to Him, you could enter heaven much quicker than if we give little. The secret to possess God and heaven is nothing else but how much love we give Him. If we give Him little of our love if ever we are saved then it is most certain that we will spent many years in purgatory. The secret to enter heaven quickly is simply by giving all or most of our love for Him.)

Final thoughts for our inspiration was the revelation from a great saint why the Catholic Church produced hundreds of thousands saints was their daily Mass attendance and their reception of Holy Communion where the real Body, Blood, Soul and Divinity of Christ were consumed fulfilling Christ's promise that those who consume His Flesh and Blood will have eternal life. Catholics believed it and in concluding the Apostle's Creed, we believe in LIFE EVERLASTING

AMEN.

END

Printed in the United States
By Bookmasters